Piagetian Research

Volume Six

PIAGETIAN RESEARCH:
Compilation and Commentary

Volume Six

The Cognitive-Developmental Approach to Morality

Sohan Modgil, PhD and Celia Modgil, MPhil

Foreword by Professor Bärbel Inhelder
The University of Geneva

NFER Publishing Company Ltd

1116

Published by the NFER Publishing Company Ltd.,
2 Jennings Buildings, Thames Avenue,
Windsor, Berks. SL4 1QS
Registered Office: The Mere, Upton Park, Slough, Berks. SL1 2DQ
First Published 1976
© Sohan and Celia Modgil, 1976
ISBN 0 85633 106 6

Printed in Great Britain by
Staples Printers Ltd., Rochester, Kent.
Distributed in the USA by Humanities Press Inc.,
Hillary House—Fernhill House, Atlantic Highlands,
New Jersey, 07716, USA.

Contents

To Gita and Ramayana

With Love

FOREWORD

I most sincerely thank Dr Sohan and Celia Modgil for asking me to write a foreword to the series of eight volumes which they are at present compiling. We all know the interest that was shown in, and the success of, the previous book, *Piagetian Research: A Handbook of Recent Studies*. Now, two years later, eight follow-up volumes are being published. We are well aware of what this represents in terms of continuity and devotion to such a long-term task.

The rapid extension of Piaget-inspired research is very impressive; in this series 3700 references are mentioned. It would seem that such an extension is explained by the need for a general theory in fundamental psychology. Another possible explanation is the growing awareness of the gaps in strictly behaviourist theory, on the one hand, and on the other, the continued emergence of new applications for the work carried out in Geneva in the fields of education and psychopathology. Recent studies confirm this trend.

Pleasing though this extension is, however, we are somewhat disturbed by the fact that the replication of our experiments does not always show a sufficient understanding of Piagetian theory on the part of the authors of these new works. We are of course the first to admit that such understanding is not easy to acquire, especially since this form of psychology is closely linked to a certain form of epistemology. Once understood, this form of epistemology appears to be that which best suits genetic psychology, as both are essentially constructivist. Constructivism implies that knowledge is not acquired merely under the impact of empirical experience, as suggested by behaviourist theory, although of course such impact is not entirely excluded from the process. It is also opposed to innate theory, to which, it seems, recourse is frequently had today (maturation being a factor which intervenes, but not exclusively). Constructivism emphasizes the child's or the subject's activity during the course of cognitive development: in other words, everything derives from actions and is eventually translated into coherent and logical thought operations.

In order to promote the necessary understanding, Sohan and Celia Modgil have systematically encouraged the reader to return to the original texts. If authors who have an excellent knowledge of the work of Piaget and his colleagues slightly misunderstand our theoretical position — which is in no way maturationist but rather epigenetic — one can easily imagine the misunderstanding of researchers who are less well informed and further away from Geneva. It is one thing to recognize the necessary sequence of the stages, but another thing altogether to explain them by invoking an innate 'programme'. Piaget's explanation, which is best presented in constructivist terms, deals with the sequence of stages by a process of equilibration or autoregulation. This regulatory activity enables the subject truly to construct knowledge — something which simple maturation does not do.

This point of view is fundamental to the understanding of Piagetian psychology; but more than that, it seems to us to constitute a particularly useful approach to questions of educational application since this form of autoconstruction corresponds more than any other perspective to the ideal called 'the active school', an ideal rarely carried out in practice.

In a constructivist perspective of this kind, it is clearly the sequence of stages which is important and not the chronological ages; the latter vary considerably from one environment to another and also depend on the experimental procedures being used. It is not astonishing that Bryant obtains convservation responses at earlier ages than those noted by us: we ourselves have obtained notable accelerations using operatory learning procedures developed in collaboration with H. Sinclair and M. Bovet (1974). We have recently published the results of a study (Inhelder *et al.*, 1975) which show stable acquisition of conservation notions as of age 5 if the following procedure is used: rather than merely deforming an object such as a ball of clay or modifying a collection of discrete elements, one removes part of or an element of the object(s) and moves it to another spot. In this case conservation appears earlier because the child understands two things he did not grasp during the simple deformations: firstly, that changes in shape are the result of displacements, and secondly, that in the course of these displacements what appears at the end is identical to what was removed at the start (this is what Piaget calls 'commutability'). We highlight this piece of work in order to show the much lesser importance of chronological age which can so easily be accelerated or delayed according to circumstances. The main point is the mode of construction which obeys constant laws and this characteristic is best exemplified by constructivism as we have defined it earlier.

We would also like to add that the recent discoveries of T. Bower and others concerning the innateness of certain behaviours which Piaget had not observed at the sensorimotor level do not contradict constructivism, since these primitive reactions do not directly result in higher-order behaviours but are reconstructed on different levels. These reconstructions are themselves not innate, but evidence of the constructive activities we have already observed elsewhere.

I should like to congratulate Dr Sohan and Celia Modgil on their fine effort in bringing together in these eight volumes the numerous pieces of work, thus rendering them accessible to researchers. We sincerely hope that this will encourage further progress in genetic psychology and all its applications.

Bärbel Inhelder,
University of Geneva

PREFACE

The eight volumes in the present series, *Piagetian Research*, together with the previous publication, *Piagetian Research: A Handbook of Recent Studies*, 1974, are intended to serve a wide range of needs for both teacher and learner at all levels: for university and college lecturers; post-graduate research students; those training to be educational psychologists; teachers and others following a wide range of advanced diploma courses; and education and psychology students at undergraduate level, following Educational and Developmental Psychology options. Research projects have been included which have implications for psychiatrists, paediatricians, rehabilitation and social workers.

In one sense, there are many authors to these volumes. The research evidence included is dependent on the countless efforts of Piaget's followers. In fairness, our gratitude is extended to those followers whose researches contribute immeasurably to the contents of these volumes. In particular, we acknowledge the cooperation of the many researchers personally communicating and forwarding papers for inclusion. Some collaborators have contributed material previously unpublished. These contributions, together with their accompanying correspondence, have resulted in a more comprehensive output.

We owe a very special debt of gratitude to Geneva University, and to universities here and abroad. Likewise, the inspiration of Professors Piaget and Inhelder, together with the general support of Professor Ruth Beard, Dr Gordon Cross, and Professor Marcel Goldschmid, are acknowledged.

It is an honour to have received such distinguished recognition for the volumes from Professor Bärbel Inhelder's gracious Foreword. We offer sincere thanks and gratitude for her interest and involvement and for the pleasant meeting in Geneva.

Enver Carim, an author in his own right as well as a perceptive editor, has provided the expertise necessary for such an ambitious series. Further to these more direct qualities Enver Carim has a profound philosophy with respect to a number of areas of knowledge including psychology and unusual drive and energy. We are indebted to him for all his support and acknowledge with gratitude the tremendous contributions he has made to this series.

Sohan Modgil
Celia Modgil
July 1976

INTRODUCTION

The eight volumes in the present series *Piagetian Research* together with the previous publication *Piagetian Research: A Handbook of Recent Studies*, 1974, are designed to make available a substantial number of Piaget-oriented researches that may be useful for immediate information as well as for long-term reference. The accelerating expansion of Piagetian research has led to an acute need for a source book more comprehensive than the ordinary textbook but more focused than the scattered periodical literature. More specifically, it should give the reader access to source materials that elaborate upon most Piagetian topics. Likewise, such volumes should offer students examples of a variety of approaches utilized by researchers in their efforts to investigate cognitive development. The numerous researches assembled present experimental subjects whose chronological ages range from birth to 98 years. The intended readership is therefore broad, from those interested in the very young, in adolescents, in the elderly.

The present volumes, as well as recording the replications and extensions of Piaget's work, include reflections on, speculations about, and analyses of the various problems of the theory. Hopefully, this should in turn provide inspiration for further elaboration, extension and revision. The research worker is provided with a broad spectrum of original sources from which an appreciation in depth of the theoretical, methodological and practical questions relevant to a Piagetian framework can be obtained. While it is conceded that a secondary source is not the ideal way to comprehend the theory, nevertheless it can provide the reader with a basic direction to the problem at hand.

The material gathered has been heavily drawn from University degree theses, published and unpublished researches up to and as recent as July 1976.* It became apparent that the subject matter was voluminous and that there were many ways to subdivide the Piagetian cognitive researches. In choosing the articles, the criteria were made as

---

* The authors have been alert to studies appearing up to August 1976 (after the completion of the main manuscript) and brief details of further selected researches have been added in order to enrich particular areas of inquiry and discussion. Hopefully, researches within this category will receive full treatment in anticipated follow-up volumes.

objective as possible, while recognizing that a personal slant is bound to influence the selection. Despite an extensive search it is not unlikely that valuable articles have been overlooked. To these researchers apologies are extended. In assembling these researches the principal objective was to include only those which satisfy one of the following criteria: Piaget-oriented (replications or extensions); developmental in nature; or those which have discussed their findings within the Piagetian framework.

The tables of content reflect a broad range of studies, and represent most of the major subdivisions of Piagetian literature. It must be pointed out that while some articles fall naturally into certain specific volumes, others would have fitted simultaneously into more than one volume, this being in part due to the inability to distinguish between the analytic and synthetic. Consequently, it was difficult to select one single scheme that would satisfy all readers and many arbitrary decisions had to be made. There is obviously considerable reliance on the use of cross references.

The compilation covers fifteen areas, assembled in eight volumes — each volume focuses on one/two major aspects of Piaget's work. The main areas covered are: Piaget's Cognitive Theory and his major works, Sensorimotor Intelligence, Conservation, Training Techniques, Logic, Space, Handicapped Children, Cross-Cultural Research, The School Curriculum, Morality, Socialization, Test Development, Animism, Imagery and Memory.

Each volume consists of an integrated review of the range of recent studies followed by abstracts of these researches arranged, in the main, alphabetically. Where details of early research are essential to illustrate the evolution of a particular area of study, these are not represented by a full abstract, but are included in the introductory review. Although many cross references to related abstracts are included, the reviews preceding the abstracts are not intended to be fully critical of the validity and reliability of experimental design. This is partly due to the fact that, unless full details are available (sometimes these have neither been published fully, nor the definition of concepts made meaningful), this would be inimical, and partly because the amount of work involved in a critical evaluation of every study in a work of this breadth would be prohibitive.

In comparison to most publications, an unusual amount of detail of researches is made available, and to accompany this with an equal amount of discussion, although essential, could introduce complexity in the aims of the volumes. Some of the abstracts (indicated by an asterisk) have been written by the authors themselves and reproduced in their entirety. It is realized that some abstracts are of only marginal importance, yet their inclusion is essential to show general developmental patterns.

It is the authors' intention that the reader, having investigated the range of available material, would then consult the original research according to his specific interests. Advanced research depends a great deal on what sources and data are available for study, and there is a consequent tendency for some parts of the field to be ploughed over and over again, while others remain virtually untouched.

The list of references included at the end of each volume together form a comprehensive bibliography encompassing over 3,500 references. Volume One additionally includes a comprehensive survey of Piaget's works, arranged chronologically.

Every care has been taken to report the results of the researches as accurately as possible — any misinterpretation of the results is accidental. It must be conceded that all the studies included do not receive equal coverage. While the overall response to the circulated requests was excellent, some shortcomings in the volumes are due partly to some failure of response. While deficiencies of the final product are our own responsibility, they exist in spite of a number of advisers who gave their time generously.

The Cognitive-Developmental
Approach to Morality

a. Introduction

Theoretically and methodologically, investigations of children's moral development are polarized in either behavioural or cognitive systems incorporating psychoanalytical, learning and cognitive-developmental approaches. Hoffman (1970) traces this diversity historically to three philosophical doctrines. The doctrine of *original sin*, resting on the importance of the intervention by adults and being represented in modified form by Freudian theory, has led to the research interest in the production of guilt when moral standards are violated. The doctrine of *tabula rasa* assumed that the child is neither corrupt nor pure and also put stress on the importance of intervention by adults. These principles are embodied in the learning theory approach which regards morality in terms of specific acts learned on the basis of rewards and punishment with little accompanying rationale. The third doctrine, *innate purity*, stressing the corrupting influence of society (especially adult society), can be associated with Piaget's insight into the development of morality. He writes of the heteronomous nature of adult-child relations and stresses the importance of social interaction among peers, together with the development of cognitive processes for moral maturity.

Having associated Piaget with an early doctrine, attention must be drawn to his lack of allegiance to any school of psychology, together with his rejection of *a priori* moralizing about the child's notions of right and wrong. Arising mainly from his general theory of the development of the child's conception of the world (Piaget, 1928), his objective was to study the mental processes and thought structures underlying judgments concerning a variety of problematical situations.

The first part of Piaget's investigation *The Moral Judgment of the Child* (1932) was into the attitudes of different-aged children toward the origin, legitimacy, and alterability of rules, based upon a game of marbles: a situation natural and familiar to his Genevan subjects. Piaget's approach was to conceal his knowledge of the rules and to probe the child's understanding while the game was played. As a result, Piaget, distinguished a tendency in young children to regard rules as being sacred and to be obeyed without question, even though during the course of play there was an inclination for rules to be bent for self-advantage, together with little concern if both players were declared to have won. This 'moral realism' gradually becomes more flexible and Piaget attributed the establishment of 'cooperation and the development of the idea of justice' to intellectual growth and experiences of role taking in the peer group. Piaget states that children require nothing more for this development than 'the mutual respect and solidarity which holds among children themselves'. Additionally: 'The collective rule is at first something external to the individual and consequently sacred to him; then as he gradually makes it his own, it comes to that extent to be felt as a free product of mutual agreement and an autonomous conscience'.

In alignment with his general cognitive-developmental stage sequence approach, Piaget outlined four successive stages in the marble play. In the 'motor' stage, (that is, up to about three years of age) the child plays individually and rules are irrelevant. Characteristic of the following 'egocentric' stage (approximately between the ages of three and seven years), play is to a certain extent individual, although parallel, and rules are followed to the extent that they can be recognized. 'Towards the age of 7 to 8 appears the desire for mutual understanding in the sphere of play'. Piaget continues: 'As a criterion of the appearance of this stage we shall take the moment when by "winning" the child refers to the fact of getting the better of the others, therefore of gaining more marbles than the others and when he no longer says he has won when he has done no more than knock a marble out of the square, regardless of what his partners have done . . . In seeking to win the child is trying above all to contend with his partners while observing common rules'. However, Piaget elaborates by indicating that the children of this stage do not yet know the rules in detail and different children within the same group may give contradictory accounts. 'Children of the fourth stage, on the contrary have thoroughly mastered their code and even take pleasure in juridical discussions, whether of principle or merely of procedure, which may at times arise out of the points in dispute'. Piaget gives 11 or 12 as the average age at which the fourth stage develops.

Within the consciousness of rules, Piaget outlines three stages: the first stage corresponds to the purely individualistic stage referred to in connection with the practice of rules, the child seeking merely to satisfy his motor interests. However, Piaget believes that the origins of the consciousness of rules, even in so restricted a field as that of the game of marbles, are conditioned by the child's moral life as a whole;

'even if it has never seen marbles before, it is already permeated with rules and regulations due to the environment'. A second stage 'sets in from the moment when the child, either through imitation or as the result of verbal exchange, begins to want to play in conformity with certain rules received from outside'. He then 'regards the rules of the game as sacred and untouchable; he refuses to alter these rules and claims that any modification, even if accepted by general opinion would be wrong'. It is not until about the age of six that this attitude appears clearly and explicitly. Piaget characterizes the third stage (after the age of 10 on average) as 'autonomy follows upon heteronomy: the rule of a game appears to the child no longer as an external law, sacred in so far as it has been laid down by adults; but as the outcome of a free decision and worthy of respect in the measure that it has enlisted mutual consent'.

Piaget therefore describes three kinds of rule: the motor rule, 'relatively independent of any social contact'; the coercive rule, 'due to unilateral respect' and the rational rule, 'due to mutual respect'. However, Piaget discusses the coercive rule in the following terms: 'On the one hand, the child knows that there are rules, the "real rules", and that they must be obeyed because they are obligatory and sacred; but on the other hand, although the child vaguely takes note of the general scheme of these rules. . . . he still plays more or less as he did during the previous stage, i.e. he plays more or less for himself, regardless of his partners, and takes more pleasure in his own movements than in the observance of the rules themselves, thus confusing his own wishes with universality'. In connection with rational rules, Piaget explains that the moment children really begin to submit to rules and to apply them in a spirit of genuine cooperation, they acquire a new conception of rules. They become something that can be changed if it is agreed that they should be, for the truth of a rule rests on mutual agreement and reciprocity. Piaget adds that mutual respect and cooperation are never completely realized. 'Even the most rational of adults does not subject to his "moral experience" more than an infinitesimal proportion of the rules that hedge him round'. It is upon the distinction between constraint and cooperation that Piaget's whole theory of moral development rests.

In the second section of *The Moral Judgment of the Child*, Piaget presented children with hypothetical situations in the form of stories and attempted to examine the criteria upon which the child made moral judgments. Within the chapter entitled 'Adult constraint and moral realism', Piaget examines objective responsibility incorporating clumsiness, stealing and lying. The chapter 'Cooperation and the development of the idea of justice' includes experiment and discussion concerning the problem of punishment, collective and communicable responsibility, three forms of justice (immanent, retributive and distributive), together with equality and authority. In the final chapter Piaget discusses the two moralities of the child and types of social relations, reviewing his own conclusions in the light of the theories of Durkheim, Fauconnet, M. Pierre Bovet and J.M. Baldwin.

Piaget refers to moral realism as 'the tendency which the child has to regard duty and the value attaching to it as self-subsistent and independent of the mind, as imposing itself regardless of the circumstances in which the individual may find himself'. Moral realism possesses three features: duty as viewed by moral realism is essentially heteronomous; secondly it demands that the letter rather than the spirit of the law shall be observed and thirdly, it induces an objective conception of responsibility.

Piaget encouraged children to compare stories involving two kinds of clumsiness, 'one entirely fortuitous or even the result of a well-intentioned act, but involving considerable material damage, the other, negligible as regards the damage done but happening as the result of an ill-intentioned act'. When studying problems related to stealing, the aim was to discover whether the child paid more attention to the motive or to the material results; consequently, the problems were confined to the comparison of selfishly-motivated acts with those that are well-intentioned. Concerning lying, Piaget's investigation included the definition of a lie: 'responsibility as a function of the lie's content and responsibility as a function of its material consequences'. Additionally, he questioned the children with regard to the acceptability of children lying to one another. Piaget found that the child's judgments tended to be centred on the amount of damage done by the action, but that this 'objective responsibility' diminished as the child reached the age of 10 years. Piaget felt that adult constraint is to a certain extent responsible for this 'objective' response: 'It is very easy to notice — especially in very young children, under 6—7 years of age — how frequently the sense of guilt on the occasion of clumsiness is proportional to the extent of the material disaster instead of remaining subordinate to the intentions in question'. He continues, 'there is no doubt that by adopting a certain technique with their children, parents can succeed in making them attach more importance to intentions than to rules conceived as a system of ritual interdictions'. With regard to lying, the child's judgments were objective in the sense that he evaluated the lies, not according to the intentions of the liar, but according to the greater or lesser likelihood of the lying statement — 'the more a statement departed from the truth, the more it would seem to the child to be a lie'. It was noticeable that judgments in terms of intentions became more frequent at approximately nine years of age. Piaget detected three stages in the attitude to lying: in the first stage it is regarded as wrong because it is punished; secondly, it is seen as a fault in itself and would remain so even if it were not punished; and eventually (at about 10 to 12 years) because 'truthfulness is necessary to reciprocity and mutual agreement'. Younger children considered that lies between children are allowed but lying to adults is worse than lying to peers. Piaget concludes that 'the consciousness of lying gradually becomes interiorized and the hypothesis may be hazarded that it does so under the influence of cooperation'. He continues: 'If we attribute the advance to the child's intelligence alone, which is constantly improving his understanding of what he originally took in a purely realistic sense, we are only shifting the question. For how does psychological intelligence advance with age if not by means of increased cooperation?'

In the section dealing with the child's ideas about punishment and justice, Piaget used essentially the same techniques, except that, in the stories concerning punishment, three alternative forms of punishment were given in connection with the wrongdoer. The child was requested to say which was the fairest punishment and then the most severe in order to determine whether the child evaluated the punishment in terms of its severity or in accordance with some other criterion of retribution. The suggested punishments were either 'expiatory' (i.e. no relation between the content of the guilty act and the nature of its punishment) or 'punishments by reciprocity' (misdeed and punishment are related both in content and nature). Piaget found a marked development from expiation responses to reciprocity responses as age increased and he finally concludes this section by emphasizing: 'the law of reciprocity implies certain positive obligations in virtue of its very form. And this is why the child, once he has admitted the principle of punishment by reciprocity in the sphere of justice, often comes to feel that any material punitive element is unnecessary, even if it is "motivated", the essential thing being to make the offender realize that his action was wrong, in so far as it was contrary to the rules of cooperation'.

Relating to the question of 'collective' (or 'communicable') responsibility ('collective punishment has long been resorted to in the classroom and in spite of the many protests that have been raised against this practice'), Piaget administered stories involving situations in which the adult punishes the whole group for the offence committed by one or two of its members; secondly, where the adult attempts to discover the transgressor who is not owning up and the group refuses to reveal his identity; and finally, where the adult is attempting to discover the transgressor, who is not prepared to own up, while the group is ignorant of his identity. In each of the three cases the child was asked whether it is fair to punish the whole group and why. In the first instance even the younger children showed no trace of collective

responsibility. To the second situation the reactions were indeter-
minate. There was however, a tendency for the younger children to say
that everyone should be punished as each individual is guilty because of
the failure to reveal the transgressor. The older children tended to offer
the response that everyone should be punished because of the solidarity
of the group in deciding not to reveal the offender. Children of
approximately an intermediate age felt that 'no one should be
punished; partly because it is right not to "tell" and partly because the
guilty one is not known'. In the third situation, the younger children
accepted collective punishment, because the guilty one is unknown and
'there must be a punishment at all costs'. (The necessity of punishment
is the fundamental fact). The older children considered general
punishment as a greater injustice than the impunity of the guilty. In
conclusion, Piaget discusses that in none of the three situations is any
judgment found comparable to the classical notion of collective
responsibility, but in situations two and three, the reactions can be
regarded as bearing upon communicable responsibility.

A problem connected with that of punishment is immanent justice.
Piaget hypothesized that during the early years of his life, the child
would affirm the existence of automatic punishments which emanate
from things themselves, while later, under the influence of factors
affecting his moral growth he is likely to abandon this belief. Piaget's
hypothesis was confirmed and he found belief in immanent justice to
decline with age.

Piaget then approached the analysis of the conflicts that can take
place between distributive or equalitarian justice and retributive justice.
Three stories were administered, asking each time whether or not it was
fair to favour the well-behaved child. The first situation mentioned no
special fault and established the conflict between retributive and
distributive justice in the abstract; the second introduced only
negligible faults and minor punishment; the third, brought in a
punishment which might strike the child as very severe. The younger
children reacted in the form of punishment outweighing equality,
whereas the opposite was the case for the older children. Concerning
the relation between equality and authority, Piaget was intent to
discover whether the subjects would place the adult in the right, out of
respect for authority or whether they would defend equality out of
respect for an inner ideal, even if the latter was in opposition with
obedience. As expected, there was a predominance of the first solution
among the younger children and as the age of the subjects increased
(about 11 to 12 years) there was a definite progression in the direction
of the latter. Piaget was able to distinguish three broad stages in the
development of distributive justice in relation to adult authority. In the
first stage, justice is not distinguished from the authority of the law;

during the second stage, equalitarianism grows in strength and comes to outweigh any other consideration; and during the third stage, equalitarianism makes way for a more subtle conception of justice which 'we may call "equity" and which consists in never defining equality without taking account of the way in which each individual is situated'. In the domain of retributive justice, equity consists 'in determining what are the attenuating circumstances'. In the domain of distributive justice, equity consists 'in taking account of age, of previous services rendered etc.'. With respect to adults and children being served in shops, even the majority of the six-year-old children responded that each should be served in turn. Responding to questions in connection with cheating and tale-telling, there was again a gradual diminution in the pre-occupation with authority and an increase in the desire for equality.

In summary, Piaget views moral development as the result of a process involving the development of cognitive processes in conjunction with experiences of role-taking in the peer group, allowing the movement from moral realism to autonomy. In connection with the sense of justice, Piaget concludes that 'though naturally capable of being reinforced by the precepts and the practical example of the adult (it) is largely independent of these influences and requires nothing more for its development than the mutual respect and solidarity which holds among children themselves. It is often at the expense of the adult and not because of him that the notions of the just and unjust find their way into the youthful mind'.

b. Replications of Piaget's Investigations

Although not falling strictly under the designation of this section, it is perhaps pertinent to draw attention to a number of early studies described by Johnson (1962) as 'adding force in their buttressing of Piaget's position'. Taking into account that the studies were carried out nearly 40 years before Piaget's work, they yield similar results and, as they apparently took place independently, they can be considered to support Piaget. Johnson cites three main studies — Barnes (1894, 1902) and Schallenberger (1894) — all of which obtained 'written responses to questions from extremely large samples of children at various ages'. From the responses of children aged seven to 16 years, to questions asking for descriptions of just and unjust punishments, Barnes (1894) concluded that punishments are usually considered to be just, since they come from adults. Further, children believe that offences can be paid for with pain. This view was found to decrease with age. Schallenberger (1894) after analysing the written responses of children aged six to 16 years, to a story involving a child painting 'all the chairs in the parlour, so as to make them look nice for her mother', found that the younger children most frequently said that the mother should punish the child harshly. At the older level there was an emphasis on explanation as to why the chairs should not have been painted. Schallenberger concluded: 'Younger children judge actions by their results, older children look at the motives that prompt them'. Barnes (1902) replicated Schallenberger's work with English children as opposed to American, and again revealed that punitive measures were most often suggested at younger age levels. Expiatory punishment was found to occur before restitutive, and older children often emphasized the importance of explanation as to why the deed was wrong. He described a correlation between the 'explanation' responses and the highest intelligence levels. English children were found to be more mature in their earlier rejection of punitive punishment but not differing in the more mature forms of response. These studies can therefore be said to add support to Piaget's work in that they illustrated the young child's moral realism and the increasing concern for motives with increasing age; they reveal the younger child's belief in the justness of adult punishment and the expiatory value, together with the younger child's belief in severe punishment. The major changes in age also occurred at about 12 years of age.

Among early studies which can be considered as replicating Piaget's work is Harrower's (1934) investigation. As a result of responses obtained from working class and upper-middle class children, Harrower queried the existence of stages and considered that the children were merely reflecting different kinds of experiences. She suggested that mature responses are learnt from parents. Attention is drawn to a comprehensive review by Medinnus (1959) of the early literature relating to the development of immanent justice, in children, namely, Lerner, Abel, Dennis, Liu, Havighurst and Neugarten and MacRae.

Lerner (1937) investigated the relationship between social status, parental authority and moral realism. With a sample of children between the ages of six and 12 years, belonging to two contrasted status groups, Lerner showed that high-status parents used fewer coercive techniques in child-rearing and that there was less tendency in their children (as compared with the low status children) to see principles as external and unvarying. The findings agreed with Piaget's in showing a decrease with age in the number of children expressing a belief in immanent justice. Lerner considered that middle class children passed through the earlier stage more quickly. Abel (1941) adopted Piaget's approach to study the moral judgments of mentally retarded girls. The subjects were 94 subnormal girls, CA 15—21 years, with mental ages of six to 11. Comparing the institutionalized girls with those living in the community, it was found that approximately twice as many of the former gave responses which indicated a belief in immanent justice. Dennis (1943), in his work with Hopi Indian children, although mainly concerned with the concept of animism, also investigated immanent justice. In his sample of 98 subjects, aged 12 to 18 years, Dennis found that 64 per cent of his youngest subjects indicated a belief in the immanence of punishment. This figure decreased markedly with age and among the 16-year-old and 17-year-old subjects was only nine per cent. Dennis attributed the differences in the findings of these early investigators to a variety of cultural factors specifically unidentifiable, but contended that development was universal in all societies.

In connection with immanent justice, Liu (1950) found a decrease in belief in immanent justice responses at the ages of six to 12 years, but at each level, more non-Chinese children than Chinese revealed a belief in immanent justice. Liu concluded that decreasing moral realism is not due to age maturity alone. Havighurst and Neugarten (1955), in a large investigation involving 902 Indian children from six Indian tribes and aged from six to 18 years, showed that there was either an increase or no change with age in the children's belief in immanent justice for most of the groups studied. Except for one group, 85 per cent of the 12- to 18-year-old subjects indicated a belief in immanent justice. Within the younger age groups the percentage tended to be smaller. It was considered that these findings supported Piaget's hypothesis that children in primitive societies become more rigid in their moral development as they increase in age, due to constraints being placed on them. There is, however, a discrepancy with the findings of Dennis in which he found a decrease with age in belief in immanent justice in his Hopi Indian subjects. When comparing differing degrees of acculturation, Havighurst and Neugarten found that there was no significant differences in immanent justice responses and they concluded that rather than measuring the degree of influence from modern societies, environmental factors within each cultural group must be investigated in depth. Medinnus (1959) draws attention to Thompson's (1948) view that the basic orientation of primitive people is deeply rooted in the tribal past and it persists regardless of changes in the group's economy or exposure to white cultures. This can be considered as accounting for the lack of relationship between the degree of acculturation and belief in immanent justice. In a study of immanent justice among West African children, Jahoda (1958) aimed to replicate the work of Havighurst and Neugarten and confirmed the prevalence of immanent justice responses among young African children but questioned the inclusion of 'acts of God' in the category of immanent justice responses. He emphasized that this inclusion leads to a much less marked decrease among older children. In a study among Lebanese children and adults, Najarian-Svajian (1966) confirmed his hypothesis that the Lebanese culture would reinforce the belief in immanent justice in adults of little education. He concluded that educational and social factors were effective in changing thinking connected with immanent justice.

MacRae (1954) found in general 'a decrease over the age range in the children's belief in immanent justice, the trend was not consistent. For both stories a smaller percentage of the five- and six-year-olds gave responses which were scored as indicating a belief in immanent punishment than the nine- and 10-year-olds', (Medinnus 1959). The latter, considering that research findings of the various studies on the whole support Piaget's conclusions that there is a decrease with age of children's belief in immanent justice, was intent to further replicate this area of Piaget's theory. In discussing his findings, he drew attention to the importance of the context and content of the story. Grinder

(1964), in his investigation into behavioural and cognitive dimensions of conscience, also found that the influence of the morality of constraint on children's moral judgments decreased with age. Brennan (1962) confirmed 'movement away from moral realism' but found that CA and MA were significantly related to moral judgment only up to 9.5 years.

Turning to punishment, Durkin's (1959a) subjects substantiated Piaget's contention of a relationship existing between age and concepts of justice but also found, contrary to Piaget, that only between the years seven and 10 was there evidence of an increasing acceptance of reciprocity: even the 13-year-old subjects tended to seek justice in the authority person. However, it was evident that older children were more aware of the complexity of the situation. Whelan (1975) reviewing Piaget's stages of development in justice and authority examined them as logical, natural developments of the child's growing awareness of himself and of society, and suggested the educational implications of this developmental process. (Details are given later.)

Results essentially in agreement with Piaget's with respect to the child's conception of lying were obtained from the Medinnus (1962) questionnaire consisting of stories drawn from Piaget. Again modelled on Piaget's approach, Kane (1970) also investigated children's attitudes to lying.

The development of moral judgments in children was studied by Lydiat (1973). A mixed sample of 368 schoolchildren aged seven to 12 years were given six tests of moral judgment patterned after Piaget (1932). There were two tests in each of three areas: clumsiness, stealing, and lying. 'Generally, immature forms of moral judgment were replaced in older children by more mature forms, but elements of immature judgments could still be discerned in children up to 12 years of age . . . the bulk of this immature residue was concentrated in the responses of a small number of children aged 11 and 12 years (N = 16). Similarly, a small group of younger children (N = 16; ages seven and eight years) was isolated, where responses showed consistent evidence of mature judgment . . . No significant differences could be established between the patterns of response of boys and girls . . . children of above average ability performed best and children of below average ability performed worst at all age levels', p. 376. (Details are given later.)

Bobroff (1960) observed and assessed the practice and consciousness of rules during a game of marbles, following Piaget's approach. His results were generally consistent with the findings of Piaget. The group of mentally retarded children were found to follow the same sequence of developmental stages as normal children. Piaget's contention that, by the age of 12 years, children judge behaviour according to interiorized rules rather than mere conformity to rules was not supported by

Medinnus (1966) in his behavioural and cognitive measures of conscience development inquiry. (Further details of the earlier studies are
given in Modgil, 1974.)

c. Developments from Piaget's Approach

Strauss (1954) studied the growth of the awareness of rules governing transactions, particularly purchasing, and disregarded the importance placed by Piaget on 'special kinds of' social relations (i.e. parent/child, child/peers) concerning the conceptions of rules, viewing rules rather in terms of sets of relations that exist among general roles. The effects of participation in rule formation on the moral judgment of children were studied by Merchant and Rebelsky (1972). The subjects were 50 kindergarten and first grade children who each took part in making up game rules, while 50 matched children were each taught the rules made up by their matched counterparts. 'Participation Ss showed greater flexibility about changing the rules given mutual agreement at the .01 level of significance, and this effect generalized to a different kind of rule at the .11 level of significance. First grade Ss were not more flexible than kindergarten Ss', p. 303. (Details follow.)

Armsby (1971) emphasizes that 'the story-pairs used by Piaget to test the shift in moral judgment reveal that they do not clearly differentiate accidental from purposive behaviour. For example, in Piaget's cup-breaking story pair, one boy accidentally breaks 15 cups while the other boy breaks one cup while attempting to get some jam'. Armsby points out that in both stories the damage done is accidental and in order to make a valid assessment of the development of intentionality it is surely necessary to devise moral judgment stories that contrast an accidental act with a purposive act. He also thought it important to provide written copies of the stories to reduce the confounding factor of memory ability. As a result of these innovations, Armsby concluded that children make moral judgments based on intentionality at an earlier age than Piaget and other experimenters have suggested and, although there is an age progression, there is no clear age level at which the morality of constraint ceases to operate. Breznitz and Kugelmass (1967), when attempting to contrast a more adequate measure to assess the sequential structure of the principle of inten-

tionality through adolescence, considered: 'what is it in the use of
intentionality that would characteristically be acquired in the later
years of childhood and adolescence'. They hypothesized that 'as the
child matures and broadens his range of experience, it is possible for
him to respond to a wider range of situations' and that 'an
intentionality-oriented response might be the predominant type of
response in increasingly more spheres of life'. Thus development would
tend to be a quantitative change. Secondly, when the range of stimuli
to which the same type of response is given is sufficiently broad, a
cognitive principle to abstract all specific relations may need to be
developed. Breznitz and Kugelmass considered that the interrelation of
these two processes was highly complex and they therefore concentrated solely on the cognitive principle. The analysis following the
administering of the final construction of the measure indicated that
the emergence of a cognitive principle underlying the use of intentionality in moral judgment goes through four successive stages. Breznitz and
Kugelmass comment that a highly developed principle of intentionality
could be termed essentially similar to Inhelder and Piaget's 'formal
operations'. McKechnie (1971) found in a pilot study that, if the
structure of Piaget's stories were reversed and the ill-intentioned act led
to greater material damage, then the frequency of 'subjective responsibility' responses increased. The study also suggested that the size of
consequence may influence the judgment and that it might be
expedient to look at 'good' and 'bad' intentions separately. He also
noted that Durkin (1959b, 1961) and Boehm and Nass (1964) drew
attention to children making different judgments depending on the
characteristics of the situations described in the stories. He therefore
designed a study to investigate further the influence of story structure
and context on the moral judgment of the child. He confirmed his
further hypothesis that the structure of Piaget's stories masked the
development taking place between the two extremes Piaget detected:
'the two moralities are only end-points of a developmental process in
which consequences originally dominate the complex of factors and
eventually give way to the increasing importance of intentions in the
mind of the child'. Irwin and Moore (1971) attempted to measure the
degree to which pre-school children make conventional judgments
concerning, among other aspects, accidental and intentional misdeeds.
The outstanding feature of this study was the use of illustrated
material, thus reducing the necessity for a verbal response. The older
pre-school children understood notions of justice better than the
younger ones. The understanding of guilt, innocence, apology and
restitution was clearer than intentionality. The data were consistent
with Piaget's theory that the concept of intentionality is slow to
develop compared with the notion of restitution.

A quantitative methodology to examine the development of moral judgment was undertaken by Buchanan and Thompson (1973) among 48 boys aged between six to 10 years who made two quantitative moral judgments about characters in stories where levels of damage and intent differed systematically. Damage was the most important factor in moral decisions for younger children while intent information was more important to older subjects. However, unlike Piaget's clinical procedure, the E's methodology permitted substantiation of the ability of children to simultaneously weigh damage and intent information when making a moral judgment. (Details are given later.)

Gutkin (1972) with respect to the concept of intentionality constructed story pairs 'in which the two salient variables of moral intentionality items, intentions and damage, and their two respective values (good-bad, high-low) were arranged in the six different possible combinations'. Judgments were scalable and suggested a four-stage developmental sequence: '(1) intentions irrelevant, (2) intentions relevant but damage more important, (3) intentions more important than damage but damage still relevant, (4) intentions alone relevant'. (Details are given later.)

The concept of moral intentionality was further analyzed by Gutkin (1973) and shown to be concerned with the more general ethical problem of responsibility. It was concluded that 'empirical studies that make use of various levels of intention are needed and that the consequences of actions have moral importance despite the misleading impression created on this issue by some of the work in the area'. (Details are given later.)

Children's level of moral intentionality was compared by Gutkin (1975) to their mothers' self-reports on how they would treat the children in situations involving intention and damage (Bandura and McDonald, 1963; and Gutkin, 1972 *op. cit.*). The amount of punishment mothers reported they would give was significantly negatively related to intentionality in their children, although there was no correlation observed between the extent to which mothers reported intentional responding to their children and the children's level of intentionality. That power-assertive discipline by parents may be associated with less advanced moral development in children was lent further credence. (Details follow.)

The effects of provocation, intentions, and consequences on 128 eight- and 12-years-old Dutch boys on their moral judgments were examined by Hewitt (1975). Ss read brief stories (modeled after Rule and Duker, 1973) about a harmdoer whose intentions were either good or bad and whose actions resulted in either minor or serious injury to a victim. The harmdoer had previously been either strongly provoked or not provoked by the victim. Results showed that the older boys differentiated their evaluations of the harmdoer's naughtiness on the basis of provocation and intentions, in contrast to the younger boys who failed to differentiate their evaluations of the provoked harmdoer on the basis of intentions. Ss in both eight and 12 year groups differentiated their judgments of the victim's naughtiness on the basis of his role as provoker, except when the victim was seriously injured by a bad-intentioned aggressor. (Details follow.)

Intentionality, degree of damage and moral judgments were studied in 153 first grade children through the administration of Piagetian moral judgment problems by Berg-Cross (1975) employing a new simplified methodology as well as the usual story-pair paradigm. 'The new methodology involved making quantitative judgments about single stories and evaluated the influence of level of intentionality and degree of damage upon absolute punishment ratings. Contrary to results obtained with a story-pair methodology, it was found that with single stories even six-year-old children responded to the level of intention in the stories as well as the quantity and quality of damage involved. This suggested that Piaget's methodology may be forcing children to employ a simplifying strategy while under other conditions they are able to perform the mental operations necessary to make complex moral judgments', p. 970. (Details follow.)

The understanding of motives and intentionality and moral judgments were assessed for children (N = 72) of different ages with four types of situations by Berndt and Berndt (1975). The children watched films and heard stories which portrayed an actor who intentionally or accidentally injured another for either good or bad motives. Following the film or story, children were questioned to determine their understanding of the actor's motives and the intentionality of his act and their moral judgments. The concepts of motive and intentionality were comprehended by children of all ages. However, that the ability to make accurate inferences about motives and intentionality developed with age. Motives affected children's evaluations at all ages, but intentionality affected only grade school children's evaluations. Berndt and Berndt discussed the results of moral judgment in terms of a theory which included features of both cognitive-developmental and social learning explanations of moral development. (Details follow.)

In a study entitled, 'The modification of age-specific expectations of Piaget's theory of development of intentionality in moral judgments of four- to seven-year-old children in relation to use of puppets in a social (imitative) learning paradigm', Reeves (1972) through a pre-test screening, selected 80 middle class children enrolled in nursery, kindergarten, and grade one classes. Ss were randomly assigned to one of eight treatment conditions. A pre- and post-test 2 x 2 factorial experimental design (treatment vs. control and four to five vs. six to seven age level) was employed for data analysis. 'As dependent variables, immediate post-test and delayed post-tests were separately analyzed for statistical significance by two-way analysis of covariance with age and treatment as the main variables, and with pre-test scores as covariates'. Reeves concluded that the use of the film promoted moral development and both the immediate and delayed post-test results afforded a basis for questioning the age-specific expectations of Piaget's theory. (Details follow.)

The relationship between level of moral development as conceived by Piaget and children's appreciation of humour based on varying levels of quantity and intentionality of damaging outcomes was examined in three related studies by McGhee (1974). In the first two studies, second grade Ss at both the heteronomous and autonomous level of moral development were used to investigate the relationship. Study three drew Ss from grades four and eight and from college, assuming progressively greater lengths of time for functioning at the autonomous level. Results demonstrated that 'heteronomous children consistently found stories with highly damaging outcomes funnier than stories with less damaging outcomes. For autonomous children, this trend was found only when damage occurred unintentionally . . . autonomous children found accidental damaging outcomes funnier than intentional ones. It was concluded that while increased naughtiness or moral unacceptability of an outcome or event adds to its funniness for heteronomous children, it detracts from humour appreciation in adults and morally more mature autonomous children', (*ibid.*, p. 514). (Details follow.)

In Nesdale, Rule and Mcara's (1975) study 128 women 'read a transcript of an interview which described either an attractive or unattractive male interviewee who aggressed against another with either a good or bad intention and with mild or severe consequences for the victim . . . Aggression committed by an attractive person and also by one who had good intentions was judged more favourably than was aggression committed by an unattractive person and by one who had bad intentions . . . an unattractive aggressor was seen as more likely to aggress again when his intentions were bad rather than good whereas little difference due to varying intentions was seen in the probability of an attractive person's future aggression. However, the corresponding prediction that attractiveness would interact with intentions to affect moral judgments of aggression was not supported,' p. 339. The authors further maintain that, 'The fact that intention rather than consequences produces an effect on judgments of aggression is consistent with an attributional viewpoint. In addition, the finding is consistent with Piaget's (1932) suggestion that, while children make moral judgments on the basis of outcomes rather than intentions, more mature persons (presumably at higher stages of moral development) are more responsive to the nature of intentions rather than behavioural outcomes. This notion has also received support from several studies which have examined age trends in the influence of intentions and consequences on children's moral judgments of aggression (Costanzo, Coie, Grumet and Farnill, 1973; Gutkin, 1972; Hebble, 1971; Rule and Duker, 1973; Shantz and Voydanoff, 1973)', (*ibid.*, p. 346). (Details follow.)

Durkin (1959b) questioned her subjects about violations of justice other than physical aggression in order to evaluate still further the applicability of Piaget's theory concerning 'the increasing acceptance with age, of reciprocity as a justice-principle'. The results indicated that, when justice-violations were described in terms of violations of property and character rights, the acceptance of reciprocity was negatively related to CA. Contrary to Piaget's suggestion, it was the seven-year-old children rather than the children of 13 years who saw restoration of justice in terms of reciprocity. Specificity of judgment was indicated in that only four subjects out of a total of 101, consistently gave reciprocity responses for all four stories. This suggests a further weakness in Piaget's theory in that his investigation in this respect was based on responses to only one kind of violation. She emphasizes the complexity involved in arriving at a reliable theory of the development of justice in children. In a further study (1961), Durkin systematically examined the specificity of the judgments given by the subjects in the previous study and examined the reasons they gave for their judgments as an attempt to explain the specificity. The 'findings indicated that a child's judgments about the restoration of "right order" in various situations was affected by the particulars of each situation'. She reported that the 'phenomenon of specificity can be said to place limitations on the general applicability of Piaget's theory of the development of concepts of justice in children'. Closer analysis of responses revealed that apparently identical responses were fundamentally different when further details were sought.

Aldrich (1976) determined from a study involving the portrayal of transgressions through film and investigating the child's differential reaction to adult chastisement, that children place an increased emphasis on motives in determining moral culpability as they increase in age; that contextual cues influence the degree to which negative adult sanctions are treated by older children as constituting morally relevant information and younger children view a child's compliance to adult prescriptions as being mandatory, whereas older children do not — they evaluate a child's behaviour toward an adult in terms of whether the child's behaviour is congruent with the principle of reciprocal social interaction. (Details follow.)

Morris (1958) attempted to gain further insight into the behaviour which young people expect of their contemporaries by devising, 'Piaget-style', a number of everyday problem situations. There was also an attempt to assess any differences between what adolescents thought should be done in the problem situations and what they thought would actually be done. Although there was a tendency to greater reciprocity and equity with increasing age, the study drew attention to individual differences in moral development and the social influences.

A wide survey by Johnson (1962) attempted to determine the degree of interrelation within and between areas of moral judgment together with the investigation of the relation of various antecedent conditions to moral judgment. The stories were modelled closely to those of Piaget, but new questions were devised to suit the adolescent subjects and to allow the test to be administered in pencil and paper form. The results indicated some consistency of response between areas of moral judgment and the experimenter considered that a general factor of moral judgment could be said to exist.

Hogan (1974) outlined an alternative viewpoint on moralization which attempted systematically to incorporate a dialectical perspective. The paper defined the concept of the dialectic and placed it 'within the context of a well-defined methodology, i.e. that of organicism, which contrasts markedly with the logical empiricism of much contemporary psychology'. The paper also pointed out the relevance of a dialectical perspective for developmental psychology by summarizing and re-viewing three standard models of moral development (those proposed by Freud, Mead and Piaget) using the definition of dialectic. The paper further promotes the view that 'a viable society may need its immoralists'. (Further details of the earlier studies are given in Modgil, 1974.)

d. Associated Factors

i. Relations with other cognitive measures

Generally, research indicates that intelligence is associated with mature moral judgment. However, Durkin (1959a, 1959b) found the relationship of intelligence and kind of justice response conflicting throughout different age levels. Boehm (1962) observed that academically gifted children mature earlier in their moral judgments concerning distinctions between intention and outcome of an action, than children of average intelligence. In a later analysis Boehm (1962b), in relation to recognizing the distinction between motivation and results of an action, found that gifted upper middle class children, irrespective of type of school, scored higher at an earlier age than their counterparts of average intelligence. Gifted working class children also scored higher than their peers. With respect to independence from adults and peer reciprocity, gifted working class children and upper middle class children scored higher than their counterparts of average intelligence. Johnson (1962) found IQ to be positively correlated with mature moral judgment in all the aspects investigated. Whiteman and Kosier (1964) revealed 'systematic increases in mature responses in association with increases in age and with IQ at each age'. Combining the verbal and numerical raw scores of the Differential Aptitude Test to represent the intelligence level, Porteus and Johnson's (1965) investigation indicated that intelligence seemed to be the most important variable for measures of both 'cognitive and affective zones' of conscience development. The hypothesis that the more intellectually able children, as measured by the WISC vocabulary, are also more mature in moral attitudes was supported by Harris (1970). More recently, the effect of age, sex, IQ and SES on children's moral judgments was studied by Rawan (1975) in 160 subjects, 40 at each of four age levels seven, nine, 11 and 13. The four areas of moral judgment included: intention versus consequence; solution to transgression, immanent justice; and meaning of rules. The intellectual functioning of the Ss was assessed by the administration of the Goodenough Harris Drawing Test. Age was positively correlated to moral maturity but not to immanent justice. IQ and SES were positively and significantly related to both moral maturity and immanent justice. No such relationships were noted with sex. In the areas of intention versus consequence, solution to transgression, and meaning of rules, it was noted that Afghan children showed generally less maturity than Piaget's Swiss children. In the area of immanent justice the difference in developmental maturity was greater. (Details are given later.)

MacRae (1954) reported that children of above-average intelligence respond more maturely to cognitive aspects of moral development. He maintains that cognitive responses are based on knowledge of adult expectations and are due to 'cultural indoctrination and learning of norms'. He believes that the bright child and the child of the upper social class internalizes parental rules more strongly and remains dependent upon parents longer than children of average intelligence and lower class. However, Boehm's findings (*op. cit.*) did not bear out MacRae's study. Bull (1969) concludes that 'intelligence is a leading constituent factor in moral judgment; and that, as such, it facilitates development in moral judgment. But is not by any means the only factor. Intelligence *per se* does not guarantee higher levels of moral insight and action'. Although finding significant association between moral judgment and intelligence at earlier ages Bull reports no positive associations at 17 years.

Ugurel-Semin (1952) concluded that the progress of moral thought is characterized by five different tendencies whose common trait is found in the change from centralization to decentralization. Likewise, Stuart (1967) drew attention to the importance of the ability to 'decenter' in the development of moral judgment. When the moral and causal judgments of high and low decentering subjects were contrasted, high decenterers were significantly superior. A traditional measure of IQ was found to be a significant influence in the two moral judgment areas and decentration.

Role taking and moral judgment in five- and seven-year-olds were studied by Ambron and Irwin (1975) who argued that research on role taking (Flavell *et al.*, 1968) and moral judgment (Kohlberg, 1969; Piaget, 1932) has focused on middle childhood and adolescence with little attention to young children. 'Additionally, the results of these studies often conflict because role taking and moral judgment have been treated as single dimensions rather than as summary variables representing multidimensional constructs', p. 102. The three dimensions of role taking (perceptual, cognitive, and affective) and two dimensions of moral judgment (intentionality and restitution) were studied in 72 children aged from five to seven years. Each S was tested on 32 role taking items and 24 moral judgment items. There was a significant correlation (r = .36, p<.001) between role taking and moral judgment. Ss high and low on moral judgment and those high and low on role taking demonstrated significant relations between cognitive role taking and moral judgment (p<.05 for cognitive role taking stories and p<.01 for the cognitive role taking game) and border-line significance between total moral judgment and role taking (p<.10). Seven-year-olds performed at higher levels than the five-year-olds on all areas of role taking except the perceptual tasks, and further on total moral judgment and intentionality but not on restitution. No sex differences were observed on the moral judgment dimensions. However boys performed significantly better than girls on the perceptual role taking task. The results receive substantiation from the findings reported by Irwin (1973) who employed similar measures . . . 'This study highlights the need for precise definitions of moral judgment and role taking and the use of common instruments if research in this area is to make any progress', (Ambron and Irwin, *op. cit.*, p. 102). (Details follow.)

Mischio (1976) in an investigation of the triadic relationship between moral judgment, role-taking and social participation confirmed that cognitive-functioning was essential to moral growth. Although the triadic relationship was not confirmed, role-taking was found to be significantly related to moral judgment. Young retarded children proceeded through the Piagetian moral stages at a slower rate, corresponding to their stage of Piagetian intellectual development rather than CA. (Details follow.)

To determine if there were a relationship between moral judgment, causal thinking and moral reasoning, Brooks-Walsh and Sullivan (1973) tested 28 children of mean age nine years two months and a mean IQ of 115.7 on Piaget's items for the rules of the games of marbles to determine the level of moral judgment; A General Reasoning Task; and the Causal Judgment Task (Laurendeau and Pinard, 1962). A significant relationship was computed between the general reasoning task and the causal judgment task with no significant relationship being observed between general reasoning and moral judgment. Likewise, no significant results were yielded between the relationship of causal judgment and moral judgment. (Details follow.)

Hardeman (1972) among 142 first grade children using moral reasoning stories from Piaget (1932) and conservation (Almy *et al.*, 1966) and class-inclusion (Miller, 1966) tasks, found no direct relation between conservation and moral reasoning and class-inclusion and moral reasoning, but identified greater variation in moral reasoning scores for children who succeeded in all conservation tasks, than for those who succeeded in none: suggesting that the ability to give structure of an operational kind to inanimate visible objects may be a prerequisite to the ability to give a corresponding structure to moral situations. (Details are given later.)

Early conceptions of positive justice as related to the development of logical operations were examined by Damon (1975) in 50 children within the age range from four to eight years. A 'positive justice' interview (Ugurel-Semin, 1952; and Kohlberg (1958) and five of Piaget's concrete-operational mathematical and physical tasks were given. Results demonstrated (a) a strong association between the level of a child's reasoning about positive justice and the level of his reasoning about mathematical and physical problems; (b) 'in the great majority of Ss, there was close synchrony (i.e. little segregation) between parallel levels of reasoning in the two domains; and (c) there was little evidence in support of the notion that one type of reasoning (e.g. mathematical– physical) provides a necessary condition for the development of the other (e.g. justice)'. (Details follow.)

Breznitz and Kugelmass (1967) suggested that there was a cognitive principle underlying the use of intentionality in moral judgment through four successive stages. A highly-developed principle of inten-tionality could allow abstract activity which can be seen to be synonymous with Inhelder and Piaget's 'formal operations'. Johnson (1962), however, found concreteness and abstractness to be only slightly related to moral judgment responses. It should perhaps be pointed out that the measure used was Gorham's Proverbs Test. (See also Stephens, Miller and McLaughlin, 1969 and Chapter 7 'The Development of Reasoning among Handicapped Children' in Modgil, 1974).

To examine moral judgments, behaviour and cognitive style in young children, Schleifer and Douglas (1973) carried out two studies. Study one comprised 29 subjects, mean age six years eight months and study two involved 72 children ranging in age from three years two months to six years. Children in study one were read Piaget-type stories (1932), administered the reflection-impulsivity test (Kagan *et al.*, 1964); the Peabody Picture Vocabulary Test (Dunn, 1965); the field-independence test (Karp and Konstadt, 1963); and for each child the teachers completed the Pupil Personality Evaluation Form (Sutherland and Goldschmid, 1971). Children in study two were shown films designed to test moral judgments adapted from Piaget-type stories. The Beller Rating Scale, the Early Childhood Familiar Figures Test, and the Early Childhood Embedded Figures Test were administered, the latter two patterned after Banta (1968). Among the six-year-old children, the level of moral maturity related to the cognitive styles of reflection – impulsivity and field dependence – independence, but not to verbal intelligence. Ss characterized as immature in their moral judgments tended to be impulsive and more field-dependent. Children performing at the higher levels of moral judgment were rated as more attentive and more reflective by their teachers. Pre-school subjects performing at the higher levels of moral maturity were seen as less aggressive. (Details follow.)

In order to assess the notion of generalized cognitive developmental levels, the generality of altruistic behaviour, and the degree to which cognitive-developmental level predicted altruistic behaviour, Rushton and Wiener (1975) studied the interrelationships between a number of age-related cognitive tasks (role taking ability, egocentricity, cognitive complexity, and conservation) and three different behavioural measures of altruism in seven- and 11-year-old children (N = 60). Highly significant age differences were computed on all cognitive tasks. Likewise, the 11-year-olds were significantly more altruistic than were the seven-year-olds. Some generality emerged across altruistic be- haviours. However, no such generalities emerged either between the cognitive measures themselves or between the cognitive measures and altruism (Details follow.)

A cognitive-developmental analysis of achievement and moral judgments was undertaken by Weiner and Peter (1973) among 300 Ss aged four to 18 years in 16 situations. The situations varied according to the intent (effort) and ability of the person being judged and in the objective consequences of the behaviour. Results showed that the three variables of intent, ability, and outcome were employed systematically in both achievement and moral appraisal. Highly significant age trends were also computed. In both the achievement and the moral conditions subjective intent replaced objective outcome as the main determinant of judgment. 'However, after the age of 12 years in the achievement context objective outcome again became the more important deter- minant of evaluation. It is contended that society reinforces this more "primitive" developmental stage. The sequence of evaluative stages in the moral and achievement situations was identical across racial and sex groupings . . . the data strongly supported the position that achieve- ment strivings were maintained primarily by social reward while moral behaviour is controlled primarily by social punishment', p. 290. (Details appear later.)

More recently, in a study by Salili, Maehr, and Gillmore (1976) entitled, 'Achievement and morality: a cross-cultural analysis of causal attribution and evaluation', the authors were intent to determine how sociocultural factors might influence the judgmental patterns outlined by Weiner and Peter (1973) by essentially replicating their study in the manifestly different cultural context provided in Iran. Important discrepancies with Weiner and Peter were found by Salili, Maehr and Gillmore which the latter authors attributed to sociocultural factors. 'However, the cognitive-developmental framework proved generally valuable in working toward a comparative understanding of social-ization patterns extant in the two cultures', p. 327. (Details follow.)

Weiner's (1973) aim was to document the role that effort plays as a perceived determinant of achievement performance and achievement evaluation. He elaborates that this involves a cognitive-developmental analysis of achievement motivation and some proposed similarities between the development of achievement striving and the development of morality. He argues that 'a moral social system, as envisioned by Karl Marx, and a moral individual, as characterized by Jean Piaget, acknowledge the inadequacies of employing ability rather than effort (intent) ascriptions as the basis for social evaluation'. Weiner considers that we must turn our attention from the measurement of ability toward the analysis of intention and the promotion of effort.

That twins with relatively more mature judgments on the Baldwin measure (1970) would show relative to their co-twins, better cognitive functioning (WPPSI) and relatively longer attention in play and a more stable temperament (Wilson *et al.*, 1971) was studied by Brown, Matheny, and Wilson (1973) in 16 pairs of twins. Generally, the responses were comparable to Baldwins' kindergarten sample. Fourteen pairs were discordant on the kindness measure. 'For the discordant pairs, WPPSI intelligence test scores were analyzed for within-pair differences. The twins with less adultlike responses on the measure scored lower than their co-twins on several verbal and performance subtests. These twins, as reported by their mothers, were also relatively more temperamental and less attentive than their co-twins'. The authors discussed the results in terms of Piaget's concept of the parallel development of the cognition of the impersonal and interpersonal worlds. (Details follow.)

Seltzer (1969) addressed his inquiry to the development of the child's ability to conceptualize time, and its relationship to the development of his ability to make mature moral judgments. Further-more, he investigated the hypothesis that the child's moral conduct is significantly related to his ability to accurately perceive the passage of time. Both hypotheses were substantiated. In Brennan's (1962) research high perspective (the cognitive aspect of social adaptation) was associated with low 'moral realism', though this was significant only at the nine-and-a-half year level.

(Details of the approach of Kohlberg and his colleagues to cognitive aspects of moral development are given later.)

(Further details of the earlier studies are given in Modgil, 1974).

ii. Social factors

Boehm and Nass (1962) failed to confirm their hypothesis that middle class children will be more concerned with underlying motives and working class children with the amount of physical injury in response to a physically aggressive situation. However, the authors cast doubt on the assigned socioeconomic status of the children in the sample. Boehm, in her 1962 study, revealed class differences to the extent that working class children (at two intelligence levels) showed earlier peer reciprocity and adult independence than upper middle class children. However, with respect to distinctions between intention and outcome of an action, upper middle class children develop earlier than those of working class background. Harris (1970) concluded that both White and Negro children of higher social class groups were more mature in moral attitudes than children of lower social class groups. When subjects were classified into rich, middle class and poor groups, Ugurel-Semin (1952) found that the poorer children were generous as often as the rich, more often equalitarian and less often selfish. Bull (1969) found throughout his research with children aged seven to 17 years that for boys, socioeconomic class had a close association with moral judgments. Likewise, Rawan (1975) reported SES to be positively and significantly related to moral maturity and immanent justice. (Details have been discussed earlier).

Ugurel-Semin (*op. cit.*) also demonstrated that the child of the larger family was moderately more often generous than the only child. With respect to peer group conformity, Morris (1958) revealed differences between Grammar School and Secondary Modern pupils: Grammar School pupils indicated less conformity to friends.

The results of the Boehm (1962) research did not support Piaget's belief that maturity of moral judgment increases as the child becomes independent of adults and achieves peer reciprocity. There was little relation between responses involving right and wrong and responses revealing adult independence. Bandura and McDonald (1963) report the influence of the adult of the child: children's judgments were modifiable through cues given by the adult models. McKechnie (1971) interprets his findings that the child learns to evaluate bad behaviour before good, in terms of the disciplinary approaches used by parents and teachers. Similar contentions were expressed by Piaget. From 45 correlations of dominating, possessive and ignoring parental attitudes with maturity of moral judgments, Johnson (1962) reports significant findings for only eight. MacRae (1954) did not generally find retardation in moral development in children whose parents were authoritarian but he reports associations between parental authority and 'violation of norms regarding lying and stealing'. Piaget's contention that the authoritarianism of the adult retards moral development was therefore not entirely upheld by MacRae and Johnson.

A reflection on the possible differences in social development between American and Swiss children is offered by Boehm (1957). She reports that the American child becomes less parent-dependent and more peer-dependent at an earlier age. As a result, 'the American child's conscience becomes less egocentric and interiorizes earlier than does that of the Swiss child'. Also worthy of note in this section are Najarian-Svajian (1966) and Jahoda (1958).

Kohlberg (1958, 1964) reports that children involved in more extensive social participation (middle class and popular children) tended to be more mature in moral judgment.

(Further details of the earlier studies are given in Modgil, 1974.)

iii. Sex differences

Durkin (1960) addressed her inquiry specifically to investigating sex differences in children's concepts of justice, but statistically significant differences were not revealed. She concluded that, unlike other aspects of socialization, moral training pressures are not exerted differently towards boys and girls. Whiteman and Kosier (1964), in their investigation relating to age, sex, IQ and personal-experiential variables and the development of children's moral judgments, hypothesized that 'girls because of maturational advantages during later childhood and parental and social pressures relating to impulse control, would manifest superior ability to formulate mature judgments when compared with boys of the same age'. The authors report a trend in the hypothesized direction but it was not significantly supported. Boehm and Nass (1962); Irwin and Moore (1971); Jensen and Hughston (1971); Medinnus (1962); and Ugurel-Semin (1952) all report no highly significant differences between responses from boys and girls, although some trends in favour of girls were found. Morris (1958) reported generally no differences between boys' and girls' responses to problem-situations. However, some tendency for girls' values to be slightly more developed than boys', and a greater discrepancy between 'should' and 'would' were noted. Grinder (1964) found some greater sophistication for girls with respect to resistance to temptation at early ages, but these differences were eliminated by 11 or 12 years. Grinder elaborates: 'behavioural and cognitive characteristics of the mature conscience especially in boys may develop independently of one another'. Girls showed greater moral maturity than boys in a study reported by Porteus and Johnson (1965); their responses also revealed less consistency with respect to the 'cognitive' and 'affective' stories. Bull (1969) found girls in advance of boys in all the areas of moral judgment studied.

Magowan and Lee (1970) consider that differences found by investigators between the sexes 'may be an artifact of the measuring instrument'. (See also Kohlberg 1964b; and Keasey, 1972.)

(Further details of the earlier studies were given in Modgil, 1974.)

iv. Religious influences

With respect to recognizing the distinction between the motivation and the results of an action Boehm (1962b) confirmed that 'Catholic children, regardless of socioeconomic class or intelligence level, scored higher at an earlier age than public school children'. She concludes that this difference can be explained by the encouragement given to Catholic children towards confession and the insight gained into the motivation of actions. Some superiority was shown by Jewish children compared to Catholic children in response to the 'Fight' story in Boehm's 1963 study. Boehm explained this in terms of the greater emphasis on guilt made by exponents of Catholicism. The immature responses of the Jewish children to the 'Scout' story were attributed to the strong traditional belief in authority and the Jewish child therefore chose to follow the advice of a teacher. Boehm's (1963) findings were interpreted as reflecting the influence of specific religious/moral philosophies, 'and she did not explore differences in educational practice or attitudes to discipline. Her general conclusion was that the schools produced variations in the "content of conscience". But even this vague statement is subject to caution as subsequent research indicates that the concept of intentionality is greatly influenced by subtle differences in methodology (e.g., Armsby, 1971)', McCann and Bell (1975, p. 63).

To examine the development of moral concepts in two types of schools of different educational orientation, one based on the theory of Freinet (1960), the other conventional Catholic schools, McCann and Bell's study involved two matched samples of 20 French-Canadian children aged between six years seven months and 11 years three months. The groups were matched on: CA, IQ, school grade, sex, religious affiliation, occupational level of father, and number of children in family and birth order of subject. Four moral conflict stories were used, adapted from the stories employed by Piaget (1932). The stories differed in the presence or absence of authority figures and peers, and were set either in the home or the school. Children attending the Freinet school demonstrated the more higher levels of moral judgments for all stories combined. Stories involving peers only elicited more mature judgments than those involving authority figures. Democratic group self-discipline was encouraged more in children from Freinet schools and provided varied role taking opportunities. Such practices enhanced moral development. (Details follow.)

While a higher percentage of Catholic children made intentionality judgments to the standard Piaget stories in Armsby's (1971) study, there was no significant difference between the percentage of Catholic and public school children who made intentionality judgments in response to the revised stories. Armsby offers the explanation that in the standard Piaget stories, the supposedly purposive act was often accidental, damage resulting while a child was disobeying his mother. The revised stories, on the other hand, compare clear accidental behaviour with clear intentional behaviour; obedience is therefore not an intervening factor. Armsby hypothesizes that the greater emphasis on obedience and the more authoritarian approach to education in the Catholic schools sensitized the Catholic school children to make judgments in terms of whether a child was obeying his mother or not. Obedience was not so important to the public school children, so when obedience factors were minimized there were no differences. Armsby concludes that Catholic training does not foster earlier mature moral judgment although it may more successfully train obedience. Armsby also criticizes Boehm's samples in that the Catholic and Public school samples were drawn from two distinctly different areas. MacRae's (1954) sample of parochial school children showed more moral realism with regard to authority, a more extended belief in immanent justice and selected more severe punishment for breaking of norms and rules. (Kohlberg, 1964, found no differences in the development of moral judgment between Protestants and Catholics.)

Whiteman and Kosier (1964) found slight trends in favour of members of Sunday Schools and Scout groups relating to moral judgments, but they were not statistically creditable. Bull (1969) found 'scattered, unpatterned and inconsistent' associations between moral judgments and church affiliation. The 'lying' situation and the 'value of life' test elicited the strongest associations.

Pertinent here also is Attfield's (1976) paper the aim of which was to discuss the degree of moral readiness required for the satisfactory comprehension of Biblical material — 'what is needed to prevent certain crudely understood Scriptural ideas from distorting ethical development'. Referring to Goldman's (1964) research he focuses on the finding that the moral development found in responses to religious material, correlates with the Piagetian schema of growth in general moral thinking. Attfield considers that psychological inquiry into means to achieve the prerequisites of moral development, is as necessary to Religious Education as it is to Moral Education. Further, 'to come to Biblical material . . . too early may impede the growth of moral thinking. Certain moral criticisms of sacred history are precluded at early stages in moral thought. This could be to the possible disadvantage of children later, in not being able to accept or reject belief in God on proper grounds and for relevant reasons because the children's minds had already been confused or prejudiced when they had been subjected to such stories as the Burning Bush or Crossing the Red Sea too soon in terms of their coming to reflect ethically. And this sad result, illustrated by Goldman's findings in applying Piagetian

psychology to the Bible basically springs from the conceptual requirements of moral rationality,' p. 32. (Goldman's work is discussed more
appropriately in Volume 4 in the present series *Piagetian Research*.)
    (Further details of the earlier studies are given in Modgil, 1974.)

v. Consistency across moral attributes

    Piaget speculated about the developmental relations between child-
ren's behavioural resolutions of actual moral conflicts and cognitive
processes and regarded further research into the question as of
'fundamental importance in human psychology'. Attention has frequently been drawn to the necessity for evidence concerning the
relation of judgments upon hypothetical moral situations and actual
behaviour in concrete moral situations (Aronfreed, 1961; Bull, 1969;
Grinder, 1964; Medinnus, 1966; Pittel and Mendelsohn, 1966; Ugurel-
Semin, 1952; Wright, 1971). An extensive early study by Hartshorne
and May (1928-30) involved the devising of ingenious tests to measure
actual moral conduct in concrete situations together with tests to assess
moral conduct. There was considerable doubt expressed at the time of
the analysis concerning a general factor in moral development, but
Burton (1963) in a re-analysis of the data has reported more generality
than was first indicated. Peck and Havighurst (1960), in a longitudinal
study involving the population of 'Prairie City', produced evidence for
generality rather than specificity in moral behaviour. Basing the study
upon a 'motivational definition of character', it was found that
inconsistency was characteristic of all subjects but that, nevertheless,
there was a consistent pattern of behaviour which was maintained
throughout maturation. However, there have generally been few studies
investigating an individual's theoretical morality and the way he
actually behaves in moral conflict situations. It is obvious that
feasibility and reliability are the inhibiting factors. A recent attempt
involving the relationship between moral judgment, egocentrism, and
altruistic behaviour was undertaken by Rubin and Schneider (1973) in 55
seven-year-old children who were administered cognitive measures of
communicative egocentrism and moral judgment together with providing two opportunities to demonstrate altruistic behaviour − (a) to
donate sweets to poor children and (b) to assist a younger child
complete a task. 'Success on the two cognitive measures was positively
correlated with the incidence of altruistic behaviour in both altruism
conditions. With mental age partialled out the correlations between the
cognitive measures and donating candy were significantly lower than
the correlation between the cognitive measures and helping. The
difference between the correlations was accounted for by the fact that
only in the candy donation were there cues that helped the subject
attend the possibility of emitting an altruistic act. Finally, the

communicative and moral judgment measures were significantly correlated', p. 661. (Details appear later.) Rubin and Schneider assert, 'Apparently only the classical Hartshorne and May (1930) study has related moral cognition and altruistic behaviour. However, the correlations between their eight subscales of "moral knowledge" and "helpful behaviour" (Hartshorne and May, 1930, p. 203) were generally lower than those found in the present study. We believe that our higher correlations were, in part, a function of differences in the measures used to define moral judgment. In the present study, only Lee's (1971) three "authority vs. altruism" and her three "peer vs. altruism" situations were read to the children. Thus the measure of moral judgment was specific to altruism. However, Hartshorne and May's moral knowledge measures were general, tapping many aspects of moral cognition (e.g., honesty, good manners, bravery, and prejudice). The present results are consistent with more recent research which indicates a positive relationship between levels of moral judgment and other moral behaviours, e.g., resistance to temptation (Krebs, 1967) and children's adherence to rules in the absence of authority (Kohlberg, 1964)', p. 664. (Details follow.)

An argument for the plausibility of an intrinsic altruistic motive is presented by Hoffman (1975) based on psychological research and inferences about human evolution. A theoretical model for the development of this motive is outlined. 'The central idea of the model is that a person's empathic response to another person's distress, interacting with his cognitive sense of the other person, provides the basis for a motive independent of egoistic motivation to help the other person. Empathic distress and three steps in the development of a sense of the other are discussed, along with empirical evidence for the approximate ages at which they occur. A theoretical account of the interaction between these affective and cognitive processes is then presented, followed by an attempt to assess the evidence for the theory.' (Details follow.)

'Rationale content', an assumed cognitive determinant of resistance to deviation in children, was investigated by LaVoie (1974) using a standard punishment paradigm with 7-, 9-, and 11-year-old children. The data suggested that level of moral judgment influences moral behaviour. (Details follow.) (See also Schleifer and Douglas, 1973.)

Ugurel-Semin (1952) was interested in Piaget's hypothesis that the child would demonstrate moral judgment in action far earlier than in speech and devised his 'sharing investigation, designed, among other purposes, to assess the relationship between moral behaviour and moral judgment. Among the children who shared equally and children classified as generous, some consistency between moral conduct and moral judgment was apparent. Grinder (1964) concluded that children's resistance to temptation occurs more as a result of social-learning experiences than from changes in the cognitive structure and that maturation of the cognitive processes does not guarantee alteration of behavioural habits established by social reinforcement. He therefore considers 'that behavioural and cognitive characteristics . . . may develop independently of one another'. Medinnus (1966) reported results indicating little association between behaviour and verbal responses. (See also Stephens, Miller and McLaughlin, 1969.) Porteus and Johnson (1965), using stories to measure cognitive and affective aspects of moral development, together with sociometric ratings to assess behaviour, found a significant relation between responses to cognitive and affective measures, especially for boys, although these were 'not of any great magnitude'. The relation between the affective measure and nominations for moral behaviour was insignificant. It was concluded that popularity was a major factor in determining moral nominations. The authors drew attention to the need to develop reliable measures of actual behaviour and cited the contribution of Grinder (*op. cit.*). Ward (1965) found small positive correlations between moral judgment and moral knowledge.

On the basis of prior research (e.g. Boehm, 1962; Piaget, 1932; Ugurel-Semin, 1952), Dreman (1976) 'predicted that both reciprocity, like justifications, and the ability to judge moral judgment stories on the basis of intentionality would increase with age as the child develops an autonomous morality based on cooperation and reciprocity,' p. 187. In an earlier study, Dreman and Greenbaum (1973) found 'that middle class kindergarten boys donated more in a situation where the recipient would know who gave the gift, thus permitting reciprocity in the future, than in a situation in which the recipient would not know who gave the gift.' The purpose of Dreman's study was therefore to extend the earlier work by systematically 'investigating the joint effects of prior help and future expectations of reciprocity.' The study employed a 3 x 3 x 2 factorial design which included three age levels (ages six to seven, nine to 10 and 12–13); 'three levels of prior help; and two levels of expectations of future reciprocity.' The three levels of prior reward by the intended recipient included 'Recipient to S, Recipient to Other, and No Donation', the two levels of expectations of future reward from this recipient, 'S Identified and S Anonymous.' Following developmental expectations, donations over all conditions increased as a function of age. 'On the basis of social learning theory it was predicted that Ss would contribute the most in the condition in which they both had received a reward in the past and had expectations of obtaining reciprocation in the future (Recipient to S, S Identified). Contrary to this prediction Ss contributed the second smallest amount of candies in this condition, and an interaction was obtained between prior reward and future expectation of reward conditions,' p. 186. A relation between moral judgment and behaviour was found.

(Further details of the earlier studies are given in Modgil, 1974.)

vi. Investigations within different cultures

Dennis (1943) contended that moral development with respect to immanent justice was universal in all societies but that differences in ages at which moral maturity is reached are due to a specifically unidentifiable variety of cultural factors. Liu (1950) in an investigation involving Chinese and non-Chinese children concluded that decreasing moral realism is not due entirely to increase in age. Havighurst and Neugarten (1955) considered that their findings, from the responses given by children from six Indian tribes, supported Piaget's hypothesis that children in primitive societies become more rigid in their moral development as they increase in age, due to greater constraints being placed upon them. However, when investigating differing degrees of acculturation, Havighurst and Neugarten found no significant differences in immanent justice responses and they concluded that environmental factors within each culture should be investigated in depth rather than measuring the degree of influence from modern societies. Dennis (*op. cit.*) found a decrease with age in belief in immanent justice in his Hopi Indian subjects, and Jahoda (1958) confirms the prevalence of immanent justice responses among young African children but states that if 'acts of God' are included as immanent justice responses (Piaget is rather ambiguous in this respect) then the decrease among older children is less marked. He considers that neither his African sample nor Havighurst and Neugarten's Indian subjects were entirely representative of a primitive population, and further, that Havighurst and Neugarten's claim to have confirmed Piaget's hypothesis was due to a faulty methodology and their evidence must therefore be discounted. Njarian-Svajian (1966) reports cultural influences affecting the development of moral realism.

Although all studies carried out other than in Geneva can be considered within the category of investigations within different cultures, mention is made of Boehm (1957) as she specifically addressed her inquiry to a comparison between American and Swiss children in 'content of conscience' according to differences in the cultural pattern. Harris (1970), in her comparison between White and Negro boys, concluded that social class had a slightly greater and more consistent influence on maturity of moral attitudes than race. Attention should also be drawn to Seltzer's 1969 study involving a Negro sample.

Evidence for or against cultural factors stimulating or retarding age trends of development on the Piaget dimensions remains inconclusive.

(Further details of the earlier studies are given in Modgil, 1974.)

vii. Training techniques in the inducement of moral concepts

Piaget has shown that age changes in moral judgment occur but he has not indicated exactly what influence various factors have in producing this change. Various training studies have attempted to accelerate or change the orientation of the developmental sequence, thereby aiming to determine the crucial factors involved in maturation.

Bandura and MacDonald (1963) predicted that children's moral orientations can be altered and even reversed by 'the manipulation of response-reinforcement contingencies and by the provision of appropriate social models'. The experimental conditions utilizing adult modelling procedures alone were the most effective in modifying children's judgments as opposed to a combination of modelling/reinforcement and conditioning alone. In a replication of Bandura and MacDonald, Cowan *et al.* (1969) concluded that neither their study nor that of Bandura and MacDonald could be used to affirm or deny Piaget's sequential stages of moral development. Dworkin (1968), in a comparison of training techniques involving imitation, imitation/reinforcement and cognitive information, found that cognitive information was the most successful in promoting an intentional moral orientation. Further, although imitation and reinforcement were successful for younger children, the effectiveness was lost as the child gains understanding of the concept being taught. Crowley (1968) gave evidence to the effect that training which employed stories with moral content proved to be more effective than training using non-moral stories, but all the training situations used were effective in the acquisition of mature moral judgment. However, attention is drawn by the author to Turiel's explanation (1966) for the success: that it is dealing with a specific response; and further, that changes resulting from training must be interpreted as an isolated change rather than in a mental structure or stage. The failure of the discussion method to produce better results than mere labelling is explained in Piaget's terms: that assimilation of information can only take place if the relevant cognitive schemata are available.

However, Jensen and Larm (1970), in a study with kindergarten children, designed to train the concept of intentionality, asserted that 'a brief training programme can immediately produce more mature moral judgments'. They report that a discussion-type training was superior when an understanding of the underlying principle is required, and, due to the necessity for trained subjects to state verbal explanations, it seemed that the concepts were understood. Jensen and Hughston (1971), working with four- and five-year-old children, who patterned their inquiry after the programmes used by Crowley, and Jensen and

Larm and related the training to independence of sanctions, report training to be more effective for the older children. It was considered that older children are closer to moving towards higher levels of thought and are therefore more able to benefit from training. It was further acknowledged that training produced changes in moral reasoning only about the moral issues introduced.

In a study entitled: 'Stability of training effects on intentionality in moral judgment in children', Glassco, Milgram, and Youniss (1970), located 80 subjects from Crowley's (1968) study. 'Subjects who consistently judged moral acts in terms of objective consequences rather than the subjective intentions of the agents, shifted markedly to a subjective basis following training on paired stories in which the objective consequences were equalized. The primary effect of training on judgmental style six months later with several different series of moral stories was on the centering — decentering process. The long-term effects of training were more consistent with a Piagetian stage — dependent conceptualization than with a superficial verbal response set', p. 360.

A conflict procedure in which reliance on adult values was opposed to reliance on damage as a measure of blame was reported by Peterson, Peterson and Finley (1974) to enhance second grade subjects' use of intention in making moral judgments of story pairs. Conflict had no effect on the judgments of pre-school children or adults. Question wording affected adults but not second grade children. (Details are given later.)

In a study by Le Furgy and Woloshin (1969) it was found that adolescents of both sexes and varying moral orientation will respond to immediate, face-to-face peer pressures with dramatic shifts away from their initial orientations. The authors emphasize that this does not imply long-term changes.

(Further details of the earlier studies are given in Modgil, 1974.)

viii. Methodological issues

Pittel and Mendelsohn (1966), in a review and critique relating to the measurement of moral values, enumerate conceptual and methodological weaknesses. The authors consider that a number of instruments assess knowledge of 'legal, moral or ethical standards rather than the individual's attitude toward these standards'. With this emphasis on information it can be speculated that this may account for the correlations with measures of intelligence and the increase of scores with age. The scoring of some measures is based on 'normative or other evaluative standards of "correctness" determined by societally defined criteria'. The tendency is therefore to assign high scores to those responses in agreement with the norms established by the investigators.

Pittel and Mendelsohn further perpend that 'subjects are asked to evaluate abstract acts independent of the setting in which such acts occur and in which contextual factors may serve to mitigate or justify their wrongness'. Subjects are often asked to respond to situations in the test context which are unlikely to be met in 'real life'. The specificity of the investigations is also queried by the authors: 'The content typically sampled is based on categories of conventional morality or on the author's theoretical preoccupation. Many dimensions of behaviour which are potentially morally salient are thereby excluded'. The standardization, validity and reliability of the majority of the instruments can also be questioned. The authors in conclusion state that the problems seem to be the result of an 'insufficient effort to conceptualize the nature of moral values and their relation to behaviour. Perhaps the greatest single shortcoming underlying each of the specific criticisms discussed is the failure to view evaluative attitudes as subjective phenomena whose measurement is best achieved independent of a concern with the relationship of these attitudes to conventional and normative standards of moral valuation. It is important to assess at an individual level the content, strength and patterning of subjective attitudes of evaluation *per se*. Whether these attitudes would be approved or disapproved by society is a subsequent question which need not be considered in the construction of measures of evaluative attitudes'.

Purcell (1958), in a critique related to projective tests in general, also considers that defects in the experimental conceptualization of the problem can be causal to the inadequacies of the results.

Magowan and Lee (1970) in an investigation involving three story variables, conclude that the projective method 'is liable to serious imperfections and more stringent controls are urged for its future use'. (Details appear in Modgil, 1974.)

e. Relations with Other Theories

In a Paper entitled, 'Durkheim and others: some philosophical influences on Piaget's theory of moral development', Craig (1976) maintains, 'Beside Bergson and Rousseau, the thinker who influenced Piaget's view on moral development is Emile Durkheim, and the remainder of this paper will investigate the similarities between Durkheim's and Piaget's views on moral development. Piaget has been criticized for his apparent disregard for academic disciplines, for he often utilizes the method of the psychologist and at other times that of the sociologist. His interest in sociology is evident when he writes: "Whether we wish it or not, the questions we have had to discuss in connection with child morality take us to the very heart of the problems studied by contemporary sociology and social psychology, (Piaget, p. 327)". And one sociologist he has in mind is Durkheim'. (Details are given later.)

Meacham (1975) considered certain problems of moral development within a dialectical framework. 'Following a brief introduction to the dialectical model and its potential for describing mature, adult thought, the model is used to illuminate the close relations between moral judgments and the maintenance of self-esteem, and the resulting dialectical morality, one of mediation or compromise, is described ... developmental considerations, in particular the interdependence of individual and socio-historical changes are discussed', p. 159. In his concluding remarks Meacham maintained, 'Indeed there is much that can be described in dialectical terms in the theories of Freud, Mead, and Piaget, as Hogan (1974) has pointed out. Hogan (1973) has also advanced a multidimensional model of moral conduct, in which moral maturity is defined as optimal placement on each of several dimensions — this model is similar in spirit to the morality of mediation proposed ... present paper does not suggest a theory, but merely emphasizes certain aspects of moral development which are made apparent from a dialectical perspective. In particular, the interdependence of subject and object in the process of moral judgment is seen in the reciprocal interaction of moral judgment and self-esteem, and in the developmental synthesis of moral principles and self-concept within the individual. Second, a mature, dialectical morality of mediation is one in which the individual recognizes his own participation in his moral judgments, and further recognizes contradictions between moral principles and seeks to resolve these in higher syntheses. Finally, a dialectical approach emphasizes the interaction of the individual and the cultural-historical context, with the potential for development in the moral process continuing throughout the life span', (*ibid.*, pp. 168–169).

f. Kohlberg's Extension of Piaget's Schema

i. Introduction

As has been evidenced in the previous section, throughout the years following Piaget's (1932) publication, research on moral judgment has not essentially digressed from the Piagetian framework. Although Piaget's work was not the only influence on Kohlberg's comprehensive empirical research considerable inspiration was obtained from Piaget's pioneering efforts. Kohlberg, using an elaborate and detailed set of hypothetical moral dilemmas has made even more refined distinctions within an extended sequence of moral developmental stages. Over the years a 'typology of definite and universal levels' has been formulated on the basis of subject's reasoning from the dilemmas in which obedience to laws, rules or authority conflict with the needs and welfare of other people. Intent to acquire moral evaluation in addition to moral judgments, Kohlberg has probed the thinking underlying the choices of action with a series of questions. Kohlberg has therefore developed Piaget's explanation of heteronomy and autonomy as an account of moral development and sees it as more extended in developmental time and more cognitively complex than internalization of external values. Kohlberg found elements of Piaget's heteronomy in his stages 1–4, and elements of Piaget's autonomy in stages 2–6. He puts greater emphasis on the cognitive-developmental approach to stages than Piaget and considers that cognitive factors predominate whereas Piaget stressed the social determinants.

Weinrich (1975) denotes the fact that Piaget's influence in the 'moral field' is the result largely of one work, based on a single research project and that it is not often that reference is made, when discussing moral development, to the much more elaborated thinking of Piaget in other areas of cognitive growth, 'either in critiques or in attempts to formulate more advanced conceptions of moral growth'. Weinrich considers that Kohlberg does to some extent consider some of the formal qualities of Piaget's general system and 'he also returns to

Baldwin in his conception of the early modes of thinking.' More than Piaget, Kohlberg lays stress on the egocentric, the 'syntelic' aspects of the earlier stage of Baldwin's scheme, the inability of the child to differentiate between subject and object, between ideas and the objects to which they refer, and secondly, the inability to differentiate the meaning of an object to the self from its meaning to others. The second stage he regards as 'instrumental thinking', the differentiation of means and ends, and of subject and object. This conception is closer to Piaget's general formulation of cognitive growth than it is to his work on moral growth.

Weinrich further analyses that Kohlberg's first two stages do have some similarity to Piaget's heteronomous and autonomous stages, 'but depart from them in some important aspects'. She continues 'It is difficult to demonstrate the relationship of Piaget's third stage to Kohlberg's data; it is an oversimplification to say that the latter four types are subtypes of an equity-based morality because equity is firstly only one factor of many in each of the stages, and secondly equity is too general a term for the rather fine differentiations of different types of justice which were found to develop at the later stages. But it is clear that Kohlberg's work must be regarded as a confirmation and extension of Piaget's thinking, rather than a refutation of it'. Weinrich in extension of her consideration of the relationship of Kohlberg and Piaget examines the concept of stages and the nature and processes of stage development, allowing the correspondence between Kohlberg's moral development and Piaget's cognitive development to be examined. (Details are given later in this section.)

Kohlberg (1964) promotes the view that findings do not support 'the notion of Piaget that there is a general trend of moral development in childhood from an authoritarian to a democratic ethic, although they do support the notion that the child's earliest morality is oriented to obedience, punishment, and impersonal forces, and that it progresses toward more internal and subjective values'. Further, Piaget's theory of a shift from unilateral to mutual respect also has suggested a number of factors which would be associated with development on all the dimensions he has described. Kohlberg considers that research findings have not supported Piaget's theory with regard to these factors. Peer group participation although an important factor associated with general development of moral judgment, has not been found to be specifically associated with advance on measures of intentionality or reciprocity (Kohlberg, 1964a; Breznitz and Kugelmass, 1967). Parental democracy or permissiveness has not been found to relate to development on the Piaget dimensions (Johnson, 1962; MacRae, 1954).

Kohlberg further focuses on a third qualification introduced into Piaget's interpretation of his dimensions of development by research results: 'Piaget's dimensions do not represent definite unitary stages which cut across the separate aspects of moral judgment. Within age and IQ groups, a child who is at the autonomous stage on one aspect of morality (for example, intentionality) is not especially likely to be autonomous on another aspect of morality, for example, naturalistic justice or reciprocity (MacRae, 1954; Johnson 1962)'. Prior to expanding on his own research Kohlberg concludes: 'while the results of the Piaget studies provide only limited support for his theory, they do suggest the possibility of uncovering basic trends in the development of moral judgment'.

Kohlberg (1968a) emphasizes that his research suggests that attitudes of rigidity toward game rules seem to decline with age in American children of five years to twelve years, but that attitudes expressing the rigidity or sacredness of moral rules or of laws, increase in this period, rather than decline. From cross-cultural research by Kohlberg and his colleagues, Kohlberg concludes that Piaget is correct in assuming a culturally universal age development of a sense of justice, involving progressing concern for the needs and feelings of others and elaborated conceptions of reciprocity and equality. As this sense of justice develops, however, it reinforces respect for authority and for the rules of adult society; it also reinforces more informal peer norms, since adult institutions have underpinnings of reciprocity, equality of treatment, service to human needs etc.

Kohlberg (*op. cit.*), in order to give full explanation to his theory, places his argument within the context of the various psychological approaches to the broader category of moral development. Commenting that the study of moral development has long been recognized as a key problem area in the social sciences, Kohlberg suggests difficulty in making clear distinctions between moral development and the broader area of social development and socialization. Kohlberg (1964, 1968a, 1969) centres on the limitations of the study of internalized socialization in deciphering the classical problems of moral development: Internalization does not represent a clear dimension of temporal development; experimental measures of resistance to temptation (honesty) do not indicate any clear age trends toward greater occurrence of honesty from the preschool years to adolescence; projective measures of the intensity of guilt or moral anxiety also do not indicate clear age trends, except in terms of rather rapid and cognitively based age changes in the years 8 to 12, and these changes are in the direction of defining moral anxiety as a reaction to moral self-judgement rather than to more diffuse external events. Further, a distinctive set of socialization factors has not been found that can be considered as an antecedent of moral internalization: research results suggest that the conditions which facilitate moral internalization (e.g.

parental warmth) are the same conditions which, in general, facilitate the learning of nonmoral cultural rules and expectations. The findings of Hartshorne's and May's (1928–30) studies of moral character suggested that honest behaviour is determined by situational factors of punishment, reward, group pressures, and group values, rather than by an internal disposition of conscience or character. Kohlberg concludes: 'that to the extent that human resistance to temptation is not general across situations to which a moral rule pertains and must therefore be predicted by purely situational factors, it would not seem to be expedient to describe human behaviour as the result of conscience'.

Research on parental antecedents of guilt and of resistance to temptation has usually indicated that the child-rearing correlates of children's resistance to temptation in one situation are not correlates of resistance in another, and further the child-rearing correlates of projective test measures of guilt have not proved to be correlates of actual moral behaviour. Finally, projective measures of guilt have failed to consistently predict actual resistance to temptation behaviour (reviewed in Kohlberg 1963a, 1964). Kohlberg acknowledges that following Burton's (1963) analysis of honesty, however, it can be agreed that there is some personal consistency in honest behaviour or some determination of honest behaviour by general personality traits. These traits, however, do not seem to be traits of moral conscience but rather a set of ego abilities corresponding to commonsense notions of prudence and will. Findings in this context suggest that honesty can be predicted as successfully from an individual's behaviour in cognitive-task or other nonmoral situations as from situations involving honesty, leading to the implication that the study of moral behaviour in terms of early experiences centering on specifically moral training of honesty, guilt, etc., is less likely to be profitable than is a study of moral behaviour in terms of more general experiences relevant to ego development and ego control in nonmoral contexts.

Kohlberg (*op. cit.*) concludes that a more distinctive focus of analysis centres instead upon the direct study of the development of moral values, judgments and emotions. 'The study of actual conduct becomes relevant to problems of moral development insofar as research is able to find links between the child's conduct and the development of his moral values and emotions. The pursuits of the origin of distinctively moral concepts and emotions in the child; the extent to which the child's development indicates typical or regular trends of change in these concepts and sentiments; the causes of stimulation of these developmental changes and the extent to which these develop-mental changes in moral concepts and attitudes are reflected in developmental changes in the child's moral action under conditions of conflict or temptation', appear to be relevant in connection with moral development.

ii. Kohlberg's Cognitive-Developmental Theory of Moralization

For more than sixteen years, Kohlberg has studied the development of moral judgment and character, primarily by following the same group of 75 boys at three year intervals from early adolescence (10 years) through manhood (up to 28 years) supplemented by a series of studies of development in other cultures and varying environmental conditions. These studies have led to the definition of moral stages as follows derived from responses to hypothetical moral dilemmas, 'deliberately philosophical, some found in medieval works of casuistry'. (As the stages form the basis for full interpretation of Kohlberg's work, Kohlberg's own summary as given in Kohlberg, *passim,* is included.)

'Definition of Moral Stages
I.. Preconventional level

At this level the child is responsive to cultural rules and labels of good and bad, right and wrong, but interprets these labels in terms of either the physical or the hedonistic consequences of action (punishment, reward, exchange of favours), or in terms of the physical power of those who enunciate the rules and labels. The level is divided into the following two stages:

Stage 1: The punishment and obedience orientation. The physical consequences of action determine its goodness or badness regardless of the human meaning or value of these consequences. Avoidance of punishment and unquestioning deference to power are valued in their own right, not in terms of respect for an underlying moral order supported by punishment and authority (the latter being stage 4).

Stage 2: The instrumental relativist orientation. Right action consists of that which instrumentally satisfied one's own needs and occasionally the needs of others. Human relations are viewed in terms like those of the market place. Elements of fairness, of reciprocity, and of equal sharing are present, but they are always interpreted in a physical pragmatic way. Reciprocity is a matter of "you scratch my back and I'll scratch yours", not of loyalty, gratitude, or justice.

II. Conventional level

At this level, maintaining the expectations of the individual's family, group or nation is perceived as valuable in its own right, regardless of immediate and obvious consequences. The attitude is not only one of conformity to personal expectations and social order, but of loyalty to it, of actively maintaining, supporting and justifying the order, and of identifying with the persons or group involved in it. At this level, there are the following two stages:

Stage 3: The interpersonal concordance or "good boy-nice girl" orientation. Good behaviour is that which pleases or helps others and is approved by them. There is much conformity to stereotypical images of what is majority or "natural" behaviour. Behaviour is frequently judged by intention — "he means well" becomes important for the first time. One earns approval by being "nice".

Stage 4: The "law and order" orientation. There is orientation toward authority, fixed rules, and the maintenance of the social order. Right behaviour consists of doing one's duty, showing respect for authority, and maintaining the given social order for its own sake.

III. Postconventional, autonomous, or principled level
At this level, there is a clear effort to define moral values and principles which have validity and application apart from the authority of the groups or persons holding these principles, and apart from the individual's own identification with these groups. This level again has two stages:

Stage 5: The social-contract legalistic orientation, generally with utilitarian overtones. Right action tends to be defined in terms of general individual rights, and standards which have been critically examined and agreed upon by the whole society. There is a clear awareness of the relativism of personal values and opinions and a corresponding emphasis upon procedural rules for reaching consensus. Aside from what is constitutionally and democratically agreed upon, the right is a matter of personal "values" and "opinion". The result is an emphasis upon the "legal point of view", but with an emphasis upon the possibility of changing law in terms of rational considerations of social utility (rather than freezing it in terms of stage 4 "law and order"). Outside the legal realm, free agreement and contract is the binding element of obligation. This is the "official" morality of the American government and constitution.

Stage 6: The universal ethical principle orientation. Right is defined by the decision of conscience in accord with self-chosen ethical principles appealing to logical comprehensiveness, universality, and consistency. These principles are abstract and ethical (the Golden Rule, the categorical imperative); they are not concrete moral rules like the Ten Commandments. At heart, these are universal principles of justice, of the reciprocity and equality of human rights, and of respect for the dignity of human beings as individual persons.'

Porter (1972) refers to speculation by Kohlberg on the possibility of a Stage Seven, based on 'rational mysticism' traditionally examined by religion or metaphysics rather than the combined efforts of psychology and philosophy.

Kohlberg (1971) elaborates that his notions of moral categories are derived from both the Piagetian psychological tradition and from traditional ethical analysis. Piaget's structural analysis of cognitive development is based on dividing cognition into basic categories such as logic, space, time, causality, and number, which define basic kinds of judgments, or relationships, in terms of which any physical experience must be construed: that is, it must be located in spatial and temporal coordinates, considered as the effect of a cause etc. Piaget's cognitive categories derive from Kant's analysis of the categories of pure reason, who also considered an analogous set of categories of pure practical reason, or of action under the mode of freedom. Further, Kohlberg has received inspiration from Dewey's treatment of moral categories, which echoes Kant's distinction.

Any given moral judgment may be simultaneously assigned to a mode, to an element and to an issue in Kohlberg's scheme, with each mode, element, and issue being defined at each of the stages of development. Kohlberg's table of the 'Aspects of Moral Judgement' is reproduced as follows:

'ASPECTS OF MORAL JUDGEMENT'
'I. The modes of judgement of obligation and value
    A. Judgement of right
    B. Judgement of having a right
    C. Judgement of duty and obligation
    D. Judgements of responsibility — conceptions of consequence of action or of the demands or opinions of others one should consider over and above strict duties or strict regard for the rights of others
    E. Judgement of praise or blame
    F. Judgements of punishability and reward
    G. Justification and explanation
    H. Judgements of nonmoral value or goodness

II. The elements of obligation and value
    A. Prudence — consequences desirable or undesirable to the self
    B. Social welfare — consequences desirable to others
    C. Love

    D. Respect
    E. Justice as liberty
    F. Justice as equality
    G. Justice as reciprocity and contract

III. The issues or institutions
    A. Social norms
    B. Personal conscience
    C. Roles and issues of affection
    D. Roles and issues of authority and democracy, of division of labour between roles relative to social control
    E. Civil liberties — rights to liberty and equality to persons as human beings, as citizens, or as members of groups.
    F. Justice of actions apart from fixed rights — reciprocity, contract, trust, and equity in the actions or reactions of one person.
    G. Punitive justice
    H. Life
    I. Property
    J. Truth
    K. Sex'

It is emphasized that the concept of stages 'implies something more than age trends. First, stages imply invariant sequence': each person 'moving step by step through each of the kinds of moral judgement outlined', with the possibility of moving at varying speeds and becoming fixated at any level of development. Secondly, stages 'define "structured wholes", total ways of thinking, not attitudes toward particular situations'. 'A stage is a way of thinking which may be used to support either side of an action choice, that is, it illustrates the distinction between moral form and moral content (action choice)'. Kohlberg emphasizes that correlational studies indicate a general factor of moral level which cross-cuts aspect, but it should however be noted that any individual is usually not entirely at one stage. Typically, as children develop, they are partly in their major stage (about fifty per cent of their ideas), partly in the stage into which they are moving, and partly in the stage they have just left behind. Thirdly, 'a stage concept implies universality of sequence under varying cultural conditions': suggesting that 'moral development is not merely a matter of learning the verbal values or rules of the child's culture, but that it reflects something more universal in development, something which would occur in any culture'. Kohlberg claims to have validated the cultural universality of the sequence of stages from his researches in the United States, Taiwan, Mexico, Yucatan and Turkey. Kohlberg further reports that no important differences have been identified in the development of moral thinking between Catholic, Protestants, Jews, Buddhists, Moslems and Atheists.

The order of psychological adequacy of the stage is claimed by Kohlberg to have been empirically tested: the studies of Rest (Rest, Turiel and Kohlberg, 1969) 'form the core data which link' the 'psychological explanations to issues of philosophic adequacy'. In these studies, 'adolescents were first pre-tested with standard moral dilemmas, then asked to put in their own words, prepared arguments at each stage, "pro" and "con" a choice for each of two newly presented dilemmas'. It was found that adolescents distorted arguments higher than their own moral stage into ideas at their own stage or one below, in contrast having no difficulty comprehending arguments below their own modal stage. The major implication of these findings are that Kohlberg's stages 'constitute a hierarchy of cognitive difficulty with lower stages available to, but not used by those at higher stages'. This order of cognitive difficulty does not however indicate an order of moral adequacy but Rest further found that his adolescent subjects perceived the statements for each stage as 'representing a hierarchical order of perceived moral adequacy'. It was further predicted that, 'eliminating the stage at which he is, the subject should most assimilate moral judgments one stage above his own, and assimilate much less those which are two or more stages above, or one or more stages below his own'. Verification for these predictions have been obtained from the studies of Turiel (1966), Rest, Turiel and Kohlberg (1969) and Blatt and Kohlberg (1971). A recent study by Rest *et al.* (1974) lends further credence to the stage hierarchy: using Kohlberg's moral stages, statements were written to exemplify stage characteristics. Subjects were asked to select the statement defining the most important issue in a moral dilemma. The importance attributed to principled (Stages 5 and 6) moral statements evidenced developmental trends, differentiating student groups of varied advancement and correlating in the 60s with age, comprehension of social-moral concepts and Kohlberg's scale, together with attitude measures. The more advanced subjects attributed more importance to higher stage statements and further, the correlations suggested that as subjects develop cognitively they come to define moral dilemmas more complexly and come to place greater importance on principled moral thinking than do the less cognitively advanced subjects.

Kohlberg emphasizes that a cognitive-developmental theory of moralization claims that there is a 'sequence of moral stages for the same basic reasons that there are cognitive or logico-mathematical stages, that is, because cognitive-structural reorganizations toward the more equilibrated occur in the course of interaction between the organism and the environment'. 'The psychological assumption that moral judgment development centrally involves cognitive development is not the assumption that this is an increased "knowledge" of rules found outside the child, in his culture and its socialization agents. Studies of "moral knowledge" such as the Hartshorne and May study (*op. cit.*) indicate that most children know the basic moral rules and conventions of our society by the age of six to seven years'. 'By insisting on the cognitive core of moral development, is meant rather that the distinctive characteristic of the moral is that it involves active judgment . . . Judgment is neither the expression of, nor the description of, emotional or volitional states, it is a different kind of function with a definite cognitive structure'. Kohlberg elaborates that this structure of judgment has been studied 'as the child's use and interpretation of rules in conflict situations, and his reasons for moral action, rather than as correct knowledge of rules or conventional belief in them'. Kohlberg (1971) describes his cognitive hypothesis to be basically 'that moral judgment has a characteristic form at a given stage, and that this form is parallel to the form of intellectual judgment at a corresponding stage. This implies a parallelism or isomorphism between the development of the forms of logical and ethical judgment'. By this it is meant that 'each new stage of moral judgment entails a new set of logical operations not present at the prior stage. The sequence of logical operations involved is defined by Piaget's stages of logico-mathematical thinking.'

With respect to cognition and affect, Kohlberg considers that such discussions 'usually founder under the assumption that cognitions and affects are different mental states . . . ' However, 'the cognitive-developmental view holds that "cognition" and "affect" are different aspects, or perspectives, on the same mental events, that all mental events have both cognitive and affective aspects, and that the development of mental dispositions reflects structural changes recognizable in both cognitive and affective perspectives'. Kohlberg affirms that it is evident that moral judgments often involve strong emotional components, but this in no way reduces the cognitive component of moral judgment, though it may imply a somewhat different functioning of the cognitive component than is implied in more neutral areas. Kohlberg concludes that 'the quality (as opposed to the quantity) of affects involved in moral judgment is determined by its cognitive-structural development', and is an inseparable component of the general development of the child's conceptions of a moral order.

'The centrality of role taking for moral judgment is recognized in the notion that moral judgment is based on sympathy for others, as well as in the notion that the moral judge must adopt the perspective of the "impartial spectator" or the "generalized other" . . . ' Kohlberg's empirical claims include the underlining of opportunities for role taking, operating by stimulating moral development rather than producing a particular value system. Holstein (1971) 'found that the amount of parental encouragement of the child's participation in discussion (in a taped "revealed-differences" mother-father-child discussion of moral conflict situations) was a powerful correlate of moral advance in the child. An explanation of differential moral advance in terms of role taking is an explanation in terms of social cognition which differs from an emotional interpretation of differential moral advance' is the clarification given by Kohlberg.

Kohlberg (1964) discusses that affectional relationships (or identification) with parents are important in moral development, more because positive and affectional relations to others are generally conducive to ego development and to role taking and acceptance of social standards than because they provide a unique and direct basis for conscience formation.

'Role taking tendencies' and the 'sense of justice' are interlocked. 'While role taking in the form of sympathy often extends more broadly than the sense of justice, organized or "principled" forms of role-taking are defined by justice structures.' 'In order for roles and rules to represent socio-moral order, they must be experienced as representing shared expectations or shared values and the general shareability of rules and role expectations in an institution rests centrally upon a justice structure underlying specific rule and role definitions ... Because the central mechanisms of role taking are justice structures of reciprocity and equality' it can be suggested therefore, 'that institutions better organized in terms of justice provide greater opportunities for role taking and a sense of sharedness than do unjust situations'. The concepts of role-taking and justice, 'provide concrete meaning to the cognitive-developmental assumption that moral principles are neither external rules taken inward, nor natural ego tendencies of a biological organism, but rather the interactional emergents of social interaction'. In Piaget's theory, closely followed by Kohlberg, 'the notion that logical and moral stages are interactional is united to the notion that they are forms of equilibrium, forms of integrating discrepancies or conflicts between the child's schemata of action and the actions of others. Opportunities to role take are opportunities to experience conflict or discrepancy between one's own actions and evaluations and the action and evaluations of others. To role take in a moral situation is to experience moral conflict': the conflicts of the wishes and claims of the self, the other and a third party or more. However, exposure to higher stages of thinking presented by significant figures in the environment is probably neither a necessary nor a sufficient condition for upward movement: the studies of Turiel, and Rest, Turiel and Kohlberg (*op. cit.*) have led Kohlberg to presume that movement to the next stage involves internal cognitive reorganization rather than the mere addition of more difficult content from the outside. Turiel (1969) postulates that cognitive conflict is the central 'motor' for the internal cognitive reorganization that upward movement to the next stage involves. Turiel is conducting a series of experiments presenting children with 'varying combinations of contradictory arguments flowing from the same stage structure'. Turiel hopes to show that exposure to the next stage up, effects change 'not through the assimilation of specific messages, but by providing awareness that there are other, better, or more consistent solutions than the child's own, forcing him to rethink his own solution', thereby proving to be one of the environmental events promoting cognitive conflict. Exposure to real or verbal moral conflict situations not readily resolvable at the child's own stage, and disagreement with, and among significant others about such situations are other environmental effects being empirically tested in the moral discussion classes conducted by Blatt (Blatt, 1969; Blatt and Kohlberg, 1971). Blatt's findings suggest that 'the effects of naturally occurring moral discussions upon moral judgment be understood in the theoretical terms . . . outlined, those of inducing cognitive conflict in the child, and subsequent reorganization at the next level of thinking.'

Kohlberg's cognitive-developmental theory can be summarized as claiming that '(a) moral judgment is a role-taking process, which (b) has a new logical structure at each stage, paralleling Piaget's logical stages; this structure is best formulated as (c) a justice structure, which (d) is progressively more comprehensive, differentiated and equilibrated than the prior structure'. Kohlberg claims that evidence has been presented of a 'culturally universal, invariant moral sequence, as well as evidence that this sequence represents a cumulative hierarchy of cognitive complexity perceived as successively more adequate by non-philosopher subjects'.

iii. The implications of Kohlberg's genetic studies for philosophic ethics

Kohlberg (1971) focuses on the 'epistemological blinders' worn by psychologists, which have hidden from them the fact that the concept of morality is itself a philosophical (ethical) rather than a behavioural concept. He considers that it was due to his awareness of the necessity for orienting to philosophic concepts of morality when starting his psychological research that he has uncovered facts not previously noted. There was a failure to anticipate, however, that an empirical developmental study could contribute to the solution of distinctively philosophic problems in both normative ethics and meta-ethics. It was because of a practical concern to develop his research implications into an active programme of moral education (Kohlberg, 1970a, 1970b;

Blatt and Kohlberg, 1971) that he worried about the implications of his moral research for a definite ethical position. Kohlberg's 1971 paper is therefore addressed to 'From is (the facts of moral development) to Ought (the ideal content and epistemological status of moral ideas)'. Kohlberg claims that his earlier, philosophic claim that the stimulation of development is the only ethically acceptable form of moral education, can be upheld regardless of his more controversial claim, namely: that 'the common assumption of the cultural relativity of ethics' is in error, promoting instead, that ' "ethical principles" are the end point of sequential "natural" development in social functioning and thinking; . . . the stimulation of their development' being 'a different matter from the inculcation of arbitrary cultural beliefs'. This cultural relativity, on which almost all contemporary social scientific theorizing about morality is based, has influenced the sociological-role theorists, psychoanalytic theorists and learning theorists to view moral development and other forms of socialization as the direct internalization of external norms of a given culture. A second assumption, closely linked to the assumption of ethical relativity, being that morality and moral learning are fundamentally emotional and irrational processes based on mechanisms of habit, reward and punishment, identification and defense. (Kohlberg's full consideration of the empirical propositions derivable from the relativity postulation as being factually correct statements about variations in human moral behaviour and judgment, appears in Kohlberg, 1971, pp. 155–63 and *passim*.) In contrast to 'extreme' and 'sociological relativism', Kohlberg has empirically demonstrated that there are universal moral concepts, values, or principles, and there is less variation between individuals and cultures than has usually been maintained, in the sense that: 'almost all individuals in all cultures use the same thirty basic moral categories, concepts or principles; . . . all individuals in all cultures go through the same order or sequences of gross stages of development, though varying in rate and terminal point of development'. The marked differences between individuals and cultures which exist are differences in stage or developmental status.

Kohlberg affirms that his psychological theory as to why moral development is upward and sequential is broadly the same as his philosophical justification for claiming that a higher stage is more adequate or more moral than a lower stage. Both psychological and philosophical analyses suggest that the more mature stage of moral thought is the more structurally adequate. This greater adequacy of more mature moral judgment rests on structural criteria more general than those of truth value or efficiency. These general criteria are the formal criteria which developmental theory holds as defining all mature structures, the criteria of increased differentiation and integration:

these formal criteria which philosophers of the formalist school have held to characterize genuine adequate moral judgments. From Kant to Hare, formalists have stressed the distinctively universal and prescriptive nature of adequate moral judgments. The increasingly prescriptive nature of more mature moral judgments is, Kohlberg stresses, reflected in the genes of differentiations described throughout the theory, 'which is a series of increased differentiations of "is" and "ought" (or of morality) as internal principles from external events and expectations'. The claim of principled morality is that it defines the right for anyone in any situation: in contrast, 'conventional morality defines good behaviour for a Democrat but not for a Republican, for an American but not for a Vietnamese.' Conventional morality is not fully universal and prescriptive, and leads to continual self-contradiction; in contrast, principled morality is directed to resolving these conflicts in a stable, self-consistent fashion.

Kohlberg claims that the higher moral stage is the philosophically better although he accentuates that ' "claims of superiority" for higher stages are not claims for a system of grading the moral worth of individual persons, but are claims for the greater adequacy of one form of moral thinking over another.' In Kohlberg's view, the basic referent of the term 'moral' is a 'type of judgment or a type of decision-making process, not a type of behaviour, emotion, or social institution'. Kohlberg (1970) elaborates: 'for one man, a prohibition of parking is a moral norm, for another a mere administrative regulation. What makes it moral is not the legislation of the rule but the individual's attitude towards it'. Kohlberg (1971) emphasizes that Stage-6 is a deontological theory of morality. He elaborates that 'the three primary modes of moral judgment and the corresponding types of ethical theory, deal with (a) duties and rights (deontological), (b) ultimate aims or ends (teleological) and (c) personal worth or virtue (theory of approbation)'. Kohlberg emphasizes that 'claims of superiority, then, are claims for the superiority of Stage-6 judgments of duties and rights (or of justice) over other systems of judgments of duties and rights. We make no direct claims about the ultimate aims of men, about the good life, or about other problems which a teleological theory must handle. These are problems beyond the scope of the sphere of morality or moral principles, which we define as principles of choice for resolving conflicts of obligation', pp. 214—15.

Kohlberg continues: 'the general criterion we have used in saying that a higher stage mode of judgment is more adequate than a lower stage is that of morality itself, not of conceptions of rationality or sophistication imported from other domains'. Kohlberg acknowledges that 'a philosopher may not judge Stage-6 as more adequate than lower stages because it is not more scientifically true, is not more instrumentally efficient, does not reflect more meta-ethical or epistemological sophistication, or is not based on a more parsimonious set of normative ethical postulates. Only a philosophical formalist who views morality as an autonomous domain, with its own criteria of adequacy or rationality, is likely to evaluate moral arguments by moral criteria rather than by philosophical criteria of rationality imported from nonmoral domains'. In further explanation, Kohlberg states: 'we are arguing that a criterion of adequacy must take account of the fact that morality is a unique *sui generis* realm. If it is unique, its uniqueness must be defined by general formal criteria, so our meta-ethical conception is formalistic. Like most deontological moral philosophers since Kant, we define morality in terms of the formal character of a moral judgment, method, or point of view, rather than in terms of its content. Impersonality, ideality, universalizability, pre-emptiveness, etc. are the formal characteristics of a moral judgment. These are best seen in the reasons given for a moral judgment, a moral reason being one which has these properties. But we claim that the formal definition of morality only works when we recognize that there are developmental levels of moral judgment which increasingly approximates the philosopher's moral form. This recognition shows us (a) that there are formal criteria which make judgments moral, (b) that these are only fully met by the most mature stage of moral judgment, so that (c) our mature stages of judgment are more moral (in the formalist sense, more morally adequate) than less mature stages' (Kohlberg 1971, p. 215).

Kohlberg therefore claims that 'developmental theory assumes formalistic criteria of adequacy, the criteria of levels of differentiation and integration. In the moral domain, these criteria are parallel to formalistic moral philosophy's criteria of prescriptivity and universality. These two criteria combined represent a formalistic definition of the moral, with each stage representing a successive differentiation of the moral from the nonmoral and a more full realization of the moral form'.

With respect to principles of justice Kohlberg expounds that 'the whole notion that there is a distinctively moral form of judgment demands that moral judgment be principled, that is, that it rely on moral principle, on a mode of choosing which is universal, which we want all people to adopt in all situations'. Mature principles are 'neither rules (means) nor values (ends) but are guides to perceiving and integrating all the morally relevant elements in concrete situations'; guiding the resolving of claims which compete in a situation. All principles can be reduced to the single principle. (Kohlberg promotes eight 'steps of argument' for justice as the basic moral principle in Kohlberg, 1970a, p. 65 and 'six arguments' in Kohlberg, 1971, p. 229.)

In final summary, Kohlberg delineates that what is being claimed with respect to the relation of 'is to ought' in moral development is that scientific facts reveal 'a universal moral form successively emerging in development and centering on principles of justice'. Science can test whether 'a philosopher's conception of morality phenomenologically fits the psychological fact' but cannot 'justify that conception of morality as what morality ought to be' because 'the rules of scientific discourse are not the rules of moral discourse'. However, 'science can contribute to a moral discourse as to why one moral theory is better than another'. The scientific theory as to 'why people factually do move upward from stage to stage and why they factually do prefer a higher stage to a lower, is broadly the same as a moral theory as to why people should prefer a higher stage to a lower'. 'We have argued for a parallelism between a theory of psychological development and a formalistic moral theory on the ground that the formal psychological developmental criteria of differentiation and integration, of structural equilibrium, map into the formal moral criteria of prescriptiveness and universality . . . In essence there is a "deep logical structure" of movement from one stage to the next; a structure tapped by both a psychological theory of movement and by families of philosophical argument. If these contentions are correct, they provide a new definition of the moral philosopher's task, a definition more exciting than that implied by much recent philosophic work'.

iv. 'From thought to action'

Kohlberg postulates that maturity of moral thought should predict maturity of moral action: 'that specific forms of moral action require specific forms of moral thought as prerequisites'. The 'judgment—action relationship' can be described as 'the correspondence between the general maturity of an individual's moral judgment and the maturity of his moral action'. Kohlberg's initial study (Kohlberg, 1958) produced a product moment correlation of .46 between moral judgment scores and ratings of conscience. Experimental studies by Krebs (1967) and by Brown *et al.* (1969) bear these correlation trends out by revealing that principled subjects appear much less likely to cheat than conventional subjects. Conventional subjects referred to cheating in terms of maintaining social expectations and order, which carried no force when no longer supported by the group; the principled person defines the issue of cheating as one of inequality, of taking advantage of others, of deceptively obtaining unequal opportunity, that is, in terms of justice. Kohlberg claims that 'this interpretation implies that moral judgment determines action by way of concrete definitions of rights and duties in a situation'.

Kohlberg argues that 'moral judgment dispositions influence action through being stable cognitive dispositions, not through the affective changes with which they are associated.' He is claiming that the moral force in personality is cognitive. 'Affective forces are involved in moral decisions, but affect is neither moral nor immoral. When the affective arousal is channelled into moral directions, it is moral; when it is not so channelled it is not. The moral channelling mechanisms are cognitive principles defining situations, sorting out conflicting claims without distorting or cancelling them, leaving personal inclination as the arbiter of action.' 'The study of the relation of social cognitive structures to social action seems in principle much like the study of the relation of physical cognitive structure to actions upon physical objects, including the fact that both take place in social fields'. However, Kohlberg acknowledges that the issue of sacrifice raises a fundamental difference in the moral area: 'Because much morality involves basic sacrifice, it has been consigned to the realm of the irrational by Nietszche, Freud and Kierkegaard and their followers. If, however, a mature belief in moral principle itself engenders a sacrifice of the rational ego, apart from other personality and emotional considerations, we are faced with a conception of the rational and of cognitive structure which has no parallel in the realm of scientific and logical thought'.

Further studies providing validation for Kohlberg's 'judgment–action relationship' include those of Haan, Smith and Block (1968); Rubin and Schneider (1973); Fodor (1972); and Mann (1973). Berkeley students faced with a decision to 'sit-in' in the name of political freedom of communication were administered moral judgment interviews by Haan *et al.*. Fifty per cent of Stage-5 subjects and eighty per cent of Stage-6 subjects were among those 'sitting-in', while only ten per cent of conventional level students were included. Rubin and Schneider, using Lee's (1971) adaptions of Kohlberg's moral approach reported a positive relationship between decentration skills as indicated by scores on measures of communicative egocentrism, moral judgment and altruism in seven-year-old subjects, thereby relating moral cognition to altruistic behaviour. Fodor (1972), following the administration of the Kohlberg interview to 40 delinquent and 40 non-delinquent adolescent boys, found delinquents received substantially lower moral judgment scores (significant at the .001 level) than did non-delinquents.

Kohlberg (1971a) cites that with respect to the My Lai shootings in Vietnam, the one man who refused to shoot any civilians during the massacre showed principled thinking in his reasoning about both My Lai and other moral conflicts. The public statements of other soldiers involved, indicated that they were at conventional levels, reasoning that it was necessary to shoot to obey orders. Mann (1973) reports an Australian survey of public attitudes relating to the My Lai massacre and the trial of Lieutenant Calley. Fifty-nine per cent believed that the My Lai soldiers should be 'pardoned' and thirty per cent reported they also would have obeyed orders to shoot civilians. Subjects endorsing the 'follow-orders' ideology were more likely to be older, less well-educated, at the lower end of the economic scale, politically conservative and authoritarian. Following further analysis, Mann had reasons to believe that the true level of obedience ideology in the population could be substantially higher than revealed by the data; thereby lending further credence to Kohlberg's indications that the majority of the population operate at conventional levels.

v. Critique of Kohlberg's theory

Alston (1971) commenting on an earlier version of Kohlberg's 1971 paper considers that scrutiny of Kohlberg's descriptions of stages and assignation of subjects to stages reveals that what is being classified is what might be called a person's habitual style of moral reasoning. Alston points to a fundamental conceptual point about having a concept, on the one hand, and of using a concept (or habitually or typically using a concept) on the other. Therefore, 'the hypotheses that are confirmed by empirical studies using these stage assignments, hypotheses concerning the causes and consequences of stage membership and stage transition, cannot themselves be construed as hypotheses about the causes and consequences of stages of conceptual development'. 'A more direct demonstration would require the development of a test for possession of moral concepts, analogous to the test of typical mode of moral reasoning', leading to a further question of a parallel sequence between the acquisition of moral concepts and the adoption of a mode of reasoning.

Alston with respect to Kohlberg's claim that each stage involves a differentiation of its characteristic content from that of the preceding stage would suggest that this is contemporaneous with one's adopting ('or falling into') that mode of moral reasoning as dominant. He feels that Kohlberg has not presented adequate evidence for that claim. Many philosophers who are as conceptually sophisticated as Kohlberg's Stage-6 subjects take positions in moral philosophy that reflect Stage-4 or 5.

With respect to the concept of justice as a supreme moral principle; 'a judgment based on a principle of racial destiny, or on no principle at all, can be just as prescriptive as a judgment based on an application of Kohlberg's principle of justice'. Alston considers that Kohlberg met with only partial success in showing what he set out to illustrate, 'namely, that the facts of the order of moral development and its explanation reveal his Stage-6 of moral reasoning to be a morally superior way of resolving moral problems'. The mere fact that one concept logically depends on another has no tendency to show that moral thinking involving the former is superior to moral thinking involving the latter. However . . . 'the evidence Kohlberg adduces goes far toward breaking down the popular contrast between factual and scientific judgment as objective, and moral judgment as subjective. It does at least strongly suggest that one's modes of moral judgment universally tend to develop in certain directions under the impact of objective dimensions of its subject matter'. Alston considers that Kohlberg has enriched moral psychology and has opened a number of new perspectives which 'should force psychologists to take the cognitive aspects of morality seriously as an important influence on behaviour'. However, Kohlberg 'has not been able to resist the temptation to overstate his case'; he tends to imply an insignificant role for affect in moral life and further, he gives the impression that traits based on cultural norms and the concept of habit have no place in moral psychology. Alston argues that habit concepts are indispensable in psychology, moral or otherwise and Kohlberg's evidence does not prove to the contrary. With respect to affect one can 'unreservedly embrace the thesis that any distinctive emotional state will have a cognitive side, by virtue of which it is the kind of emotional state it is, and still insist that emotional states, to which an affective side is also essential, play crucial roles in moral development and moral motivation . . . ' Alston suggests that Kohlberg's concentration on moral dilemmas in his research leads to his emphasis on reasoning as against affect and habitual response, 'both in terms of relative contributions to the determination of behaviour and in terms of phenomenological prominence . . . Thus one may see the neglect of the affective and the habitual as, in part, a sort of "methodological artifact" . . . '

In similar vein to Alston, Peters (1971), in addition to considering that Kohlberg's argument that moral development occurs as a result of interaction between the child and his physical and social environment is inadequate, refers to Kohlberg's contention that specific character traits, such as honesty, which function as habits are of little significance in the moral life. Peters considers that it parallels Kohlberg's claim that learning theorists have produced no evidence of the influence of early forms of habit training on adult behaviour (Kohlberg, 1966). 'This lack of importance assigned to habit goes against a whole tradition of thought about moral development stemming from Aristotle'. Peters expands that it is not the case that habits have to be formed by a process like that of a drill: learning habits in an intelligent way, can be regarded as providing an appropriate basis, in the moral case, for the later stage when rules are followed or rejected because of the justification that they are seen to have or lack. In addition to intelligent rule following, Peters feels that young children can become sensitive to considerations which will later serve him as principles. Justice is a difficult abstract consideration for young children and if instead of justice, concern for others was encouraged, 'it can come to function later on as one of the fundamental principles of morality'. Further, Peters considers Kohlberg nowhere deals with the development of the class of virtues involving self-control: namely to be tempted, or to be made fearful. Familiarity with such situations carry over into situations in later life when the proper reasons for being courageous can be appreciated. 'Habituation is important both in familiarizing children with the features of such situations and in developing the relevant action patterns that will enable them to deal practically with the emotions that may be aroused instead of being overcome by them. Habituation may thus help to lay down a pattern of response that may be used in the service of more appropriate motives at a later stage'. Peters asks whether Kohlberg thinks that an individual can 'adhere to his favoured principle of justice . . . without some . . . training'. Peters also refers to the 'disposition to act': on a broader view of 'reason', it becomes readily apparent that there are a cluster of 'passions' closely connected with it, without which its operation would be unintelligible. Passions such as 'abhorrence of the arbitrary, the hatred of inconsistency and irrelevance, the love of clarity and order and the determination to look at the facts'. Kohlberg's reliance, like Piaget's, on the 'instrinsic motivation which leads children to assimilate and accommodate to what is novel' reveals a 'great difference between sporadic curiosity and the passions which cluster round the concern for truth'. The question of how children come to care finds no clear answer in Kohlberg's writings.

Peters concludes that Kohlberg's account of moral development might be considered to be one-sided, in that it has been erected on the features of a limited interpretation of morality: any moral system in which justice is regarded as the fundamental principle cannot be applied without a view, deriving from considerations other than those of justice, about what is important. To propose any criteria about what is just implies evaluation and this 'opens up obvious possibilities for alternative emphases in morality in addition to those already mentioned'. Peters (1974) argues that Kohlberg's account of the development of a rational form of morality is compatible with a Skinnerian type of account of the learning of content in early childhood. He considers that Kohlberg provides conceptual levels which define the types of 'reinforcement' and instruction that are possible. He further argues that 'no adequate account can be given of the development of a rational form of morality without more attention to the learning of content than Kohlberg is disposed to give.' Furthermore, he indicates 'that there are certain ways in which content may be learnt which actively impede the development of a rational form of morality.' He defends this thesis by considering Kohlberg's thesis about stages of development with particular attention to the types of 'cognitive stimulation' that may be necessary (pp. 367—83). Peters (1971) considers that Kohlberg's findings are of unquestionable importance but 'there is a grave danger that they may become exalted into a general theory of moral development . . . ' Peters considers that Freudian theory far from providing a competing theory of moral development is providing a much needed supplement to the work of the Piaget—Kohlberg school. (Further discussion relating to Kohlberg's theory can be found in Peters, 1974.)

Simpson (1974) in considering the methodology and interpretation of findings which are specific to Kohlberg's cognitive-developmental research believes that it will serve as a focus for examining more broadly some of the problems of cross-cultural studies in any field 'not just the emotion-laden one of morality'. She considers that one of the difficulties of Kohlberg's work is that although developing parallel and in some senses, isomorphic philosophical and psychological statements of cognition and morality, he does not make clear the empirical sources of his claims to universality in the empirical realm. The distinction between normative philosophy and empirical psychology remains blurred, and normative thinking especially governs the description of what he calls empirically derived categories of 'post-conventional' or 'principled' reasoning. The related research only tentatively supports the claim of an invariant developmental sequence and Simpson does not accept the related studies of Turiel (1966, *op. cit.*) and Rest (1969, *op. cit.*) as being conclusive. She emphasizes that Kohlberg's 'cosmopolitanism is hemispheric' for his 'pluralism' is strictly confined to Western philosophy. In Simpson's view, Western and Eastern philosophies differ far more between themselves than within, both in substance and methodology, Western philosophy does not represent systems of thought common to the entire world.

Simpson considers that like each of us, Kohlberg's interest in cognitive development and moral reasoning, his choice of a Kantian or Deweyian infrastructure for his theory and his predilection for abstractions of such principles of justice, equality or reciprocity, are all in a sense accidents of time and place and the interaction of his personality with a specifiable social environment and the norms of the subgroups within that environment. His rebuttal to those who emphasize cultural differences is 'more a statement of faith than an evidence-based conclusion'. Universality is far from confirmed from the limited cross-cultural studies reported, and further, if principled reasoning as defined by Kohlberg does not occur in some cultures, then one third of the paradigm is missing and the assumption that, under different conditions, these stages would appear in these groups is not necessarily warranted. Simpson further refers to the fact that post-conventional reasoning presupposes the capacity to perform formal operations of abstract thought. She refers to the empirical parameters of formal thinking being defined by cultural manifestations and what Piaget (1972) terms 'extremely disadvantageous conditions' which may delay its appearance to 20 years of age and indeed even prevent its appearance. (Piaget, 1972 has been discussed in Volume Three in this series of *Piagetian Research*.) If formal operational thinking — a precondition for principled reasoning does not occur in every culture, it seems illogical to expect principled moral reasoning to appear universally. Simpson further focuses on findings such as those of Ross (1972) (cited in Volume Three in the series *Piagetian Research*) which point out that fewer than fifty per cent in adolescent samples are able to achieve this level of reasoning. Simpson further states: 'the ascendancy of the normative philosopher over the empirical scientist becomes very clear in Kohlberg's acknowledgement that his Stage-6 describes a utopian ideal rather than a reality'. This is in response to Kohlberg's statement: 'There is a universal set of moral principles held by men in various cultures, our Stage-6. (These principles, we shall agree, could logically and consistently be held by all men in all societies; they would in fact be universal to all mankind if the conditions for socio-moral development were optional for all individuals in all cultures.) In responding to written and oral interviews based on situations and issues, a very small percentage of subjects studied in a number of cultures utilize the reasoning processes and the principled content which I prefer to think is the highest developmental stage of which human beings are capable, and which I believe all should utilize and would under specifiable conditions'. Simpson concludes 'the preacher has succeeded the philosopher'. She acknowledges that cultures and individuals may be systematically described as to their stage or developmental status, however, 'Kohlberg leans a little farther into philosophy and assumes a judgmental, normative stance which is in danger of toppling him out of scientific psychology entirely'.

With respect to principled thinking Simpson considers that the principles displayed may simply be the learned values of a different and smaller reference group so well internalized that its members believe themselves to be functioning autonomously: 'in some groups, internality — in the sense of autonomy in respect to the dominant culture — is learned as a norm, and admission and continued membership are contingent upon that knowledge'. Further, Simpson considers that the language used in the protocols of Stage-5 and Stage-6 subjects raises other questions about the structural aspects of the moral development interviews. There is a dependence on the capacity to refer to hierarchies and principles, to universal ideas, and especially to concepts such as justice, equality and reciprocity at a high level of abstraction. Simpson finds it difficult to believe that Stage-6 subjects are not functioning independently of their socialization, that they must have been very thoroughly socialized into the company of intellectual elites who value and practice analytic, abstract and logical reasoning. Highly abstract concepts such as justice have so little commonality in meaning from one group to another as to be practically useless as cross-cultural generalizations: concept development simply does not mean the same thing from one class or culture to another; for example, the concept of equality has a wide range of specific meanings which is affected by class membership.

Further, the series of issues, selected because they are deemed to have universal applicability are questionable: the issue of property rights is prone to cultural differences as is the value of life prone to the same ambiguities; 'in every group it is not that life is valued overall or not valued, but that it is valued situationally in highly culturally-specific ways' and is not a matter of natural and universal knowledge. Simpson believes that Kohlberg's (1969) suggestion that Stages-4, 5 and 6 could be viewed as alternative types of mature moral responses, rather than as a sequence 'would relieve some of the tension caused by the attempt to define the higher three stages as culture-free and universally attained through normal development. It would also render the hierarchy a typology and represent the stages (at least above the first three) as lateral, rather than vertical growth so that the present pious loading should be shovelled off principled reasoning'.

Simpson further criticizes the lack of systematization and detail in the reporting of the methodology and focuses on the delayed publication of Kohlberg's frequently cited major works (Kohlberg, 1969 and Kohlberg and Turiel, 1971). In conclusion: 'We would do better to explore and analyze differences whenever found, to borrow and adapt, and to nurture invention and cultural mutation as it occurs than to perpetuate the ideology of a suicidal world trying to reconcile its differences through the use of a theoretical framework ill-suited for containing and ordering real human diversity'.

Weinrich (1974) states that Kohlberg's research has mapped out a broad description of moral growth, has illuminated the correlates of moral judgment development, with some awareness of the causative preconditions of moral progression. However, an understanding of the processes of moral thought remains lacking: the examination of the 'anomalies and lacunae' in the evidence may be more fruitful of explanation than the evidence which confirms the system. There are many implications arising from the failure of most people to arrive at Stage-6: the degree to which a stage of thought is functional to society may indeed affect the personal viability of that mode of thought for the individual; there may not exist the external stimulation to progress beyond a certain stage; motivation to progress is not necessarily intrinsic and while exposure to material and arguments of a subsequent stage may lead to the transition to that stage in some cases, understanding of the transition demands an understanding of the nature of the current stage and the reason why the subsequent stage is more satisfactory to the individual. Weinrich (1975) considers that despite 'the global nature of the definition of justices used by Kohlberg, there are many aspects of moral development encompassed by his own scheme which can be more adequately conceptualized by other notions than justice and furthermore, his apparent attempt to use "the sense of justice" as a motivating force seems a concession to Piaget's view that the pressure of the peer group acts as a causative agent in moral growth in later childhood. This is a view to which Kohlberg does not wholly subscribe'.

McGeorge (1974) concluded from his research with forty 12-year-old subjects and twenty-three college students, that a description of a subject's development in moral judgment, in terms only of his percentage of use of the various stages is too simple. He considers that there is a need to specify the issues involved and record profiles of stage usage on those. Further, that the most immediate need is for scoring systems which would make such precision possible and enable further research on specific mechanisms of development in moral judgment and on the relationship of this dimension to moral action. Ziv (1976) focuses on the inavailability of Kohlberg's moral judgment scale: 'To our knowledge this is the only psychological measurement instrument with which research is done and published without a publicly available administration and scoring manual,' p. 191. Ziv further attacks the content of the stories and their relevance for children.

In a paper entitled, 'An emotion – attribution approach to moral behaviour: interfacing cognitive and avoidance theories of moral development', Dienstbier, Hillman, Lehnhoff, Hillman and Valkenaar (1975) have maintained that, 'Neither Piaget nor Kohlberg has extensively addressed theoretical questions of the relationship of moral behaviour to moral reasoning, or of the relationship of affect and emotional arousal to moral reasoning. Kohlberg (1969), however, approached our viewpoint by suggesting that affective responses would progress developmentally with cognitive responses and that for the higher moral stages, guilt would be associated with different types of transgression. Thus for a Stage-6 individual, "guilt over violation of internal principles" would result; for the Stage-4 individual, guilt would imply "concern about one's responsibility according to rules"; for the Stage-3 individual, only shame would be experienced. Kohlberg's astute analysis is completely compatible with our orientation, but it is through the emotion – attribution perspective that we can address the issue of the dynamics that account for this presumed usual compatibility of affect and moral judgment in the maturing individual', p. 312.

Tomlinson (1975) casts some doubt on Kohlberg's consideration that empirical evidence for preference for the higher stages supports their being morally better. In an analysis of the potential contribution of research in moral development to political education Tomlinson considers that the 'possible role of specific attitudes and particular virtues, and of the traditionally emphasized habit and emotional variables, is played down by Kohlberg in favour of the person's construal of what sorts of questions are at stake in his situation ... even if one accepts Kohlberg's cognitive approach, a person's degree of consistency motivation is one central influence on stage development, and such motivation can vary considerably across individuals.' Further, 'any view which emphasizes thought forms and structures will be faced with the question of what it is most important to apply them to. Although Kohlberg does do this to some extent by associating certain issue — emphases with certain stages, things remain somewhat open', p. 261. Tomlinson elaborates that he agrees with Jurd (*nd*) that 'what seems to be needed is some notion which integrates the cognitive, affective and behavioural aspects of a person.' The 'sophistication of Kohlberg's cognitive approach to human action requires supplementing with a consideration of other aspects of human functioning', p. 262.

Meacham (1975) asserted that, 'Psychologists have treated the good and not-so-good motives as two separate problems — altruism and moral behaviour. The first has been concerned with kindness, generosity, cooperation, etc., but rarely has an understanding of such behaviours been sought in terms of the moral judgments of which individuals are capable. Krebs (1970), for example, in a recent discussion of altruism, mentions Kohlberg's work only as it contributes to an understanding of the attribution of altruism, but neither Kohlberg's nor Piaget theories are suggested to have value in understanding the motivation for altruistic behaviours. An exception to this lack of integration is provided by Rosenhan (1972), who suggests a parallel between Kohlberg's developmental stages and the development from normative to autonomous altruism. Similarly, the second problem, moral behaviour, has been concerned with transgression, yielding to temptation, nonconformity, etc., with infrequent discussion of the relationship between moral judgment and altruistic behaviours (but see, for example, Maccoby, 1968, p. 260). What is needed is a theory of moral behaviour which considers the relationships between moral judgments and the broad range of behaviours, both good and bad, in which the individual may engage. A dialectical approach considers the multiple aspects of behaviours and recognizes that they can be both good and bad, moral and immoral, depending upon the framework within which they are evaluated', pp. 161–162.

vi. Further empirical validation of Kohlberg's work

White (1975) maintained that 'All previous cross-cultural research on moral development has emerged entirely out of the Kohlberg laboratory and has been conducted exclusively with males. The domestic and cross-cultural research to date supports Kohlberg's hypothesis of the cultural universality and developmental status of the moral stages. However, it would seem important to validate cross-culturally the previous findings and to examine sex differences in moral development in other cultures. Previous research on sex differences in moral development in the US has been equivocal but generally suggests that adolescent males are more advanced than adolescent females, although these differences may disappear by young adulthood', p. 535. Bahamian school children (N = 134) between seven and 14 years of age were administered three of the standard Kohlberg moral dilemmas (1958). Age trend in moral development and the male—female difference at the 13- to 14-year-old age level was consistent with previous cross-cultural findings in the United States. (Details appear later.)

However, Grimley (1974), in a cross-cultural study of moral development involving subjects from Zambia, United States, Hong Kong, Japan and England, reported results confirming that sequential stages of moral development are to be found in different cultures. While the parameters in moral development (rate of development, dispersion of moral maturity scores etc.) were found to vary somewhat from one culture to another, no significant differences between nationalities were found in the development of moral judgment. Similarly religious background did not account for any significant differences in the development of moral reasoning among Catholics, Protestants, Jews, Buddhists, and Atheists. Academic performance and socioeconomic status were found to be highly significant factors affecting development, although the same sequences persisted. Holstein (1976) empirically assessed two central issues in Kohlberg's stage — sequence model through a longitudinal study among 52 adolescents and their parents: the 'stepwise, invariant sequence and irreversibility of the stages in ontogeny'. Individual developmental sequences for adolescents and adults over a period of three years supported the sequence but with respect to levels rather than stages and only for the first two levels of the three-level scheme. Some regression was found in the higher stages relating to the irreversibility issue. It was considered that measurement error cannot be dismissed as an explanation and further that stages from the conventional level up could be content-bound and used 'when and if preferred once certain cognitive prerequisites are met.' (Details follow.) Keasey (1973) modified by exposure to various conflict situations, the moral opinions and stage of reasoning of pre-adolescents at Kohlberg's first three stages of moral development. Opinion and reasoning change were found to be independent processes. The small amount of upward reasoning change induced was consistent with the cognitive-developmental view that radical changes in an individual's stage of cognitive functioning are rare and reaching a more equilibrated state depends on readiness to move upward. Graham (cited 1972) in a replication of Kohlberg's measures with British children found a correlation between verbal intelligence and moral judgment (Kohlberg global scoring) of +.53 at the age of 11 years and +.43 at the age of fourteen years, both on a sample of 40 children, 'the difference between the two coefficients being statistically insignificant.' Noting Kohlberg's report of a correlation of +.31 between intelligence and maturity of moral judgment, Graham comments: 'Naturally, one would expect to find some differences in the size of correlations when different tests of intelligence are used, with moral judgment correlating more highly with verbal than with non-verbal tests. But there does also seem to be a tendency in American studies to have a somewhat selected population, which would, of course, have the effect of decreasing the size of the correlation coefficient'. He further comments on Kohlberg's stated correlation of +.59 between moral judgment and chronological age, with intelligence held constant, arguing that intelligence cannot therefore be the only factor in the age-related developmental sequence, Graham considers: 'It may well be the case that intelligence is relevant only up to a certain point, beyond which further increases in intelligence are of little significance.'

A comparison of the effects of selective Catholic and public high schools on the moral development of their respective students (N = 630) was made by Robinson (1976). It was concluded that changes in moral development were more likely to occur in the Catholic high schools. The general findings for public schools demonstrated few significant changes occuring in the character development of students from the freshmen to senior years. Catholic high school Ss performed at the higher moral reasoning abilities than the public school Ss. (Details follow).

A curvilinear relationship between moral judgment level and overall frequency of conformity is reported by Saltzstein *et al.* (1972). Stage-3 children (so-called 'good boy, good girl, approval-seeking' morality) were more likely to conform than children at either higher or lower moral judgment levels. In particular, very few of the higher level subjects (those at Stages-4 or 5) made any conforming response. Fodor (1969) compared Negro and white male adolescents in moral judgment in accordance with the Kohlberg interview. The subjects consisted of twenty-five socially disadvantaged Negro boys together with twenty-five white boys aged 14 to 17 years selected at random. The difference between moral judgment scores for white and Negro boys was non-significant. There was a statistically significant difference on moral judgment scores between boys whose mothers had graduated from high school and boys whose mothers lacked this experience.

Selman (1971) confirmed that the development of reciprocal role taking skills related to the development of conventional moral judgment among sixty middle class children at ages 8,9 and 10. Results of a re-examination one year later of ten subjects whose role taking and moral judgment levels were low in the original study, supported the hypothesis that the development of the ability to understand the reciprocal nature of interpersonal relations is a necessary but not sufficient condition for the development of conventional moral thought. Moir (1974) concludes that moral development may be characterized in part as a gradual evolution of role taking abilities. From correlations between scores of 11-year-old girls on Kohlberg's Moral Judgment Interview and a nonmoral role taking test, the results showed that a significant proportion of the variance in moral maturity scores could be accounted for by measures of nonmoral-role taking (Details follow). Langford and George (1975) argue, 'while we may, therefore, agree with Kohlberg as to the existence of his six types of moral attitude, things are less certain when we come to his analysis of the formation and nature of the types, which he seems to regard as attitudes to social life generally. It is not clear from Kohlberg's analysis why, for instance, the moral attitudes associated with role taking (Types four and five) are any different from role taking itself, and thus from the structure and functions of the developing ego. A child plays many roles in his life; the roles of "good boy", "nice girl" and "rule-obeyer" are quite specific examples of these. Role playing has long been regarded as an integral part of ego structure and learning to take roles as an essential stage in ego development (see especially Erikson, 1950, Chapter 7)'. Keasey (1971) examined the hypothesis that higher stages of moral development would be positively associated with social participation. Extent of social participation was assessed by having subjects indicate the number of social organizations of which they were members or leaders, together with ratings by teachers and peers. The stage of moral development was found to be positively related to the extent of social participation whether judged by self, peers or teachers. Further support was therefore given to Kohlberg's report (Kohlberg *passim*) that the quality of social participation is associated with accelerated moral development and further, to his proposal that social interaction is an important source of dis-equilibration which facilitates progression through the stages of moral development together with role taking opportunities as the funda-mental social inputs stimulating moral development.

In a paper entitled, 'Level of social perspective taking and the development of empathy in children: speculations from a social-cognitive viewpoint', Selman (1975) draws from his own research as well as the theory of Baldwin (1906), Mead (1934) and Kohlberg (1968) and concludes, '. . . we have tried to make two speculative points. First, perspective-taking is not a "have it or have it not" ability but a process which undergoes life-span developmental restructuring. Just as we have found perspective-taking levels to be necessary but not sufficient for parallel developmental forms of moral reasoning (Selman, 1975a), so too would we expect such relations between social perspective-taking and empathy. Second, although each higher level of social perspective-taking may be necessary for each higher level of empathic judgment, it is not sufficient. Therefore, we cannot guarantee that a child with a high level of perspective-taking will apply his understanding in an empathic way. Both basic and educational research is needed to understand the mechanisms which stimulate the development of social perspective — taking as well as those mechanisms which will enable the child to use this underlying social-cognitive process for the positive understanding rather than the detriment of others', p. 43.

After citing Kohlberg's works (1958, 1964, 1968, 1969, 1971), Rest, Cooper, Masanz, and Anderson (1974) assert, 'People also make judgments about the moral judgment of others. When a person is faced with a moral dilemma, he often seeks the advice of others rather than acting on his own immediate solution to the dilemma. In taking or not taking another's advice, we are making judgments about his judgments. In public debate over moral–political issues we are hardly ever aware of a dilemma without also hearing someone's moral judgment of it. Democratic political process involves our reacting to the judgments of candidates for office and presumably voting for candidates whose judgments we approve', p. 491. Rest *et al.* continue, 'The methodological problems of Kohlberg's measure have also motivated the search for a different method of developmental assessment. Kohlberg's method produces material that is not strictly comparable from subject to subject; the assessments are vulnerable to interviewer and scorer biases; and scoring the material involves complex interpretations and rather great inferential leaps from the data. The test–retest reliability in several studies has been poor (Blatt and Kohlberg, in press; Guilliland, 1971; Turiel, 1966). Correlations of Kohlberg's measure with other sets of moral dilemmas that use a similar interview method and similar stage-scoring guides have been only moderate (Gilligan, Kohlberg, Lerner and Belenky, 1971; Lockwood, in press) . . . it is unclear to what extent differences in verbal expressiveness and other, test-taking sets influence scores . . . Kohlberg's measure is very time consuming', p. 492. In a study entitled 'Judging the important issues in moral dilemmas — an objective measure of development', Rest, Cooper, Coder, Masanz, and Anderson therefore used Kohlberg's moral stages which were written to exemplify stage characteristics. Ss were asked to select the statement defining the most important issue in a moral dilemma. 'The importance attributed to principled (Stages five and six) moral statements (the P score) evidenced developmental trends: the P score differentiated student groups of varied advancement — junior high, senior high, college and graduate students ($F > 48.5$): P correlated in the .60s with age, comprehension of social—moral concepts, and Kohlberg's scale — and less so but significantly with IQ. The way Ss chose important issues was not only an intellectual skill but also value related: P correlated in the .60s with attitude measures. A second student sample and an adult sample provided replications. Test—retest correlation of the P score was .81', p. 491. (Details follow.) However, McGeorge (1975) has argued in respect to the Defining Issues Test (used in the Rest *et al.* study) that while the test can be objectively scored and may be given to large groups, 'subjects simply rank and rate prepared statements, answers cannot be probed, and the question of faking by astute or lucky subjects arises', p. 108. In his study 146 college students with a mean age of 19.02 years completed the Defining Issues Test on two occasions 18 days apart. Brief instructions were devised asking Ss to fake bad, fake good, or to record their own views (standard). Ss were assigned to five treatments: (a) standard — standard, (b) standard — good, (c) good — standard, (d) standard — bad, (e) bad — standard. Ss were unable to fake high under the standard — good and good — standard conditions. Ss in the bad — standard group scored significantly lower when asked to fake bad as did those in the standard — bad group. The standard — bad group's bad scores were significantly lower than were those of the bad — standard group. The standard — standard groups scores on the two tests did not differ significantly and a test—retest reliability coefficient of .65 was obtained. No significant sex differences were observed in any of the conditions (Details follow.)

   Cognitive style and modification of moral judgment was examined by Arbuthnot (1974). It was hypothesized that as a result of a role-playing episode concerning a moral dilemma, field-dependent subjects would show greater change in maturity of moral judgment in accordance with the level of the cognitive demands of their role. Seventy-eight subjects comprised the sample and Jackson's (1956) short form of the Embedded-figures Test was used to assess level of field dependency. Kohlberg's (1971) standard moral dilemmas were employed to evaluate maturity of moral judgment, in a pre-test, immediate post-test, and one-week post-test design. Field-dependent subjects were more susceptible to both positive and negatively conducive roles on an immediate but not on a one-week post-test (Details are given later).

Arbuthnot (1975) in a further study, investigated the modifications of moral judgment through actual role playing among 96 introductory psychology students who were administered seven of Kohlberg's (1958) moral dilemmas. The pre-test composed of dilemmas three and four; dilemma three, the role playing task (of Heinz or the Druggist); dilemmas eight and ten, the immediate post-test; and dilemmas five, six, and seven, the one-week delayed post-test. The effectiveness of actual role playing in the context of a moral dilemma for producing both immediate and relatively long-term changes in the maturity of moral judgment was clearly demonstrated. (Details follow.)

Keasey (1973) examined 'The moral opinions and stage of reasoning of preadolescents (63 boys and 63 girls) at Kohlberg's first three stages of moral development were modified by exposure to various conflict situations. Opinion and reasoning change were found to be independent processes. The small amount of upward reasoning change induced is consistent with the cognitive—developmental view that radical changes in an individual's stage of cognitive functioning are rare. Exposure to a model using higher stage reasoning induced immediate change but was no more successful than other paradigms in inducing long-term reasoning change. It was concluded that children seek to resolve the disequilibrium induced by any of several paradigms. Whether their attempts at resolution reach a more equilibrated state depends largely on their readiness to move upward'.

Tomlinson-Keasey and Keasey (1974) from high correlations and systematic relationships between the stages of cognitive development (concrete and formal operations) and moral development suggest that sophisticated cognitive operations are a prerequisite to advanced moral judgments and further that there is a lag or *décalage* between the acquisition of logical operations and their application to the area of morality, thereby providing further confirmation for Kohlberg's postulations in this connection, (*op. cit*). Lee (1971) using material patterned after both Piaget's and Kohlberg's work, with children 5—17 years, identified, from factor analysis that a concrete operations component best related to a decrease of authority type responses and concomitant increases in moral modes of conceptualization. The formal operations mode of thought best predicted the increase of societal, idealist moral modes of conceptualization. Further support that cognitive and moral modes of thought covary according to their respective modes of conceptualization was found in the transition function as age progressed. Lee concluded that the findings clearly supported concomitant 'growth' of the two modes of thought.

To investigate the relation between a test of reasoning at Piaget's level of formal operations and strength of Kohlberg's various types of moral development using similar correlational techniques patterned after Lee (1971), Langford and George (1975) tested 65 girls aged from 12 to 15 years on four dilemma stories used by Kohlberg (1958). Additionally, Inhelder and Piaget's (1958) 'Law of Floating Bodies' task was administered. Langford and George concluded, 'It is suggested that while Kohlberg's (1958) stages in the development of moral judgment are descriptively more adequate than those of Piaget (1932), Kohlberg has underplayed the role of the child's attitude to power relations in the development of moral judgment. While this does not determine the form of moral judgments at different stages in the child's development, power relations are the subject matter of such judgments. The form taken by moral judgments at different stages is determined by stages in the development of both thought and ego. Existing theory and factual evidence relating to the details of this determination are examined and found to contain some contradictions . . . (our) . . . results . . . remove these contradictions but also undermine some of the positive evidence hitherto enjoyed by hypotheses in this area. (Details are given later.) Lee (1971) found small positive correlations between Piaget's Stage 2 moral attitude and formal operational thinking. This departs from those reported by Langford and George (1975) who argue, 'We can gather from Lee's Figure 7 that the relative frequency of Stage two responses to her moral dilemma stories follows a peculiar course in its relation to age of subject. Such responses first reach a peak between the ages of six and 10 years. From 11 to 14 years they decline. But between the ages of 15 and 17 years they return to their previous peak, relative to other responses. According to Piaget's view of moral development, such responses should decline continuously throughout adolescence. The fact that Lee's score for these responses follows an upward trend in this period not only goes to explain his finding of a positive correlation with formal operations reasoning, but also bears out our earlier suggestion that Piaget's sequence of stages in moral development is not adequate to deal with the period of adolescence, being derived from study of younger children'.

Kuhn, Langer, Kohlberg and Hann (1971) were intent to determine the actualization in development of the stage of formal operations; to obtain information about certain structural characteristics of formal operations; to examine closely the ontogenesis of formal operations together with the 'actualized ontogenetic relation between stages of logical reasoning and stages of development in a social domain, namely, moral judgment' among a large sample of normal adolescents and adults. A primary finding was that subjects on the average do not attain as advanced a level in the moral domain as they do in the logical domain. The data were 'evaluated in terms of their bearing on the general theoretical question of the interrelations among stage developments as they occur in different conceptual domains'. (Details follow.)

Modgil (1975) attempted to determine the empirical links which might be present among cognitive and moral factors in the adolescent's development. It was an attempt to elucidate and establish whether a relationship exists between operativity as conceived by Piaget, and moral development as postulated by Kohlberg. Piagetian stage groups of subjects (contrasted according to levels of logical reasoning) were selected and matched with respect to age, social class and measured intelligence. The four Piagetian tests comprised: 'Angles of Incidence and Reflection', 'Equilibrium in the Balance', 'Communicating Vessels' and 'The Projection of Shadows' (Inhelder and Piaget, 1958), patterned after Tisher (1962, 1971). The moral development variable served as the dependent variable, as measured by Kohlberg's Moral Judgment Interview Schedules (1971b). The results indicated that a relationship existed between Piagetian operativity and moral development. A qualitative analysis of the Piagetian reasoning tasks in relation to the stages of moral judgment gave further insight with respect to the established association. (Details follow.)

Interrelations among Piaget's formal operations, Erikson's ego identity and Kohlberg's principled morality were investigated by Cauble (1975) in 90 college undergraduates. Both formal operations and SES contributed significantly to P score variance on Rest's Defining Issues Test of principled morality. However, Constantinople's ego measure (Erikson) did not relate to any of the variables in the regression analyses. The identity questioners (Erikson) scored significantly higher than the non-questioners on formal-operations, but scored no higher on the Constantinople Inventory of Personality Development or Rest's principled morality measure. (Details are given later.)

Ego-identity status and 'level of moral judgment' were independently assessed and examined in relation to each other by Podd (1972). Subjects who achieved an ego identity were generally characterized by the most mature level of moral judgment, while those with a relative lack of ego identity were generally characterized by either the least mature level of moral judgment or a transitional period between moderate and highly mature moral judgment. People undergoing an identity crisis were found to be unstable and inconsistent in their moral reasoning.

To investigate the relationship between Erikson's stages of ego development and Kohlberg's theory of moral development, Moore's (1976) study tested 143 women between the ages of 25 and 74. The Ss who were drawn from a Roman Catholic Community of sisters and a Roman Catholic parish were administered Boyd's Self-Description Questionnaire and Rest's Defining Issues Test. The former yielded information concerning resolution of sequential ego stages and the pertinency of phase-specific ego stages. The latter assessed the level of moral development by locating the subject according to use of principled thinking. Significant correlations between ego development and moral development scores indicated that the totality of 'the positive and negative attitudes that have been incorporated into the personality is related to how one approaches a moral dilemma. A significant correlation was found between concern for the generativity crisis and moral development scores. There were also positive correlations between moral development and status as a lay or religious woman. When the effects of education were partialled, the correlation between status and moral development were negligible. Resolution of the eight stages of ego development served in the prediction of moral development scores', p. 3580–B. (Details follow).

Differences in responses between preconventional and postconventional subjects provided support for Kohlberg's characterizations of these levels as externally versus internally oriented. Weisbroth (1970) reports that identification with both parents is significantly related to high moral judgment in males, while identification with the father is significantly related to high moral judgment in females. (Cf. a theoretical paper by Frank, 1976, with respect to identification, moral character and conceptual organization). The rated and observed moral behaviour, judgment, and affect of 120 subjects (pre-adolescent) from lower class boys from 'early-divorced (before the boys were six), late-divorced (between six and 10), and parentally intact homes', were studied by Santrock (1975). Additionally, the mothers' discipline covering such facets as power assertive, inductive, and love withdrawal, and affection were investigated by questioning Ss about their mothers' methods of handling with their transgressions. Resistance-to-temptation, self-criticism, altruism, reparation, and teacher-rating measures were given to assess moral behaviour. Moral judgment was measured by administering three Kohlberg's (1958) items and moral affect was studied with two story-completion items maximizing guilt. Few differences were found between father-absent and father-present boys when IQ, SES, CA, and sibling status were held constant. However, father-absent boys were as less advanced in moral development than father present boys as reported by their teachers. The sons of the divorced women indicated more 'social deviation', but were more advanced in level of moral judgment than were the sons of widows; and according to their sons' reports, divorced women disciplined with more power assertion than widows. (Details follow.)

Tapp and Kohlberg (1971) derived a theory of legal development from cognitive-developmental theory using kindergarten to college and cross-national pre-adolescent data. Paralleling evidence on universal moral levels, the development of individual orientations *vis-a-vis* legal or rule systems revealed consistent movement from a preconventional law-obeying, to a conventional law-maintaining, to a post-conventional law-making perspective. In both the United States and cross-national samples, 'law and order' conventional reasoning is modal, reflecting that socialization experiences can accelerate, retard or crystallise the growth of legal values and roles. Tapp (1970) in an earlier report of part of this work, comments that such striking convergences across such divergent nations are 'a good sign'. The common trends of child development and the socialization goals that transcend nationality suggest that the shared values throughout our world are more compelling than diverse ideologies would imply. (A view counteracting those of Simpson, *op. cit.*, who focused on perspectives more aligned with the 'cultural relativists'.) 'If these children's wisdom could be maintained into adulthood, there might be a better chance for freedom and justice within a world society, which after all is the message of law'. Fontana and Noel (1973) investigated moral reasoning among three role groups: students, 'faculty' and 'administrators'. 'Administrators' employed law and order reasoning more than 'faculty' and students. 'Rightists' used law and order reasoning more than 'Leftists' and 'Leftists' reasoned egoistically more than 'Rightists'. Natural scientists employed more law and order and less social contract reasoning than those in the social sciences and humanities. These findings supported the hypothesis that stages of moral reasoning provide a fruitful model for conceptualizing and assessing differences in values and premises among groups and subgroups. A study related to Kohlberg's work and also to Tapp and Kohlberg (1971) by Adelson *et al.* (1969) traced the growth of the idea of law during adolescence. Depth interviews were conducted with 120 subjects, among whom significant changes in the view of law were found to take place between 13 and 15 years. The level of discourse shifted from concrete to abstract; 'a restrictive emphasis is replaced by a stress on the positive aims of law and a conception of amendment is increasingly present in the later years, as is an emphasis on the intrapsychic effects of law.' In general, 'law lost its absolutistic meanings and was seen as functional, as a tool for achieving community ends.'

Tomlinson (1975) focuses on the potential contribution of research in moral development to political education and upon the fact that the political area has so far made little use of cognitive developmental approaches. Tomlinson assesses that although a large number of the aspects listed by Kohlberg may enter into facets of political thinking, the issues of 'social norms and the legal system', 'the polity system' and 'civil liberties' are most relevant to political perspectives. The modes of moral judgment concerning rights, duties and responsibilities and the principle of justice, likewise seem to be central to political concerns. 'The sociopolitical level of discourse is recognized as a possible approach in human decisions, but it is not developed by Kohlberg, because as a moralist his focus is on overridingness in the decision-making of individuals,' p. 246. Tomlinson considers that the implications to be drawn from moral development research for the domain of political literacy present an obvious starting point for research. 'The sorts of topic requiring investigation seems to include the possibility of a cognitive developmental psychology of political literacy, and its use as an assessment framework (along with other relevant aspects) to study current states of affairs and the efficacy, from the political literacy viewpoint, of particular activities,' p. 262.

In a study entitled, 'Some relationships between sociopolitical ideology and moral character among college youth', Snodgrass (1975) attempted 'to clarify the relationship, observed in studies using Kohlberg's moral character model, between the character of college youth and their ideology'. Three of Hogan's dimensions of moral character (moral judgment, socialization, and empathy) (Hogan, 1970; Hogan and Dickstein, 1972) were administered to a student sample (N = 118) and were correlated with sociopolitical ideology defined in terms of several indices of liberalism—conservatism. 'Only the moral judgment dimension (ethics of social responsibility vs. ethics of personal conscience) as measured by Hogan's Survey of Ethical Attitudes was related to ideology. These results indicate that in accordance with an ethics of responsibility, conservatives have a greater respect for the utility of rules in regulating human conduct and a greater tendency to attribute blame to the individual rather than the societal environment. The study provided no evidence to support conservative charges that radical youth possess delinquent predispositions or liberal and radical claims that conservatives are less concerned about the welfare of others', (p. 195). (Details follow.)

Hogan and Dickstein (1970) supported the hypothesis that the ethics of personal conscience (as reflected by the Survey of Ethical Attitudes) is related to a tendency to blame and distrust institutions, while the ethics of social responsibility is associated with a suspicious attitude toward other people. Hogan and Dickstein formulate an 'orderly pattern of relationships surrounding these viewpoints': the ethics of conscience, moral institutionism, principled disobedience, doubt concerning the efficacy of the law as a means for promoting human welfare, and a tendency to regard institutions as the source of social injustice seem to be reliably interrelated. The ethics of responsibility, moral rationalism, principled rule compliance, belief in the instrumental value of the law, and a disposition to locate the roots of injustice in the actions of individuals also appear regularly to covary. Hogan and Dickstein comment that it might be argued that the ethics of conscience and responsibility merely reproduce Piaget's stages of autonomous and heteronomous moral judgment or perhaps Kohlberg's later stages. This observation would assume that the ethics of conscience is developmentally more advanced than the ethics of responsibility. However, the authors would disagree on the grounds that the viewpoints in question here are 'ideal types' derived from two fundamental traditions in social philosophy. In their pure forms, the ethics of conscience and responsibility should be morally and developmentally equivalent, paralleling for example, the Integratist and Normative conscience orientation. Secondly, the authors have found it useful to conceptualize moral development in terms of four dimensions considered in conjunction with conscience and responsibility (moral knowledge, socialization, empathy and autonomy). 'According to this view, a proper evaluation of a person's moral posture requires considerable information beyond the manner in which he reasons about moral dilemmas. The moral and developmental implications of a person's position with regard to the ethics of conscience-ethics of responsibility to continuum can be properly understood only within the context of total character structure.' (Of some interest in this context is an analysis of empathy with respect to historic and current conceptualizations, measurement and a cognitive theoretical perspective by Deutsch and Madle, 1975.)

In order to determine the degree of relationship between Hogan's and Kohlberg's theories of moral development, to compare the theories in terms of their abilities to predict which types of subjects would make ethical decisions independently of the punishment consequences of their decisions, and to establish the comparative adequacy of these two systems at predicting cheating, Gallagher's (1975) study involved 712 Ss drawn from a community and a senior college. The tests administered were the California Psychological Inventory Socialization Scale, Hogan's Empathy Scale, Barron's Autonomy Scale, Hogan's Survey of Ethical Attitudes and a shortened version of a standard Kohlberg interview involving four stories. No relationship was computed between personality type and Kohlberg's stage of moral judgment score. Punishment influenced the decisions of subjects, with subjects in the punishment condition recommending the course of action which avoided punishment significantly more often than the control condition. With respect to cheating, the result showed that subjects at higher stages of judgment cheat less often than those at lower stages. Kohlberg's system was a better predictor of non-cheating than was Hogan's. (Details follow.).

Gash (1976) investigated the relationship between Kohlberg's 'cognitive-developmental' stages and Hoffman's 'social learning' moral orientations. Kohlberg's post-conventional level was associated with Hoffman's humanistic orientation thereby substantiating the first hypothesis. Questionnaires received experimental treatment with respect to varying the distance of the interpersonal relations between principal characters in the moral problems. 'As hypothesized, there was a significant, but slight, tendency for moral dilemmas between persons with more distant personal ties to elicit the diminished role perspective of lower stages on Kohlberg's dilemmas. However, changes made to Hoffman's items were almost undetectable in the responses.' (Details follow.)

In a study entitled, 'The phenomenology and psychodynamics of moral development, Kane (1975) administered a written Kohlberg dilemma questionnaire to 12 male and female social work students followed by a five to six hours interview to gather information about their life histories and subjective experiences related to moral development. The author concluded that, 'affective factors are a significant part of moral reasoning and that efforts to look at isolated aspects of moral functioning can only result in misleading, fragmented views of the process of moral development. It was suggested that looking at moral reasoning as a discrete aspect of personality functioning was similarly unproductive and misleading. The interview findings also suggested that Kohlberg's claims for invariancy of sequence of his stages are erroneous and that stages four and five appear to be reversed. Kohlberg's tendency to ignore psychodynamic conflict and defensiveness in conscious moral reasoning were cited as reasons for this problem in stage ordering,' (p. 3049B). (Details follow.)

In order to determine whether moral judgment significantly and substantially relates to the mental health status of young adults (N = 78 community college students), Kupfersmid (1975) administered Kohlberg's moral dilemmas (1958), six measures of mental health (anxiety, self-concept, alienation, dogmatism, personality integration, and happiness), and the Otis Quick-Scoring Mental Ability Test. Generally, the results demonstrated little evidence to support the contentions that higher moral judgment is associated with more positive mental health. 'Given this situation, it was recommended that if laymen, educators, or behavioural scientists are interested in applying Kohlberg's moral maturity programme as a means to improve the mental health of participants, that implementation of the programme be deferred until evidence contrary to this study is available', p. 3516—A. (Details follow.)

Based on Kohlberg's postulation that two individuals at non-similar and non-adjacent stages of development do not agree with each other's reasoning in moral dilemma situations, Register (1976) compared two sets of stage pairings of married couples with an assessment of their marital satisfaction. One of the marital satisfaction measures supported the hypothesis that partners at similar stages of moral development would be more satisfied with their marriages than partners at non-similar or non-adjacent stages. (Details follow.)

A study of the relationship of transcendental meditation to Kohlberg's stages of moral reasoning was undertaken by Nidich (1976). The sample comprised 96 meditations, divided into six subgroups, ranging from one to three and a half years since beginning transcendental meditation, 20 non-meditators and 10 pre-meditators. Subjects ranged in age from 18 to 24 years and attended either Maharishi International University or the University of Cincinnati. Ss who practised transcendental meditation performed at the higher levels than non-meditators on Kohlberg's moral development scale. Longer term meditators did not score higher on Kohlberg's scale than shorter term meditators. That there would be no significant difference between non-meditators, not predisposed to beginning transcendental meditation, and pre-meditators interested in immediately beginning transcendental meditation, was substantiated. (Details follow.)

(Further discussion with respect to Kohlberg's earlier work, together with earlier replicatory and extension empirical studies have been included in Modgil, 1974).

vii. Kohlberg's application of his theory to the sphere of moral education.

Kohlberg (1970) considers that the issue of 'real life' brings us to what should be a central concern of moral education, the moral atmosphere of the school. He further elaborates (1971a) that to extend classroom discussions of justice to real life is to deal with issues of justice in the schools. Education for justice, requires making schools more just and encouraging students to take an active role in making the school more just. Kohlberg employs his evidence that children with extensive peer-group participation advance considerably more quickly through the Kohlberg stages of moral judgment than children isolated from such participation, for the application of environmental stimulation in the form of the enhancement of participation and role taking opportunities. Ultimate participation is participation in the structure and decisions of the school itself: 'Here the principle of participation must be integrated with our principle of stimulation by a justice-structure a stage above the child's own'.

Kohlberg (1971a) claims that the existence of moral stages offers the educator an alternative to the arbitrary indoctrination of children with the values he happens to favour. The cognitive-developmental approach to moral development involves the stimulation of natural moral development through the universal stages. The basis of the cognitive-developmental approach is that children have their own way of thinking and consequently, moral education must be based on a knowledge of their stages of development. The following propositions, basic to the cognitive-developmental approach and contrary to the propositions of ethical relativity, Kohlberg claims to be supported by clear research evidence (Kohlberg 1971a, *op. cit.*; Kohlberg and Turiel, 1971a): '(i) We often make different decisions and yet have the same basic moral values. (ii) Our values tend to originate inside ourselves as we process our social experience. (iii) In every culture and subculture of the world, the same basic moral values and the same steps toward moral maturity are found. While social environments directly produce different specific beliefs, (e.g. smoking is wrong; eating pork is wrong;) they do not engender different basic moral principles (e.g. consider the welfare of others; treat other people equally etc.). (iv) Insofar as basic values differ, it is largely because we are at different levels of maturity in thinking about basic moral and social issues and concepts. Exposure to others more mature than ourselves, helps to stimulate maturity in our own value processes. We are, however, selective in our responses to others and do not automatically incorporate the values of elders or authorities important to us', pp. 34 – 35.

Kohlberg (1971a and *passim*) reports that at certain age periods transitions to higher stages are made most easily. The first is the pre-adolescent period (10–13 years) when the transition from pre-conventional to conventional thought most commonly occurs. The level of morality at age 10 years does not indicate the level that will be attained in adulthood, but children who do not reach a solid Stage-3 or 4 level by age 13 years are unlikely to attain principled thinking in adulthood. The second transitional period appears to be in late adolescence, ages 15–19 years. Results suggest that those who do not use some (at least 20 per cent) principled thinking by the end of 'high school' are unlikely to develop principled thinking in adulthood.

The school's potential for positive influence on moral development is indicated by a variety of evidence. Bar Yam and Kohlberg (1971) showed the effect of a non-familial environment when disadvantaged adolescents in a kibbutz high school were compared with a control group of disadvantaged adolescents in the city, in moral judgment. The city children lived with their families; the kibbutz adolescents had little direct contact with their parents, yet seemed to show moral maturation. Blatt and Kohlberg (1971, *op. cit.*) indicated that more restricted educational efforts, such as Sunday School classes, to stimulate moral development can also have a significant effect on children. These studies suggest that by the use of procedures that are little different from those available to any teacher, it is possible to raise children's moral level significantly and in a way that is sustained over time.

The first principle to be embodied by teachers is for the spontaneous moral situations arising in the classroom to be embodied in a programme of moral education, for development is not achieved through direct teaching and instruction. Kohlberg's research evidence indicates that the child generates his own level of thinking and changes gradually. The task of the teacher is to facilitate the process of change.

Studies (Rest, Turiel and Kohlberg, 1969, *op. cit.*) suggest that it is not possible to encourage children to comprehend stages much higher than their own, much less to use them spontaneously. Success in stimulating change to a higher stage requires '(a) helping children to understand the next highest stage of reasoning and (b) facilitating their acceptance of that reasoning as their own, with the spontaneous use of it in new situations.' In another series of studies (Turiel, 1966, *op. cit.*) it was found to be possible to induce change in a child's thinking to the stage directly above his own. Moral reasons below the child's level are not very likely to be educational. The teacher's primary task is to help the child to focus on genuine moral conflicts; think about the reasoning he uses in solving such conflicts; see inconsistencies and inadequacies in his way of thinking and find means of resolving such inconsistencies and inadequacies (evidenced by Turiel, 1969). Kohlberg and Turiel (1971a) state that these approaches meet the criteria of being constitutional (i.e. they do not qualify as indoctrination, violate no civil rights and are independent of religious doctrines); are philosophically justified (moral philosophers throughout history have in various ways expressed principled moral judgment, moral leaders like Lincoln, Martin Luther King had an ethic based upon an advanced stage of moral development and the stages do not represent middle class bias — they are universal) and further the approaches are socially useful (persons at a higher level of moral development, not only reason better, but act in accordance with their judgments).

Therefore the aim of moral education is the 'stepwise stimulation of development toward a more mature moral judgment and reasoning, which culminate in a clear understanding of universal principles of justice, and not to develop intellectually or morally precocious children by mere acceleration. The aim is to ensure the optimal level of development in the child, to ensure that ultimately he will reach a mature level of thought and action'. (Kohlberg and Turiel, 1971a.)

Selman and Lieberman (1975) maintained that, 'According to the cognitive-developmental approach, two basic mechanisms are necessary for the development of moral reasoning. First, the child must feel some conflict or indecision over what is the right or moral action. Second, exposure to moral reasoning slightly more evolved than his own may facilitate development to the next stage or level (Kohlberg and Turiel, 1971). In intervention studies and in educational practice at the high school level, attempts to provide these experiences have in part taken the form of small group or classroom discussion of moral dilemmas (Blatt and Kohlberg, 1975). However, this approach has not, to our knowledge, been formally tested in the primary grades. While, in theory, the developmental principles of change should work regardless of the age or level of the population under study, different age groups present different problems to both research and curriculum development', p. 712. The authors therefore studied the effects of a semi-structured group discussion approach to moral education on the level of usage of the concept of moral intentionality in 68 second grade children. The medium of sound filmstrips to present moral dilemmas was used during which teachers encouraged discussion and debate among the Ss. Children in the experimental condition demonstrated higher level usage of the concept of moral intentionality on post- and follow-up testing than did a control group. The authors caution however, that due to the smallness of the participating classrooms, the results 'could not be definitively attributed to programme effects rather than to teacher effects, and conclusions must be interpreted within the context of a pilot evaluation research', (p. 712). (Details follow.)

Mosher and Sullivan (1976) describe and evaluate an experimental curriculum in moral education. Adolescents learned the process of moral dilemma discussions, developed counselling and teaching skills and then lead moral dilemma discussions with younger children. The results indicated positive changes on Kohlberg's measures of moral maturity and the Loevinger test of Ego Development.

Simon (1976) in describing the overall general process of moral development as 'consisting in the movement from heteronomy to autonomy through a period of socialization into conventional norms', focuses on the indications that parents, schools, and other social institutions are unsuccessful in enabling most youngsters to move through the stages and that the various models of moral development consist of hypothetical rather than automatic growth patterns. He continues that those involved in social (moral) education are aware of the challenges: the greatest challenge, in Simon's consideration, lying in the development of the student's ego strength in 'ways that will help him grow from a morally *reasoning* person to a morally *behaving* one,' p. 178. Leming (1976) reporting that age and empathy were the primary predictors for stage of moral reasoning and that the biographical variables (IQ, SES, age) were the primary predictor variables for choice on moral dilemmas, questions the extent to which the process of moral reasoning is readily amenable to educational intervention. He feels 'compelled to ask this question, since biographical factors are fixed and the school has little or no way of influencing them directly. It would appear that if further research supports the construct of moral reasoning suggested by this research, educators may well have to begin to reassess the viability of programmes oriented only toward in school rational activities. . . . Behaviourists and Freudians have long cautioned educators about taking too simple a view of students in an educational setting . . . Research in the area of values education, like any form of empirical research, will progress only as long as it is based on a clear and sound theoretical basis which must include some fundamental psychological assumptions about Man. A needed area of future inquiry is to develop a clear and defensible view of man as a valuing organism and to begin to derive our experimental hypotheses from this theoretical perspective,' p. 188. Mosher and Sullivan (*op. cit.*) focus on programmes of moral education currently being tested such as Grimes' (1974) classroom programme in which sixth grade students and their mothers jointly discussed and wrote moral dilemmas. Further, Stanley (1975) working with adolescents and their parents to study and change the 'justice structure' of the family in family education and counselling; Distefano (1975) teaching moral reasoning about sexual and interpersonal dilemmas to adolescents and Paolitto (1975) investigating role taking experiences for junior children and their effects on pre-adolescent moral development. Mosher and Sullivan further refer to attempts to train counsellors and social studies teachers to teach moral education through psychology and history and experiments to create just school units. They consider that the development of ways 'to educate for moral development in children and adolescents (and to empower parents as moral educators) is proceeding apace', p. 171.

Orr (1974)* has critically reviewed the prescriptions of Piaget and Kohlberg 'in their capacity as advisors concerning moral education within public schools', and Peters (1974) comments on the contributions of an educational institution to moral development, particularly with respect to development towards the autonomous stage (pp. 351—54).

viii. Moral development across the life-span

Kohlberg and Kramer's (1969) investigation of the moral judgments of 64 16- to 25-year-old males and their fathers supported Kohlberg's hypothesis that moral development is completed by post-adolescence. Papalia and Bielby (1974) focus on Kohlberg's recent (1973) acknowledgement that moral change can be a salient characteristic of adult life and his postulation relating to the existence of adulthood moral stages which represent distinct cognitive structural change. 'Alterations in adult moral ideology are said to result from "biography and common experience" (Kohlberg, 1973, p. 188) although a "different kind of experience is required for attainment of principled moral judgment than is required for the attainment of the prior stages" (Kohlberg, 1973, p. 194). Adult changes are generally due to "vicarious symbolic experience" (role taking opportunities). "Each stage is a cause and result of a wider and more adequate process of taking the perspectives of others, personal and societal, upon social conflict.",' (Papalia and Bielby, *op. cit*).

Bielby and Papalia (1975) were intent to determine the validity of Kohlberg's theorizing. Using three of Kohlberg's moral dilemmas, in a

* Gratitude is extended to Dr John B. Orr, of the University of Southern California for sending his work, which is referenced.

'cross-sectional life-span analysis of moral judgment* among 72 healthy, middle class Caucasian subjects comprising six age intervals (10—14, 15—19, 20—34, 35—49, 50—64, and 65 years and over), a curvilinear relationship between moral development and chronological age was established. 'Moral judgments rose from the lowest average stage of 2.5 in preadolescents to the highest average stage of 3.95 in the early middle-aged adults (35—49-year-olds). Thereafter, average stage levels declined; the oldest adults' average stage was 2.92. Analysis of the effects of education and sex on performance proved nonsignificant. However, inspection of anecdotal information offered by adult subjects (20—91 years) revealed that frequently close, personal experiences influenced their thinking on moral issues.' The increased variability in within-subject responses was interpreted to be a result of elderly subjects decreased ability to apply 'the environmental experiences effectively to their moral judgements.'

Podd (1972) provided confirmation of Kohlberg's (1973) hypothesis that moral development in adulthood and old age 'may parallel the ontogeny of ego development. (Podd's study is included in Modgil, 1974, p. 364.) The interrelationship was established among '134 white, middle class male college juniors and seniors'.

Holstein's (1973) sample established sex differences in moral judgment. Females characteristically remained at about stage three into middle age while adult males progressed through stages four and five. Papalia and Bielby focus on Holstein's interpretation of this pheno-menon: 'to be the result of Kohlberg's preoccupation with a moral hierarchy based on justice rather than love . . . For women, concern with the struggle for power is often irrelevant to their existence'. Bielby and Papalia's study indicated superiority among late middle-aged and elderly males when compared to females, although levels of significance were not obtained. In adulthood in general, males consistently had greater variability than females in moral stage levels. Further confir-mation was obtained from Haan *et al.* (1968).

Educational attainment does not appear to be an effective factor in moral judgments in adults and the elderly. This is considered by Papalia and Bielby to be a direct contradiction to Kohlberg and Kramer's (1969) finding that college students attained higher moral stage levels than non-college students. Papalia and Bielby comment that 'apparent-ly, adult life experiences allow the non-college student to "catch up" to the more highly educated subject. It would seem that low stage levels among the elderly are due to factors other than education since moral judgments have been strongly linked to cognitive functioning rather than educational attainment.' (Papalia and Bielby cite Tomlinson-Keasey, 1972, for evidence of this relationship — further studies in this respect have been discussed earlier in this volume). Bielby and Papalia's study reported 'a slight relationship' across the life-span between the 'conceptually related moral and cognitive (egocentrism) realms of thought.' The authors conclude that additional empirical evidence on adults, particularly the elderly, is required.

Abstracts

Observations of transgressions and a child's differential reaction to adult chastisement: effects on children's moral / person judgments
C.C. Aldrich, 1976

AIM / To attempt to validate empirically two aspects of Piaget's moral judgment: '(1) that the moral / person judgments of young children are tempered largely by consideration for the maintenance of adult authority relations, while those of older children are tempered largely by concern for reciprocal social interaction; and (2) that young children give increased attention to motives in determining moral culpability as the children increase in age.'

SUBJECTS / N = 144: 72 first and 72 sixth grade, male working class children.

METHOD / The subjects were randomly assigned to one of four experimental, or one of two control treatment conditions. The subjects assigned to the experimental treatment conditions were shown two videotape films: the first film depicting a boy involved in a situation of accidental damage being viewed by all subjects. The second film was varied in one of four different manners of response by the boy to the chastisement of his mother. The control groups viewed either only the first film or additionally that portion of the second film depicting the boy being chastised by his mother.

After viewing, the subjects evaluated the boy on a seven point goodness—badness scale (GRS); 'predicted episodes of "good" or "bad" behaviour to be exhibited by the boy' (MBPT) and further, were questioned regarding their perceptions of the stimulus film material having been presented together with their rationale for their moral / personal judgments.

RESULTS / The results indicated the MBPT to be more sensitive than the GRS. On the basis of the patterning of subjects' scores on the MBPT, the following conclusions were drawn: '(1) Children place an increased emphasis on motives in determining moral culpability as the children increase in age; (2) Contextual cues influence the degree to which negative adult sanctions are treated by older children as constituting morally relevant information; (3) Young children view a child's compliance to adult prescriptions as being mandatory; they predict a greater number of negative behaviours to be exhibited by a child who overtly counters, as opposed to a child who overtly accepts, an adult's chastisement; and (4) older children do not construe a child's compliance to adult prescriptions as being mandatory. Instead, they evaluate a child's behaviour toward an adult in terms of whether the child's behaviour is congruent with the principle of reciprocal social interaction,' p. 4123B. Further discussion of the results appear in Aldrich, *op. cit.*, p. 4123B.

Role-taking and moral judgment in five- and seven-year-olds
S.R. Ambron and D.M. Irwin, 1975

AIM / Three dimensions of role taking (perceptual, cognitive, and affective) and two dimensions of moral judgment (intentionality and restitution) were studied in young children.

SUBJECTS / N = 72, aged five and seven years.

METHOD / Each child was tested individually on 32 role taking items and 24 moral judgment items, patterned after Flavell *et al.* (1968) and Kohlberg (1969) and Piaget (1932).

RESULTS / There was a significant correlation (r = .36, p < .001) between role taking and moral judgment. Children high and low on role taking demonstrated significant relations between cognitive role taking and moral judgment (p < .05 for cognitive role taking stories and p < .01 for the cognitive role-taking game) and borderline significance between total moral judgment and role taking (p < .01). The seven-year-olds performed at the higher levels than the five-year-olds on all areas of role taking except the perceptual tasks. The seven-year-olds had higher scores than five-year-olds on total moral judgment and intentionality but not on restitution. No significant sex differences were observed on the moral judgment dimensions. However, boys performed significantly better than girls on the perceptual role taking task.

Cognitive style and modification of moral judgment
J. Arbuthnot, 1974

AIM / It was hypothesized that as a result of a role playing episode concerning a moral dilemma, field-dependent Ss would show greater change in maturity of moral judgment in accordance with the level of the cognitive demands of their role.

SUBJECTS / N = 78 female psychology students, 16 of whom served as controls.

METHOD / Jackson's (1956) short form of the Embedded-figures Test was used to assess level of field dependency. Kohlberg's (1971) standard moral dilemmas were employed to evaluate maturity of moral judgment. The pre-test comprised Dilemmas III and IV, the immediate post-test of Dilemmas VIII and X, and a one-week post-test of Dilemmas V, VI, and VII.

RESULTS / Field-dependent subjects were more susceptible to both positive and negative conducive roles on an immediate but not on a one-week post-test. 'That these effects were not observed over a one-week period (all changes became generally positive) may indicate that field-dependent Ss show more immediate response to the disequilibrium induced by role playing but resolution of this state in time tends to moderate its impact and permits a more generally positive structural change similar to that of the field-independent subjects', p. 274.

Modification of moral judgment through role playing
J. Arbuthnot, 1975

AIM / To examine the impact of actual role playing on the change of moral judgment maturity.

SUBJECTS / N = 96 introductory psychology students within the age range from 17 to 21. Of the 96 Ss, 32 served in two control groups (n = 16 in each).

METHOD / The maturity of moral judgment was evaluated by the administration in paper-and-pencil format of seven of Kohlberg's moral dilemmas. Dilemmas III and IV comprised the pretest; Dilemma III, the role playing task (of Heinz, of the Druggist); Dilemmas VIII and X, the immediate posttest; and Dilemmas V, VI, and VII, the one-week delayed posttest. (Fuller details of the experimental procedure are given in Arbuthnot, 1975, pp. 320–321.)

RESULTS / Subjects demonstrated both immediate and delayed

increases in moral judgment maturity when role playing a moral dilemma against an opponent who used reasoning above the subject's initially assessed stage. 'Change scores exceeded those of control groups who either performed extraneous tasks or who passively received role-playing arguments. More change was exhibited by subjects at the lower stages. The flexibility of subjects' responses during role playing was associated with immediate but not delayed change in moral judgment maturity. The subject did not show greater change in response to reasoning one stage higher than their own (versus two stages higher or one stage lower) as had been previously observed by Turiel. No sex differences were observed in initial stages or in amount of change', (*ibid.*, p. 319).

Intentionality, degree of damage, and moral judgments
L.G. Berg-Cross, 1975

AIM / 'The present study attempts to minimize (these) methodological flaws by presenting only single stories with clearly stated intentional factors for judgment and using both a quantitative and qualitative measure of judged naughtiness in addition to a verbal measure. It is hypothesized that with the simplified methodology . . . children will be able to make a variety of complex judgments concerning degree of deserved punishment, based on (a) the intention preceding the act as well as (b) the damage incurred. It is also hypothesized that the Ss will produce more mature responses when responding to the simple singular stories than when asked to respond to the complex story pairs', p. 971.

SUBJECTS / N = 153, with a mean age of six years seven months.

METHOD / Each subject was individually tested. Stories were read aloud to the child. 'After each story, the Ss were shown a five-point pictorial punishment scale and indicated which card they wanted to give the story character. The first card the children pointed to was their score. With increasing number of punishments depicted the score value of the cards increased from zero (no punishment) to four. After the choice, Ss explained their answers which were recorded verbatim and later scored as mature or immature according to Piaget's (1932) criteria', p. 972. (Fuller details of the experimental procedures, including story themes and damage levels are described elsewhere, Berg-Cross, 1975, pp. 971–972.)

RESULTS / Contrary to results obtained with a story-pair methodology, it was observed that with single stories, even six-year-old subjects responded to the level of intention in the stories as well as the quantity and quality of damage involved. The author contended that Piaget's methodology may be forcing children to employ a simplifying strategy while under other conditions they were able to perform the mental operations necessary to make complex moral judgments. The results are discussed with other studies: Armsby (1971); Bandura and McDonald (1963); Crowley (1968); Gutkin (1972) and Turiel (1966).

Children's use of motives and intentionality in person perception and moral judgment
T.J. Berndt and E.G. Berndt, 1975

AIMS / The study attempted to answer three specific questions: 'Do young children understand the concept of a motive as a reason for acting? Do young children understand the concept of intentionality, or the accidental—intentional distinction? When do motives and intentionality begin to affect children's evaluations?', pp. 904—905.

SUBJECTS / N = 72. Twelve boys and 12 girls at each of three grade levels, pre-school (mean age four years 11 months), second (mean age eight years two months), and fifth grade (mean age 11 years two months).

METHOD / Four types of situations were presented. Two of the situations portrayed actors with the same motive (to get a toy) who injured another either intentionally (instrumental aggression) or accidentally (accidental). Accidental injury again occurred in a third situation, however the actor had an altruistic motive (altruism). Displaced aggression was portrayed in the fourth situation. The four types of motives were presented with both films and stories in order to replicate Chandler, Greenspan and Barenboim's (1973) results that higher levels of moral judgments occur with films. Details of the experimental procedure and stimulus materials are given in Berndt and Berndt (1975, pp. 905—906).

RESULTS / Children of all ages comprehended the concepts of motive and intentionality. However, the ability to make accurate inferences about motives and intentionality developed as a function of age. Whereas motives affected children's evaluations at all ages, intentionality affected only grade school children's evaluations. Berndt and Berndt asserted, 'Either a cognitive-developmental or a social learning explanation for the development of motives and intentionality as evaluative criteria could be given. Some additional findings of the present study are relevant to this choice. First, young children used a large and varied set of evaluative criteria. In addition to intentions and consequences, children mentioned the possibility of avoiding the injury and norms of reciprocity as reasons for evaluation. The greater use of these other criteria with films affected children's moral judgments for the two media. The stories focused young children's attention on consequences, as Chandler *et al.* (1973) had found, but they also focused older children's attention on intentions. Consequently, age changes were often greater with stories than with films. The hypothesis (Chandler *et al.*, 1973; Farnill, 1974) that advanced moral judgments would be more common with films was not confirmed. When different types of stories have been used (Irwin and Moore, 1971; von Wright and Niemala, 1966), still other criteria have affected children's evaluations. Second, there was no significant interrelationship among the moral judgment measures', pp. 910–911.

The relationship between moral judgment, causal reasoning and general reasoning
I. Brooks-Walsh and E.V. Sullivan, 1973

AIM / To determine if there were a relationship between moral judgment, causal thinking and moral reasoning.

SUBJECTS / N = 28 within the age range from eight years, three months to 11 years seven months and a mean IQ of 115.7.

METHOD / The Ss were individually tested on the following tasks: (a) Piaget's (1932) items for the rules of the games of marbles to determine the level of moral judgment; (b) The General Reasoning Task was a story in the form of a riddle whose solution was operational only by those who had attained formal reasoning (Moir, 1957); and (c) The Causal Judgment Task, patterned after Laurendeau and Pinard (1962).

RESULTS / The data demonstrated 'significance between the general reasoning task and the causal judgment task . . . No significant relationship was found between general reasoning and moral judgment . . . analysis of the relationship between causal judgment and moral judgment also yielded no significant results . . . A chi-square one-sample case test was employed to analyze the relationship between relative structural level on the General Reasoning Task and the other tasks (Moral Judgment Task and Causal Judgment Task), the responses of Ss on the three tasks were scored high or low and then compared. High

GRT Ss tended to score at the same high level on CJT and MJT ... Low GRT Ss, however, scored at different levels on the CJT and MJT ...', pp. 133–134.

Baldwins' kindness concept measure as related to children's cognition and temperament: a twin study
A.M. Brown, A.P. Matheny, Jr., and R.S. Wilson, 1973

AIM / That twins with relatively more mature judgments on the Baldwin measure would show, relative to their co-twins, better cognitive functioning and relatively longer attention in play and more stable temperament.

SUBJECTS / N = 16 pairs of twins. Nine pairs were dizygotic and seven pairs monozygotic. The age range was from five to six years.

METHOD / The Ss were administered the Wechsler Preschool and Primary Scale of Intelligence (WPPSI) (Wechsler, 1949) and the Baldwin Picture-Story Measure of Kindness Concept (Baldwin and Baldwin, 1970). Usually the mother was interviewed to elicit the parent's rating of the two children, relative to one another, with respect to the attentional and temperamental variables (Wilson *et al.*, 1971).

RESULTS / Responses were comparable to the Baldwin's kinder-garten sample. Fourteen pairs were discordant on the kindness measure. 'For the discordant pairs, WPPSI intelligence test scores were analyzed for within-pair differences. The twins with less adult-like responses on the measure scored lower than their co-twins on several verbal and performance subtests. These twins, as reported by their mothers, were also relatively more temperamental and less attentive than their co-twins'. The authors discussed the results in terms of Piaget's concept of the parallel development of the cognition of the impersonal and interpersonal worlds.

A quantitative methodology to examine the development of moral judgment
J.P. Buchanan and S.K. Thompson, 1973

AIM / A quantitative methodology to examine the development of moral judgment was undertaken.

SUBJECTS / N = 48 boys between six and 10 years of age.

METHOD / Piaget's clinical method (1932) was adapted to a quantitative judgment task. The procedures used were (a) to have the S make absolute quantitative judgments rather than relative verbal judgments about naughtiness of characters in stories; (b) to have the S judge stories one at a time rather than in pairs; and (c) to have the S judge not only the Piagetian high intent–low damage (HI–LD) and low intent–high damage (LI–HD) story situations but also high intent–high damage (HI–HD) and low intent–low damage (LI–LD) story situations. 'The addition of the two new story types in the quantitative task allows for a statistical evaluation of a child's ability to use both damage and intent simultaneously making a moral judgment. The clinical method, on the other hand, since it uses only the HI–LD and LI–HD stories, can only be used to test a child's major preference for either intent or damage information. It cannot, as Piaget assumes, adequately test whether a child is employing both factors simultaneously,' p. 186.

RESULTS / Damage was the most important factor in moral decisions for younger children while intent information was more important to older children. 'However unlike Piaget's clinical procedure, the experimenter's methodology allowed substantiation of the ability of children to simultaneously weigh damage and intent information when making a moral judgment', p. 186.

Interrelations among Piaget's formal operations, Erikson's ego identity, and Kohlberg's principled morality
M.A. Cauble, 1975

AIM / To investigate the interrelations among Piaget's formal operations, Erikson's ego identity and Kohlberg's principled morality, together with the effect of sex, CA and SES on the comprehension of principled moral judgments.

SUBJECTS / N = 90 college undergraduates.

METHOD / The tasks administered included three Piagetian formal operations tests; Rest's Defining Issues Test of principled morality, and two Eriksonian measures — Constantinople's Inventory of Personality Development and Marcia's identity status interview.

RESULTS / Both formal operations and social class contributed significantly to P score variance on Rest's Defining Issues Test 'while Constantinople's ego measure did not relate to any of the variables in

the regression analyses. The identity questioners . . . scored significantly
higher (p < .05) than the non-questioners on formal operations, but
scored no higher on the Constantinople Inventory of Personality
Development or Rest's principled morality measure. Looking at the
highest stage of substantial usage on Rest's Defining Issues Test
suggested movement from Stage 5A to Stage 5B in principled morality
is accompanied by increased ego development (Constantinople) without
increased formal operations capability', (*ibid.*, p. 773—A).

Durkheim and others: some philosophical influences on Piaget's theory
*of moral development**
R.P. Craig, 1976

Jean Piaget has been influenced by many thinkers, and the Institute
Jean-Jacques Rousseau, where Piaget is the Director of Studies, bears
the name of one such influence. Rousseau, like Piaget, claimed that
verbal understanding and conceptualization come toward the end of a
process which necessarily begins with manipulation of objects. Since
motivation is internal, Rousseau believed that values needed to be
concrete before the individual internally develops moral truth. But the
value must in no way be imposed on the child by an adult authority,
for Rousseau felt this would only retard the intrinsic moral development of the child. The adult needs to recognize the autonomy of the
various stages of moral growth the child develops; and each of these
stages are intrinsically worthwhile and necessary in the maturity and
self-reliance of the child. The influence of Rousseau on Piaget is evident.
Piaget's theory of cognitive and moral development is genetic as
opposed to logical. Thus, Piaget is more closely indebted to Henri
Bergson than to Kant, for it was Kant who developed a logical
epistemology of human growth. According to Kant, the mind does not
conform to objects, but the objects conform to man's mind. Therefore,
space and time, as well as the categories of the understanding are part
of the sequence and development of the mind. The Kantian view
implies much adult intervention to ensure the correct logical development of the individual.
A genetic epistemology differs greatly from a logical one, for a
genetic epistemology presupposes a dynamic evolutionary theory as its
basis. The evolution of the cognitive and moral aspects of development
occur in spite of adult prescriptions. Piaget (1932) writes:

* Published with the kind permission of the author. Gratitude is expressed to Dr
Robert Paul Craig, Philosophy and Education Departments of St Mary's
College, Michigan.

' . . . the sense of justice, though naturally capable of being reinforced by the precepts and the practical example of the adult, is largely independent of these influences, and requires nothing more for its development than the mutual respect and solidarity which holds among children themselves', p. 198.

A genetic view, then, allows for more freedom of development and expression on the individual's part. In the final analysis, the goal for man is self-reliance.

Beside Bergson and Rousseau, the thinker who influenced Piaget's views on moral development is Emile Durkheim, and the remainder of this paper will investigate the similarities between Durkheim's and Piaget's views on moral development.

Piaget has been criticized for his apparent disregard for academic disciplines, for he often utilizes the method of the psychologist and at other times that of the sociologist. His interest in sociology is evident when he writes:

'Whether we wish it or not, the questions we have had to discuss in connection with child morality take us to the very heart of the problems studied by contemporary sociology and social psychology', (*ibid.*, p. 327).

And one sociologist he has in mind is Durkheim.

Yet much of what Durkheim has to say is often neglected by students of moral development, because Durkheim's insights appear too much like common sense. Plus, Durkheim's theory that society is the only source of morality is disputed by such thinkers as Lawrence Kohlberg who finds this kind of thinking similar to the second level of moral development. (Kohlberg, 1971)

According to Durkheim, morality consists of three elements: (1) Discipline, (2) Attachment and (3) Autonomy. (Kay, 1968) Each of the above get their meaning from society, thus, discipline, for example, is not to be viewed as merely a system of self-regulation. Durkheim (1960) writes:

'The domain of the genuinely moral life only begins where collective life begins — or in other words, that we are moral beings to the extent that we are social beings,' p.64.

At this point there would be agreement by such diverse thinkers as Aristotle and John Dewey. 'Man is a social animal,' Aristotle claimed.

For Durkheim, attachment is also basically social, for it is through attachment that one identifies oneself with a social group. Thus, 'discipline is merely the name given to the relationship when society takes the initiative; and attachment is the name given when the individual establishes the bond,' (Kay, 1968, p. 147).

The third characteristic of morality, autonomy, is seen by Durkheim as also indispensible to moral development, for real moral behaviour is not synonymous with external compulsion. Thus, one does not act morally when under group restraint; rather, one acts morally when the compulsion is within. The individual needs to have some understanding (personal judgment) of the particular moral issue at hand. 'It is this understanding that makes this social conduct autonomous,' Kay (1968, p. 148).

This understanding of moral issues and this sense of autonomy and moral responsibility is reflected in Piaget's theory of moral development. The following quotation could have been written by Piaget:

> 'A society like ours cannot therefore, contend itself with a complacent possession of moral results that have been handed down to it. It must go on to new conquests; it is necessary that the teacher prepares the children who are in his trust for these necessary advances. He must be on his guard against transmitting the moral gospel of our elders as a sort of closed book. On the contrary he must excite in them a desire to add a few lines of their own and give them the tools to satisfy this legitimate ambition', Durkheim (1960, pp. 13–14).

Piaget is obviously indebted to Durkheim, for Piaget contends, 'It is this consciousness of obligation which seems to us, as to Durkheim, to distinguish a rule in the true sense from mere regularity,' (Piaget, *op. cit.*, p. 23). Again, agreeing with Durkheim, Piaget writes:

> 'All morality consists in a system of rules and the essence of all morality is to be sought in the respect which an individual acquires for these rules', (*ibid.*, p. 1).

Durkheim and Piaget on authority

The final section of this brief paper will dwell on both Durkheim's and Piaget's ideas on authority. And Piaget's thoughts follow his moral theory rather directly, for Piaget contends ' . . . there existed at least two extreme types of rules and of authority — rules due to unilateral respect and rules due to mutual respect', (Piaget, *op. cit.*, p. 362).

The rule of constraint, then, which is tied to the notion of unilateral respect, is considered transcendent and sacred by the child. But rules which are due to mutual cooperation tend to be part and parcel of an autonomous individual. Piaget then wants to consider how far this theory of moral development is rooted in sociology, especially rooted in Durkheim.

Piaget finds that far too often contemporary society is substituting constraint for cooperation, although he does claim that this is not the case in the theories of the sociologists. The concern with democracy means an emphasis on cooperation, for democracy can only continue if the people cooperate (*ibid.,* p. 363).

Thus, democracy should be initiated in the schools; and each teacher ought to encourage participation and dialogue. Piaget makes the following important comment.

'The sense of a common law, which, as we have shown in connection with the rules of a game, is possessed by children of 9—12, shows clearly enough how capable is the child of discipline and democratic life, when he is not, as at school, condemned to wage war against authority', (*ibid.*, p. 364).

Piaget, unlike Durkheim, is in favor of the Activity School 'in which the child is not made to work by means of external constraint, but where he works of his own free will,' (*ibid.*, p. 364). Thus, even though Piaget has been influenced tremendously by Durkheim, he disagrees with him on one essential point: cooperation and mutual respect are not as superficial as Durkheim suggests. In fact, their development implies a minimum of societal influence, as they imply 'the complete autonomy of reason,' (*ibid.*, p. 371).

Durkheim suggests that the individual himself cannot create morality, but true morality is societal. Piaget disagrees, for he recognizes personal reason as developing apart from a social context. Or, to put it differently, society, with its rules and regulations, is one step in the moral development of individuals, and indeed a necessary step. But, it is a rather limited sense of moral development, according to Piaget. He writes:

'Nothing could be truer than to say that autonomy presupposes a scientific knowledge of social as of natural laws and the ability to recognize these laws at work. But social laws are unfinished and their progressive formation presupposes the unfettered cooperation of personal reason', (*ibid.*, p. 370).

Piaget views Durkheim's sociological theory with both optimism and pessimism. It is true, according to Piaget, that morality is basically social and the development of morality is tied into the development of collective groups. But this is the optimism, for Piaget disagrees that this is the extent of morality. Durkheim does not distinguish properly between the morality of constraint and the morality of cooperation. Piaget writes:

> 'Hence Durkheim's illusion that an education which makes use only of unilateral respect can lead to the results that are peculiar to the morality of mutual respect', (*ibid.*, p. 371).

For Piaget, heteronomous morality and autonomous morality differ greatly, and one cannot be taught through the methods peculiar to the other. Autonomy can never result through heteronomous standards and methods. Constraint and cooperation differ, and Durkheim is incorrect if he supposes that even in developing cooperation a certain amount of external discipline and constraint is necessary. Piaget seems to be making a rather strong claim. True cooperation and the development of autonomy is a rather 'natural' process which occurs to the extent that adult intervention is barely negligible.

As a teacher of philosophy I am especially interested in the fact that Piaget bases much of his theories on philosophical theories. Behaviourism seems to be a peculiar American phenomenon! Piaget is even proud of his knowledge of philosophy, and he is certainly correct that a psychological epistemology needs to be thoroughly grounded in philosophy. Likewise I find his interdisciplinary sense very positive, for to consider moral development a certain amount of sociology is necessary. We have so much to learn from Piaget, as he has learned from his predecessors.

Early conceptions of positive justice as related to the development of logical operations
W. Damon, 1975

AIM / To investigate the relation between the development of justice conceptions and the development of mathematical and physical conceptions.

SUBJECTS / N = 50 within the age range from four through eight years.

METHOD / The justice interview comprised of (a) an open-ended interview focusing on sharing and a sharing problem modelled after Ugurel-Semin (1952) and (b) four dilemmas of the kind used by Kohlberg (1958). Additionally, five tasks, comprising of problems in mathematical and physical logic, were administered (Inhelder and Piaget, 1964; Piaget, 1951; and Piaget, Inhelder and Szeminska, 1960).

RESULTS / A strong relationship between the level of a child's reasoning about positive justice and the level of his reasoning about mathematical and physical problems was computed. ' . . . in the great majority of Ss, there was close synchrony (i.e. little segregation) between parallel levels of reasoning in the two domains; and . . . there was little evidence in support of the notion that one type of reasoning (e.g. mathematical—physical) provides a necessary condition for the development of the other (e.g., justice)', p. 301. Damon presented an analysis of logical relations between parallel levels in the two domains.

A comparison of Hogan's and Kohlberg's theories of moral development
M.J. Gallagher, 1975

AIMS / Three objectives were formulated: first, to determine the degree of relationship between Hogan's and Kohlberg's theories of moral development; second, to compare the theories in terms of their abilities to predict which types of subjects would make ethical decisions independently of the punishment consequences of their decisions; and third, to establish the comparative adequacy of these two systems at predicting cheating.

SUBJECTS / N = 712, drawn from a community and a senior college.

METHOD / Following Hogan's procedure, the tests employed were the California Psychological Inventory Socialization Scale, Hogan's Empathy Scale, Barron's Autonomy Scale, and Hogan's Survey of Ethical Attitudes. 'Ss were divided into high and low groups on each of these variables using norms established by Hogan and Gough. Then eight personality types were formed on the basis of all the possible combinations of high and low scores on socialization, empathy, and autonomy. Each of these eight personality cells was filled with 16 subjects' typical of a particular personality type. In addition, half of the Ss in each cell had scored high on the Survey of Ethical Attitudes while the other half had scored low. This group of 128 Ss constituted the sample for the remainder of the experiment. Each of the 128 Ss was then interviewed individually and placed in one of two treatments. Half the Ss within each personality type were given a shortened version of a standard Kohlberg interview involving only four stories. The other half received the same stories, but the fourth story informed the Ss that the recommendation of a particular course of action would result in punishment for the fictional character in the story. In addition, all Ss received a spurious test of intelligence under conditions of low surveillance. Procedures were utilized which permitted the detection of cheaters with a high degree of accuracy. The order of presentation of the two tasks was systematically varied within treatment and personality type'.

RESULTS / No relationship was computed between personality type and Kohlberg's stage of moral judgment score. Of Hogan's four personality variables only empathy correlated with stage of moral judgment. Punishment influenced the decisions of subjects, with subjects in the punishment condition recommending the course of action which avoided punishment significantly more often than the control condition. 'Contrary to expectations, Ss who scored high on stage of moral judgment were just as influenced as those who scored low. However, there were too few Ss at stages five and six to draw any definite conclusions about the implications of this finding for Kohlberg's system. Hogan's system was not much better at predicting resistance to the influence of punishment. However, this was due to the fact that the autonomy measure lacked predictive validity. By disregarding autonomy level, it was found that high socialization and empathy were predictive of resistance to the influence of punishment. Also, punishment did not cause subjects to use lower stages of judgment. Consequently, Kohlberg's contention that higher stages integrate lower stages received some support. With respect to cheating, the results showed that subjects at higher stages of judgment cheat less often than those at lower stages. None of Hogan's personality types were related to non-cheating. Of Hogan's four personality variables, only high empathy was predictive of non-cheating. Further, the results indicated that Kohlberg's system was a better predictor of non-cheating than was Hogan's'.

Moral judgment: a comparison of two theoretical approaches
H. Gash, 1976

AIMS / To investigate the relationship between Kohlberg's 'cognitive-developmental' stages and Hoffman's 'social learning' moral orientations. Further, on the speculation that persons with close personal ties are more likely to take each other's perspective in their moral thinking than persons without these close ties, to change the dilemmas used by Kohlberg and Hoffman in order to vary the closeness of the relationship between the principal characters.

SUBJECTS / N = 90 middle class males: 23 ninth, 26 tenth, 22 eleventh and 19 twelfth grades.

METHOD / The Ss were administered four moral judgment questionnaires during a period of six weeks: an original and altered Kohlberg
questionnaire and an original and altered Hoffman questionnaire in
counterbalanced order. The questions used by Hoffman were designed
to force the Ss to choose between the humanistic and conventional
norms stressed in society: the original and altered questionnaires varied
the distance and closeness of the relationships. The responses were
scored as humanistic conventional or externally oriented. Four of
Kohlberg's moral dilemmas together with probing questions describing
close personal relationships between the principal characters were used
in the form of a questionnaire: the altered questionnaire reduced the
closeness of relationships. Scoring procedures followed Kohlberg's
recommendations, (See pp. 97–100).

RESULTS / 'The first hypothesis on the nature of the relationship
between Hoffman's categories and Kohlberg's levels was confirmed;
that is, post-conventional reasoning (on the original Kohlberg questionnaire) was found to be significantly associated with humanistic
reasoning (on the original Hoffman questionnaire)'. However, there
were some reservations when other more detailed analyses of associations were made at other levels (p. 109). 'The second hypothesis on
the effects of changing the original questionnaires received some
support . . . there was a significant difference between mean moral
maturity scores obtained from the original and altered Kohlberg
questionnaires supporting the hypothesis that dilemmas between
principal characters with close interpersonal relations would elicit
higher stage responses', (p. 110) although this difference can in part be
attributed to order effects. Changes made to Hoffman's items were
almost undetectable in the responses. It was concluded that it will
require further research to determine whether the humanistic orientation has a stage developmental character and whether the effects of
changing Kohlberg dilemmas can be replicated.

*The effect of systematic story changes on intentionality in children's
moral judgments*
D.C. Gutkin, 1972

AIM / The author focuses on the relatively little attention that has
been paid to the role that systematic differences in the items used to
assess moral intentionality might play. The study was concerned with
the ability of children to use intentionality in making moral judgments

on items of systematically varying difficulty.

SUBJECTS / N = 72: 24 children (12 boys and 12 girls) from each of grades one, three and five.

METHOD / Piaget and subsequent researchers have been concerned with the variable of intention (good or bad) against the variable of damage (high or low) in their investigations into intentionality. Gutkin considered that these two variables and their two respective values could be arranged in other combinations. The six possible combinations and story types generated were: Type—A, following Piaget, in which good intentions go with high damage and bad intentions go with low damage; Type—B, in which the amount of damage was held constant and low across the pair of stories, while intentions vary; a Type—C story pair was the same as a Type—B pair except that damage is held constant across the two stories at a high level; in Type—D, the intentions were held constant (at the 'good' value), while the amount of damage varied; Type—E story pairs were identical with those of Type—D except that, in Type—E, intention was held constant at the 'bad' value; finally, in Type—F story pairs, good intentions and low damage within one story were opposed to bad intentions and high damage within the other. The hypotheses formulated included: 'Type—B story pairs will elicit a greater number of intentional judgments than will Type—A story pairs'; 'Type—C story pairs will elicit a greater number of intentional judgments than will Type—A story pairs'; 'Type—A story pairs will elicit a greater number of intentional judgments than will Type—D story pairs;' 'Type—A story pairs will elicit a greater number of intentional judgments than will Type—E story pairs;' and finally, 'Type—F story pairs will elicit about the same number of intentional judgments as will Type—A story pairs.

Following the results of a pilot study, each subject was tested on six items which consisted of the same two story pairs presented in Types—A, —B, and —E.

The data were scored by the investigator into three categories: intentional, damage-based, and transitional. The great majority of the data (97 per cent) was scored as either intentional or damage based.

RESULTS / The results of a scalogram analysis suggested that the development of moral intentionality goes through four stages of progressive refinement in terms of the story-types. In the first stage, intentional judgments do not appear at all, for the child does not believe intentions are relevant. In the second stage, intentional judgments are made only to items of Type—B: the child believes that intentions have some relevance in the assessment of moral worth but not as more important than damage factors. Intentional judgments are made both to items of Type—B and Type—A but not to Type—E in the third stage: thereby believing that intentions are more important than damage but still that damage is important. Finally, in stage four, the child makes intentional judgments on items of Types—B, —A, and —E: it is intentions alone that count in such judgments.

The results of the pilot study suggested that Type—F was the functional equivalent of Type—A, that Type—C is the equivalent of Type—B and Type—D is the equivalent of Type—E.

It was further concluded that 'it is easier to make an intentional judgment to an item as Type—B than to an item as Type—A'.

An analysis of the concept of moral intentionality
D.C. Gutkin, 1973

The author focuses on the little attention which has been paid to the nature of the concept of intentionality. The aim of his paper was therefore to examine the concept of moral intentionality critically in the hope that such an examination may throw light on the data from previous studies as well as suggesting new areas that merit investigation.

Inherent in questions about moral intentions is the more general problem of responsibility: the problem is to know for what we are entitled to hold a person responsible. 'In turn the question of whether the person intended the consequences which his action brought about suggests itself as an important consideration in judging his responsibility.'

The author gives four story examples to illustrate what sort of factors seem important in deciding questions of responsibility. Four levels of intention or responsibility were specified: (1) completely innocent accident; (2) accident due to slight carelessness; (3) accident due to recklessness and (4) consequence resulting from fully intentional purposive act. He emphasizes that there are many examples from everyday life in which people are held responsible for consequences that they did not intend as goals. In such cases the concepts which are invoked to show the fairness of ascribing responsibility are ideas such as 'recklessness, criminal negligence or dereliction of duty and assumed obligation'. Not desiring a certain result as an end 'does not necessarily exonerate one from responsibility for that result'.

Following further analysis the author concludes that there are many degrees of responsibility or intention that can be studied and that in fact what people are held responsible for are the consequences of their actions. Research in psychology has been content to deal with just two values of intention (intentional and not intentional). Gutkin hypothesizes that it is reasonable to suppose that a child might go through a stage of moral judgment when he over-emphasizes intention in the same way that he goes through a stage of over-emphasizing damage. After the child has learned that intentions are more important than damage he still has to learn to discriminate among various levels of intention in order to make what adults would consider really correct moral judgments. 'Gutkin (1972) concluded that more mature subjects (who were at most 11-years-old) considered damage totally irrelevant as a moral criterion. This conclusion is justified within the narrow context of his study. But it is not true as a general conclusion about the nature of consequences and responsibility. For the process of determining moral responsibility includes a careful analysis of the likely consequences of an action. Thus in a broader sense consequences such as damage are relevant to moral judgment'. The results of the analysis were further used to help resolve an apparent contradiction between Hoffman's (1970) findings and the results of the work on intentionality. The research on intentionality has found that more mature children are concerned with intentions as revealed in actions. Hoffman's findings show that less morally mature children are especially sensitive to internal impulses apart from considerations of action. 'These findings are not incompatible since intentions and impulses are not at all the same thing'.

Maternal discipline and children's judgments of moral intentionality
D.C. Gutkin, 1975

AIM / Whether the behaviour that mothers report they would use in situations involving intent and damage bears a relation to the kind of judgments that their children make about similar situations.

SUBJECTS / N = 120, forty children from each of grades one, three, and six.

METHOD / Each S was tested individually on four story-pairs, three patterned after Bandura and McDonald (1963) and one modelled after Gutkin (1972). Four of the story-pairs (Bandura and McDonald) formed the basis of the items administered to the mothers. 'There were four different story-types, resulting from pairing each of two values of intention (good and bad) with each of two values of damage (heavy or light). Thus there were items in which the child acted from good intentions and caused heavy damage (G—H items), items in which he acted from good intentions and caused light damage (G—L items), items in which he acted from bad intentions and caused heavy damage (B—H items), and items in which he acted from bad intentions and caused light damage (B—L items)', p. 56. Mother's punishment responses were based on the intent shown by the child in the stories. This measure was reported by Hebble (1971). (Fuller details are given in Gutkin, 1975, pp. 56—58.)

RESULTS / No relation was computed between the intentional level of children and the extent to which mothers reported that their discipline practices would be determined by considerations of intention. This departs from the findings reported by Bandura (1969). The majority of the mothers reported that they would be influenced by their children's intentions rather than by the amount of damage they caused, thereby supporting Cowan *et al.'s* suggestion that parents do not provide their children with consistent models for damage-based responding. The conclusion that power-assertive discipline by parents is associated with less advanced moral development in children was given further credence.

Children's moral reasoning
M. Hardeman, 1972

AIM / To test Piaget's hypothesis of a parallel relationship between moral concepts and logical structures in human development.

SUBJECTS / N = 142 first grade children, all of middle socio-economic background. Their mean IQ was 110, the standard deviation 14.13.

METHOD / A moral reasoning interview schedule (Piaget, 1932) consisting of 18 items was administered, aimed at eliciting children's reasoning about moral values in five different areas, so that a judgment could be made concerning their relative maturity or immaturity in such reasoning. 'In Area I, three items presented situations in which the intentions of the characters were held constant, and the amount of damage varied . . . In Area II, three pairs of stories were adapted from Piaget . . . in which both the intentions of the characters and size of the consequences varied . . . Six items (Area III) were direct questions designed to find out whether the child manifested the ability to maintain or "conserve" values in the moral area in spite of perceptual distractions introduced by the size of the persons involved or by their social distance . . . Four items (Area IV) were concerned with children's reasons for obligations . . . Two items were included as a measure of the child's egocentricity (Area II)', pp. 52—53. Three conservation problems (Almy *et al.*, 1966) and four class-inclusion tasks (Miller, 1966) were also administered.

RESULTS / Piaget's hypothesis of a developmental parallelism in children's logical ability and their moral concepts was not substantiated. However, a significant difference in the spread of moral reasoning scores, between conservers and non-conservers, suggested that the ability to advance structure of an operational kind to inanimate, visible objects might possibly be a prerequisite to the ability to give a corresponding structure to moral situations. The authors conclude with the implications for theoretical issues concerning moral concept development and bearings on the education of children.

The effects of provocation, intentions, and consequences on children's moral judgments
L.S. Hewitt, 1975

AIM / To study the effects of provocation, intentions, and consequences on children's moral judgments.

SUBJECTS / N = 128 Dutch boys aged eight and 12 years with middle class background.

METHOD / Three stories, patterned after Rule and Duker (1973), describing roller-skating, and television-watching situations were used. The stories described various situations involving harmful behaviour. 'One boy (A) was portrayed as transgressing (high provocation) against a second boy (B) in half the stories and as committing no transgression (low provocation) in the remaining stories. Subsequently, B attempted either to hurt A (bad intention) or to teach A how to do something (good intention). The action of B then resulted in either serious injury (negative consequence) or minor injury (less negative consequence) to A', p. 541.

RESULTS / Older Ss differentiated their evaluations of the harm doer's naughtiness on the basis of provocation and intentions, while the younger boys failed to differentiate their evaluations of the provoked harm doer on the basis of intentions. Ss in both the eight- and 12-year-old groups differentiated their judgments of the victim's naughtiness on the basis of his role as provoker, except when the victim was seriously injured by a bad-intentioned aggressor. 'The . . . data appear consistent with notions expressed by Piaget that the ability to make differentiated inferences about the motivational determinants of behaviour shows developmental increases', p. 543.

Developmental synthesis of affect and cognition and its implications for altruistic motivation
M.L. Hoffman, 1975

Hoffman (1975) 'presents an argument, based on psychological research and inferences about human evolution, for the plausibility of an intrinsic altruistic motive, following which a theoretical model for the development of such a motive is outlined.'

The author claims that the model 'may provide an integrative framework for ordering existing knowledge on helping and related behaviour, as well as generating hypotheses for further research.'

Several assertions about sympathetic distress and its relation to helping behaviour follow from the theory:

'(a) People should generally respond to another's distress with an affective response as well as a tendency to help.

(b) The intensity of the affect and the speed of the helping response should increase with the salience of the pain cues.

(c) The affect should tend to subside more quickly when the observer engages in helping behaviour than when he does not.'

The theory also leads to the expectation that young children would experience empathic or sympathetic distress, even before acquiring the necessary cognitive skills. Other findings relating to the theory include evidence that helping correlates positively with role taking ability and is increased by role taking training. Further, that people are more apt to help another when their emotional needs are satisfied. There would be a general expectation that children are easily involved in helping behaviour (borne out to a certain extent by 'altruistic model' researches). ' . . . the assumed synthesis between the affect aroused and the observer's cognitive sense of the other is, as discussed earlier, in agreement with the recent research both on emotions and on the structure of the brain.'

The author states that a true assessment of the model depends on empirical validation of predictions derived from it. For example: 'the presumed interaction between empathic distress and cognition suggests that training in role taking, or exposure to information regarding the life condition of others, should be especially effective in producing helping behaviour when it directs the subject's attention to feelings and when the subjects are empathic to begin with . . . and similarly, the arousal of empathic distress should result in more helping in children who are cognitively able to take the other's role than in those who are not. The theory would also predict that certain socialization experiences would enhance the child's naturally developing motivation to help others in distress. For example, altruism should be more prevalent in children whose empathic proclivities have been strengthened by being allowed the normal run of distress experiences, rather than being shielded from them, since this would help provide a broad base for empathic and sympathetic distress in the early years ... It would also follow from the theory that when a discrepancy exists between the various cues indicating another person's distress (e.g., when the cues indicating the victim's immediate distress are at odds with the available information regarding his general life condition), the observer will ordinarily react in terms of the more inconclusive distress index.'

The author adds the proviso that the relation between the arousal of the motive (sympathetic distress) and relevant behaviour (helping behaviour) is not guaranteed, however, any more than it is for other motives. Among many factors, one, of particular interest here, likely to have an effect, is the extent to which the observer has the cognitive and coping skills required for appropriate action. (Further discussion, together with supporting references can be found in Hoffman, 1975.)

Irreversible, stepwise sequence in the development of moral judgment: a longitudinal study of males and females
C.B. Holstein, 1976

AIMS / To evaluate empirically the cognitive-developmental position (Kohlberg, *passim*), that 'changes in moral judgment follow a stepwise, invariant sequence of six irreversible stages, structurally defined and content-free.' Further, the claim for 'universal stepwise invariant sequences.' To undertake a longitudinal study of American adolescents and their parents and to compare the results with the longitudinal study of Kramer (1968).

SUBJECTS / N = 53 upper-middle class families, each with a 13-year-old son (N = 24) or daughter (N = 29). Selection criteria included being Caucasian, having an IQ over 100 (California Test of Mental Maturity) and constituting an intact family. Nearly all of the fathers (mean age = 44) were college graduates (87 per cent) with careers in business, management, or the professions. Most of the mothers (mean age = 41) were college graduates (65 per cent) or had attended college (30 per cent).

METHOD / A three-year interval, modelled after Kohlberg and Kramer (1969) was followed for re-testing. Five of Kohlberg's moral judgment dilemmas (I, III, IV, VII, VIII) were used for both testings.

Details of testing procedures are given in Holstein, p. 53 and scoring details, p. 54.

RESULTS / The author focuses on the limitations of the study while interpreting the results: the sample was self-selected and homogeneous; the three-year test—retest interval was too long for younger subjects who may have passed through stages they appeared to have skipped and 'short-term intraindividual fluctuation, in the sense of state as opposed to trait variability, might account for some stage movement found during the 3-year test—retest period.' Individual developmental sequences supported 'the stepwise sequence requirement, but only in the movement from level to level rather than stage to stage, and only for the first 2 levels of the 3-level scheme. With respect to irreversibility, regression is found in the higher stages.' Holstein comments 'If the regression found in higher-stage subjects reflects real change in moral judgment maturity, then irreversibility, a major requirement of Kohlberg's stage theory, has not been met. However, the possibility of measurement error cannot be eliminated as an interpretation for these findings', (*ibid.*, p. 60). The sequential movement found for young people from the preconventional to conventional level supports the developmental scheme. There was also evidence that moral justifications tend to stay at the conventional level over time.

The phenomenology and psychodynamics of moral development
M.H. Kane, 1975

AIM / To investigate the personality organizations related to various styles of Kohlberg's moral reasoning.

SUBJECTS / N = 12 male and female social work students.

METHOD / The Ss were administered a written Kohlberg dilemma questionnaire followed by an interview of five to six hours to obtain information about their life histories and subjective experiences related to moral development. Three Ss each were placed at Kohlberg stages two, three, four, and five.

RESULTS / Stage two Ss organized moral reasoning around a generalized sense of deprivation. 'They experienced their parents as having been unconcerned for their safety and as narcissistically preoccupied and uninterested in rules or principles. Hence moral situations were approached in terms of maximizing gratification with no concern for moral principles. The stage three subjects tried to please authorities by avowing concern for others. Underlying this was a covert rebelliousness and anger at authorities for failing to live up to expectations. They experienced parents as being overprotective and unresolved oedipal conflicts were prominent in their histories. The stage four subjects were dedicated to abstract principle and strove to maintain a sense of moral integrity. They took responsibility for their actions and tended to defend the rights of others. They were more independent than other subjects and recalled their parents as being loving, respectful, but also demanding of responsible behaviour. The stage five subjects tended to offer abstract moral arguments focusing on devotion to social welfare but in actual moral dilemmas consistently violated their principles by pursuing narcissistic goals which were then justified *ex post facto* with moralistic rationalizations. They experienced parents as being morally perfectionistic and opposed to narcissistic gratification. They experienced severe oedipal conflict within their families and found themselves consistently conflicted between the expression or suppression of narcissistic impulse. In general the fives resented the demanding principles they were forced to internalize and seemed to need to find ways of covertly rebelling against these principles', (*ibid.*, p. 3048—B).

The development of formal operations in logical and moral judgment *
D. Kuhn, J. Langer, L. Kohlberg and N.S. Haan, 1971

AIM / To obtain normative data on the actualization of formal operational thought in adolescence and adulthood thereby obtaining information about 'certain structural characteristics of formal operations, primarily by examining subjects' patterns of performance over a series of problems, and to examine closely the ontogenesis of formal operations by carrying out a short-term longitudinal study of a subsample of younger subjects'. Additionally, to examine the actualized ontogenetic relation between stages of logical reasoning and stages of development in moral judgment.

PART ONE

Study One

SUBJECTS / N = 265. Subjects consisted of family groups, 130 of the parent generation, who were approximately 50 years of age, and 135 of their children, between the ages of 10 and 30, and were from

* Gratitude is extended to Professor Deanna Kuhn of California State University for sending the work to be abstracted. (Now at Harvard University)

'diverse but predominantly median socioeconomic level'. Subjects were divided into four major age groups: 10—15 years, 16—20 years, 21—30 years, and 45—50 years.

METHOD / The pendulum and correlation problems were presented individually to each subject, adapted from Inhelder and Piaget, 1958. The scoring system represented a further delineation and more operational specification of the criteria described by Inhelder and Piaget, although closely following their conceptualization of the structural development underlying the behavioural stage progression for each of the problems.

RESULTS / No age group completely achieved the transition to formal operations. The development of formal operations in the pendulum problem appeared to typically occur during early adolescence, while in the correlation problem formal operational development is typically not completed until late adolescence or early adulthood. When composite scores were considered the 10- to 15-year-olds and 16- to 20-year-olds showed the highest proportion of Stages I, II, and II (III) performance. At the three most advanced stages, 21- to 30-year-olds showed the highest proportions of performance, 45- to 50-year-olds slightly lower ones, and the two younger groups the lowest. A detailed analysis of the results is provided in Kuhn *et al.* (1971).

Study Two

SUBJECTS / N = 75 fifth through seventh graders of ages 10 through 12 years. Forty-nine were from an upper middle class suburban population and 26 from a middle class city population. Subjects were divided into three age groups.

METHOD / Each subject was tested individually on four logical problems: the pendulum, correlation, combination of chemicals and verbal reasoning (Piaget, 1928) problems. A short-term longitudinal design was employed: subjects were presented with the set of problems, a second time, nine months after the initial testing.

RESULTS / An examination of changes in composite scores revealed that almost half the sample (26 Ss) showed a rise in overall composite stage level over the nine month period. All Stage I and Stage II subjects showed an increase. Ten of 24 Stage II (III) subjects showed a rise in stage level, versus three of 20 Stage III (II) subjects. Two conclusions were drawn: the change occurring most frequently among subjects in the age range sampled was the transition to a level of predominantly formal operations; subjects already exhibiting some formal operations are the ones most likely to show this change. A full analysis of the results is given in Kuhn *et al.* (1971).

PART TWO
The relation of logical operational development to the development of moral judgment.

METHOD / A measure of moral judgment was obtained from Ss from both previous studies. Subjects in Sample One received the standard moral judgment interview (Kohlberg, *passim*) with subjects in Sample Two receiving a more detailed interview, employing a smaller set of dilemmas but with an expanded set of probing questions. All moral judgment protocols were rated by a group of trained scorers and a global stage score consisting of predominant and in some cases secondary or minor, stage of reasoning was obtained for each subject.

RESULTS / Lower stage moral reasoning was found to decline with age and higher stage reasoning to increase. The overall association between age group and stage level was significant. While there was indication that the 10—12 year age period is one of pronounced change in logical operations, such pronounced change was not found to occur in moral judgment during this period. The majority of subjects who were concrete operational or below showed a level of moral judgment of predominantly Stage 3 or lower, i.e. no higher than 3(4). Almost all of the concrete operational subjects showed a moral judgment level no higher than 4(3). Among Sample One subjects at logical Stage IIIA or higher, in contrast, almost half had moral stage scores of 4 or higher and a third showed some principled reasoning. The association between logical and moral level was significant for Sample One and slightly below significance for Sample Two. The results suggested the tentative conclusion that the emergence of formal operations is a prerequisite to the emergence of principled moral judgment. The data further suggested the possibility that the emergence of formal operations is a necessary condition for the consolidation of conventional moral judgment (i.e. pure Stage 4). Discussion and detailed analysis in this respect are given in Kuhn *et al.,* 1971 together with speculation concerning the *décalage* between levels of logical and moral judgment which was considered to constitute the single most important finding. In Sample One, 85 per cent of subjects showed some formal operational reasoning and only 21 per cent showed any principled moral judgment. Most adults develop to the level of conventional moral judgment. Moral development however appears in many adults to decelerate and eventually stop altogether, although the logical structures have developed to higher levels. The longitudinal data suggested that 'deceleration' has already begun by early adolescence.

The relationship between moral maturity and selected characteristics of mental health among young adults
J.H. Kupfersmid, 1975

AIM / The study focused on the relationship between mental health and Kohlberg's moral typology.

SUBJECTS / N = 78 community college students.

METHOD / The tasks administered were: Kohlberg's moral dilemmas, six measures of mental health (anxiety, self-concept, alienation, dogmatism, personality integration, and happiness), and the Otis Quick-Scoring Mental Ability Test.

RESULTS / The hypothesis that, '... contrary to Kohlberg's expectations, there was reason to believe that moral judgment would not relate significantly ($p < .05$) or substantially ($r_{xy} = > .50$) to a global measure of mental health, a composite (multivariate) index of mental health, or add, when considered as one of several multiple predictors (along with sex and IQ), to each mental health estimate. The results suggested that the null Hypothesis (stated in accordance with the predicted hypotheses) be retained. There was no significant relationship between moral maturity scores (MMS) and a factor score (global measure of mental health). The factor score accounted for 51 per cent of the total mental health variance. Additionally, when all mental health estimates (except dogmatism), along with IQ, were considered multivariately, no relationship between moral judgment and mental health was evidenced. Likewise, when MMS was utilized as one of three predictors of each mental health characteristic, no significant multiple coefficient was obtained. The only significant relationship found in the present study was that between MMS and tolerance for ambiguity (dogmatism). However, tolerance for ambiguity did not load significantly on the primary mental health factor, nor did this variable correlate significantly with any other mental health estimate. In order to avoid possible conflict in interpretation, the data was also analyzed by means of an alternate hypothesis, i.e., that moral maturity would not account for 25 per cent ($r_{xy} = > .50$) or more of the variance of each mental health measure. Hypotheses testings suggested that the relationship between moral judgment and each mental health estimate, including tolerance for ambiguity, was significantly less than a .50 association', p. 3516—A.

*Intellectual and moral development in adolescence**
P.E. Langford and S. George, 1975

Two methods of assessing interrelations between different spheres of development are described. One is typological. The simplifying assumption is made that the child is 'at' a particular stage in each sphere and observed combinations of stages are noted. The other, in some ways more sensitive, method is to first assess the relative strengths of the various stages in each sphere and then to compute correlation coefficients between each measure of relative stage strength in one sphere and each measure of relative stage strength in the other. Relative stage strengths can be assessed from the percentage of a child's responses to a test falling into each stage category.

As applied to the assessment of relations between intellectual and moral development in adolescence, the first method was shown by Kuhn *et al.* (forthcoming) to lead to the conclusion that the attainment of thinking at Piaget's stage of formal operation is a precondition for progress to moral judgment at Kohlberg's Types 5 and 6 (judgments formed on the basis of moral principles). Using the correlational approach, however, Lee (1971) found results that appear to contradict this conclusion if we make the equation, as some authors have done, between Piaget's Stages 1 and 2 and Kohlberg's Types 1 and 2 in moral judgment and between Piaget's Stage 3 and Kohlberg's Types 5 and 6 in moral judgment. For Lee, unlike Kuhn *et al.*, used Piaget's (1932) stages in moral development, rather than those of Kohlberg (1958, 1963).

The present study adopted the correlational approach to relations between the development of formal operations reasoning and Kohlberg's types of moral judgment in adolescence. Results supported the conclusion of Kuhn *et al.* (forthcoming) that the attainment of reasoning at the level of formal operations is a precondition for the attainment of moral judgment at Kohlberg's Types 5 and 6. For this and other reasons it is suggested that Kohlberg's types are descriptively more adequate than Piaget's (1932) stages in the development of moral judgment. This is not a surprising conclusion as Kohlberg's work involved a more complete range of ages than that of Piaget.

---

* Written and prepared by the authors for inclusion in this volume. Gratitude is extended to Dr Peter Langford and Sandra George of Birkbeck College, University of London.

Development of moral judgments in children
M. Lydiat, 1973

AIM / To study the moral judgments of children.

SUBJECTS / N = 368 aged seven to 12 years.

METHOD / Six tests of moral judgment were administered adapted from Piaget (1932). The tests related to the moral dimension of objective responsibility. Two pairs of stories in each of the areas of clumsiness, stealing and lying were given.

RESULTS / 'Generally, immature forms of moral judgments were replaced in older children by more mature forms, but elements of immature judgments could still be discerned in children up to 12 years of age. In fact, the bulk of this immature residue was concentrated in the responses of a small number of children aged 11 and 12 years (N = 16). Similarly, a small group of younger children (N = 16; ages seven and eight years) was isolated where responses showed consistent evidence of mature judgment. These two groups of children formed the basis of a more detailed examination of some environmental factors which might correlate with faster or slower rate of moral development . . . No significant differences could be established between the patterns of response of boys and girls. No consistent differences could be isolated among responses to each of the three areas of moral judgment included . . . occasional significant differences appeared but never after age nine years. This trend was interpreted as evidence of the less well organized system of moral judgments possessed by younger children and their greater susceptibility to specific situational cues in making judgments. Older children appeared to have a more stable and consistent system varying less from area to area and from test to test. This greater stability of judgments in older children is one link between Piaget's theory of moral development and his more general theory of cognitive development . . . Intelligence proved to be a significant variable influencing the child's performance . . . Certain social class differences were demonstrated which suggested the advantage which middle class children have in Piagetian tests of moral judgment', p. 376.

Educational environment and the development of moral concepts
J. McCann and P. Bell, 1975

AIM / To examine the development of moral concepts in two types of schools of different educational orientation, one based on the theory of Freinet (1960), the other conventional Catholic schools.

SUBJECTS / N = 40 aged between six years seven months and 11 years three months. Children attending a Freinet school formed the experimental group and the control group was chosed from two Catholic schools. The groups were matched on CA, IQ, school grade, sex, religious affiliation, occupational level of father, and number of children in family and birth order of subject.

METHOD / Four moral conflict stories were used, followed by a questionnaire. The stories were adapted from Piaget (1932) and differed in the presence or absence of authority figures and peers, and were set either in the home or the school. The scoring criteria followed Piaget (1932) but modified after Kohlberg (1963a). This enabled classification into seven types of judgment which were reclassified into five stages reflecting ascending levels of decentration in the formation of the concept of justice or equality. (Details are given in McCann and Bell, 1975, pp. 65—67.)

RESULTS / Children attending the Freinet school demonstrated higher levels of moral judgments for all stories combined. Stories comprising peers only elicited more mature judgments than those involving authority figures. Democratic group self-discipline was encouraged by the Freinet schools' structure and furnished varied role taking opportunities. Such practices enhanced moral development. McCann and Bell concluded, 'Whether the experience of group-based self-discipline, the generally increased peer-participation activities, or the disciplinary practices of teachers are equally important sources of influence is not indicated in this study. However, it is clear that the school can be a powerful source of influence on moral development in the primary school years, even in a socioeconomically and intellectually homogeneous population', p. 70.

Susceptibility to faking of the Defining Issues Test of Moral Development
C. McGeorge, 1975

AIM / The susceptibility to faking of the Defining Issues Test of moral development was examined.

SUBJECTS / N = 146 college students, with a mean age of 19.02 years.

METHOD / Ss completed the Defining Issues Test on two occasions 18 days apart. Brief instructions were devised asking Ss to fake bad, fake good, or to record their own views (standard). Ss were assigned to five treatments: (a) standard—standard, (b) standard—good, (c) good—standard, (d) standard—bad, (e) bad—standard. No time limit was set to complete the test.

RESULTS / Ss were unable to fake high under the standard—good and good—standard conditions. Ss in the bad—standard group performed at the lower levels when asked to fake bad as did those in the standard—bad group. The standard—bad group's bad scores were significantly lower than were those of the bad—standard group. The standard—standard group's scores on the two tests did not differ significantly and a test—retest reliability coefficient of .65 was obtained. No sex differences were observed in either of the conditions. 'The results support the general theory of a sequence of cognitive stages of moral judgment such that Ss recognize stages they have passed through as immature and can respond appropriately when asked to fake low while stages higher than the S's own are inaccessible thus precluding faking upwards. Those undertaking research involving repeated measures should be alert to the possibility of faking low on the Defining Issues Test especially by Ss who have already had some experience of it', p. 108.

Moral development and children's appreciation of humour
P.E. McGhee, 1974

AIM / To examine the relationship between level of moral development (Piaget, 1932) and children's appreciation of humour based on varying levels of quantity and intentionality of damaging outcomes in three studies.

Study One
SUBJECTS / N = 80. Half of each sex Ss were functioning at the heteronomous and half at the autonomous moral level, on the basis of five moral judgment stories adapted from Piaget (1932). All Ss were drawn from second grades.

METHOD / Each S was tested individually. 'Half of the Ss tested were read the unintentional-high-damage versions first, and half were read the intentional-low-damage version first. After reading the second version of each story, the E asked the S whether he (she) thought the child in the first or second story was naughtier and why ... An

example of both versions of one of the . . . stories used follows:
(Unintentional high damage) Helen was only a little girl and had never
baked a cake before. But, she decided that she would surprise her
mother by making a delicious cake for her mother's birthday. When
Helen's sister came into the kitchen, she found Helen beating her hands
up and down on a bunch of eggs. She had made a big mess with eggs
and shells splattered all over. Helen turned to her sister and said
innocently, "I'm baking a cake and the recipe said to beat the eggs."
(Intentional low damage) Helen was only a little girl who often didn't
get along well with her mother. Her mother always made her dry the
dishes and she didn't like drying dishes. One day when her mother
asked her to help with the dishes, she got mad and decided to mess up
the table. She got an egg and started beating her hand up and down on
the egg. The egg cracked and the yoke spilled on the table. When her
sister walked in, Helen gave a sly smile and said, "I'm baking a cake and
the recipe said to beat the eggs'", p. 516. (Fuller details of the materials,
experimental procedures and the scoring techniques are given elsewhere, McGhee, 1974, p. 515–516).

Study Two
SUBJECTS / N = 112 boys. Fifty-six were heteronomous and 56
autonomous.

METHOD / The experimental procedure was identical to that used
in study one, except that the Es were two male research assistants.

Study Three
SUBJECTS / N = 168 boys. Fifty-six at each grades, four, eight and
college level.

METHOD / Materials and experimental procedures were identical to
those used in the first two studies. E was a female graduate student.

RESULTS / Heteronomous Ss consistently found stories with highly
damaging outcomes funnier than stories with less damaging outcomes.
However, for the autonomous Ss, this trend was found only when
damage occurred unintentionally. Autonomous children found accidental damaging outcomes funnier than intentional ones. McGhee concluded that while increased naughtiness or moral unacceptibility of an
outcome added to its funniness for heteronomous children, it detracted
from humour appreciation in adult Ss and morally more mature
autonomous children.

Effects of participation in rule formation on the moral judgement of children
R.L. Merchant and F. Rebelsky, 1972

AIM / The hypothesis tested was that psychological participation in forming rules leads to increased flexibility about changing rules.

SUBJECTS / N = 100 kindergarten and first grade children ranging in age from five years to seven years nine months. Subjects in the two groups were matched by age, sex, and school. 'All subjects had to have a conception of what cheating was in order to be part of this study', p. 292.

METHOD / Fifty kindergarten and first grade subjects each participated in making up game rules, while 50 matched subjects were each taught the rules made up by their matched counterparts in the first group. To evaluate psychological participation subjects were asked who made up the games. Following this each subject was administered a test of flexibility about changing rules. Each child was also administered a pre-test and post-test which measured generalization to a different kind of game rule. (Details of the various measures and the experimental procedure are described in Merchant and Rebelsky, 1972, pp. 292–295.)

RESULTS / The authors conclude, '... results of ... study show that children who are given the psychological experience of participating in making up the rules of a game show significantly more flexibility about changing the rules of that game than children who have not had this experience. These effects are felt to be due to the fact that participation in rule formation shows the child through direct experience that rules can be made and followed by people like himself who are not authorities and that they can be made by mutual agreement for co-operative purposes. It therefore follows that they can be changed by mutual agreement for cooperative purposes', p. 299.

Moral judgment and role-taking of young retarded children
G.S. Mischio, 1976

AIM / An investigation of the triadic relationship between moral judgment, role taking and social participation among young retarded children.

SUBJECTS / N = 120 educable mentally retarded children from

special education classes. Subjects were equally stratified by CA, sex and SES to form six groups, of 20 subjects each, from six to 11 years.

METHOD / The test battery consisted of Stanford-Binet Intelligence Scale, 11 Piagetian moral-judgment story situations, the Social Interaction Opportunity Scale and six Social Behaviour Rating Scales.

RESULTS / Piaget's triadic relationship was not confirmed. Role taking was significantly related to moral judgment thereby indicating that cognitive-functioning was essential to moral judgment growth. Moral judgment was found to be developmental: responses increased in maturity across chronological ages regardless of sex, religion, race or social class. Young retarded children proceeded through the Piagetian stages at a slower rate, corresponding to their stage of Piagetian intellectual development rather than CA. The author recommends that future research should extend the investigation of the triadic relationship among educable mentally retarded subjects from ages six to 17. The educational significance of the results is 'that they have implications for teacher expectations, for curriculum planning and development, and for the presentation of moral training through role-playing, less structured group experiences, and a variety of moral-judgment situations illustrated by different forms of media', (Mischio, *op. cit.*, p. 5199A).

*Piagetian operations in relation to moral development**
C. Modgil, 1975

SUMMARY / The investigation attempted to determine what empirical links might be present among cognitive and moral factors in the adolescent's development. It was an attempt to elucidate and establish whether a relationship exists between operativity, as conceived by Piaget and moral development as postulated by Kohlberg.

The sample consisted of 231 subjects; the variables controlled were: (i) CA, 14 to 15+ years (ii) subjects were selected from urban areas, and (iii) sex. Piagetian stage groups of subjects (contrasted according to levels of logical reasoning) were selected and matched on finer discriminations with respect to age, social class and measured intelligence.

The four Piagetian tests comprised: 'Angles of Incidence and

* Research conducted for the Degree of Master of Philosophy (Psychology), University of Surrey. Gratitude is extended to Professor T. Lee who supervised the research.

Reflection', 'Equilibrium in the Balance', 'Communicating Vessels', and 'The Projection of Shadows' (Inhelder and Piaget, 1958), patterned after Tisher (1962, 1971). The moral development variable served as the dependent variable, as measured by Kohlberg's Moral Judgment Interview Schedules (1971b).

Three statistical techniques were employed: (a) Student's t-test, (b) Correlations Coefficients and (c) Stepwise Multiple Regression Analysis.

The results indicated that:

1. A relationship exists between Piagetian operativity and moral development.
2. Logical reasoning is a relatively more effective indicator of moral maturity than a traditional intelligence measure.

STATEMENT OF THE PROBLEM / Post-conventional reasoning, the highest level of Kohlberg's (*passim*) hierarchy, presupposes the capacity to form the formal operations of abstract thought. The development of formal operational thinking has been shown to be prone to great variability, although replications do not detract from the essential validity of Piaget's formulations. (See Volume Three in the present series *Piagetian Research*.) It would appear that *clear* principled thinking displays a greater degree of rarity and reaches equilibrium at later ages than formal operations (Kohlberg, *op. cit.*). However, the passage from concrete to formal operations and the transitions from the various levels of moral judgment are not all-or-none phenomena and it is apparent that a study of a transitional period, within a narrow age range, with level of cognitive development being the independent variable, allowing finer degrees of measurement rather than broad categorization, from an extensive battery of formal operational tasks, would enable further illumination of the development within the logical thinking and moral areas. Further, additional data with respect to the development of formal operations among British adolescents will be of relevance together with the collection of data emanating from the application of Kohlberg's moral judgment interview to a British sample. (Graham (unpublished), Kotalawala (1971), Langford and George (1975), Weinrich (1970) are among the few British studies involving the use of Kohlberg's measures).

Therefore the problem under investigation focuses on the relations between developments in the two domains, logical and moral: examines the actualized ontogenetic relation in middle adolescence between stages of logical reasoning and stages in moral judgment. Evaluations are made on the general question of the interrelations among stage developments as they occur in different conceptual domains, involving an attempt to logically or conceptually relate developmental stages in the logical and moral domains. Further light is shed on the isomorphism of the two areas, together with further speculation with respect to the notions of the centrality of cognitive development and a *décalage* between the acquisition of logical operations and their application to other areas of development. The hypotheses tested may be stated formally as follows:

1. That a relationship exists between Piagetian operativity and moral judgment.
2. That measures of logical reasoning are relatively more effective indicators of moral maturity than traditional measures of intelligence.

OUTLINE OF INVESTIGATION /
Introduction
The overall design for investigation involved the administration of Kohlberg's Moral Judgement Interview to populations contrasted in respect of Piagetian 'concrete' and 'formal' operativity and precision matched in terms of extraneous variables, namely: IQ, age, sex and socioeconomic status.

The final sample consisted of 231 subjects (attrition of the number of subjects by 19, was due to school transfer, inconsistent attendance and incomplete responses), aged 13 years 10 months to 15 years 11 months, ranging in intelligence from below-average-minus to intellectually superior (Raven's categories 1938, 1956); representing socioeconomic classes I to IV, in accordance with the Registrar General's Classification (Registrar General, 1960), all attending secondary schools in a north London borough.

Selection of schools
In selecting the schools it was important that they should be within the same administrative unit, not only for control of environmental factors, but further, because of the current transitional nature and diversification of secondary schools organization emanating from the Circular 10 / 65, issued from the Department of Education and Science and emphasized to varying degrees by successive governments. A further factor affecting secondary schools at the time of the investigation, were preparations for and implementation of the Raising of the School Leaving-Age, which although common to all areas, was being dealt with variably by administrative units in accordance with their individual resources.

Selection of the Administrative Unit
Several London boroughs were approached through the education officials, some refusals being received on the grounds of current

pressures on secondary schools, two offering cooperation. The co-operation offered by the north London borough was accepted for the following reasons:

> The schools all followed relatively similar patterns, both in terms of general school organization and in terms of curriculum. All pupils appeared to follow a wide range of subject courses in the early years of secondary school and were only just, at the time of testing, beginning to limit subjects for study in the fourth year. General facilities, sports opportunities, extra-curricular activities and social and community activities appeared similar throughout all schools.

Measures used in the investigation
Measures used to equate (match) the various groups
(a) *Raven's Standard Progressive Matrices, Sets A, B, C, D and E. Raven, 1938, 1956.*

The Standard Progressive Matrices is a test of a person's capacity at the time of the test to apprehend meaningless figures; see the relations between them; conceive the nature of the figure completing each system of relations presented and thereby develop a systematic method of reasoning. Raven describes the scale as 'a test of observation and clear thinking' and stresses that by itself it is not a test of general intelligence, although when used in conjunction with the Mill Hill Vocabulary Scales can be considered synonymous with a single test of 'general intelligence'. The Standard Progressive Matrices Scale is intended to cover the whole range of intellectual development and to be suitable from age eight years to adult level.

Instructions and details of interpretation, including scoring, are to be found in Raven (1960).

(b) *The Mill Hill Vocabulary Scale Form One Senior (Raven, 1943)*

Like the Matrices Test, the Mill Hill Vocabulary Scale is designed to cover as nearly as possible, the whole range of intellectual development from infancy to maturity. While the Matrices Test provides a reliable index to a person's present capacity for intellectual activity, irrespective of education and language, the Mill Hill Vocabulary Scale provides a reliable index of the best intellectual level the subject has attained, whatever his present capacity for intellectual activity may happen to be. As stated above, the two tests are designed for use together, in place of a single verbal test of general intelligence, so that it is possible to assess separately and 'in a clearly defined form':

(i)   a person's present capacity for intellectual work;
(ii) the fund of verbal information he has acquired so far, and thence

his cultural level relative to other people;

(iii) the psychological significance of discrepancies between the best cultural level a person has attained, and his present capacity for intellectual activity.

Instructions and details of interpretation, including scoring, are to be found in Raven (1958, 1965).

(c) *Socioeconomic status*

A rating for each subject was obtained based upon parental occupation. The Registrar General's Classification of Occupations (Registrar General, 1960) was used as follows:

I   Professional and managerial occupations
II   Other professional and technical
III   (non-manual) Other non-manual occupations
III   (manual) Skilled manual
IV   Semi-Skilled manual

Social class III in this scale is by far the largest section of the general population and needs distinction between non-manual and manual.

Measures used to contrast the various Groups
(a) *Measures of Piagetian Operativity — The Piagetian Questionnaire (Tisher, 1962, 1971)**

Tisher (1962, 1971) has devised a pencil-and-paper test which can be used to determine a subject's stage of mental development. Criteria set out in Inhelder and Piaget (1958) were used for the construction of the test which contains 24 multiple-choice items based on four scientific phenomena or tasks: 'the bouncing ball,' 'equilibrium in a balance,' 'water levels in connected containers' and 'shadows of rings'. Fourteen of the test items can be classified as 'concrete', (that is, they would be most likely solved by pupils in the 'concrete' stage of development) and ten as 'formal'. To correct for guessing only those subjects who correctly answer five or more 'formal' items and seven or more 'concrete' items are classified as belonging to the formal stage of development.

The administration of the Questionnaire occurs in four phases, corresponding to the four sets of questions. Each phase is initiated with a demonstration of the relevant phenomenon. Tisher has compared the results obtained using the questionnaire with those obtained using the

*   Gratitude is extended to Professor R.P. Tisher of the University of Monash, Australia, and Dr L.G. Dale, Australia, for sending the relevant material.

conversation-interview technique. Additions were made to Tisher's original Questionnaire in the form of 'why do you think so', to bring it further into line with Piaget's approach. Two countersuggestion situations were also included.

References to the relevant Piagetian work upon which the Tisher Questionnaire is based are as follows:

Designation	Area of cognitive strategy*	Source
'The equality of Angles of Incidence and Reflection and the Operations of Reciprocal Implications'.	At the concrete stage, subjects establish a correspondence between slope of incidence at path and slope of reflected path. Do not construct law. At the formal stage, subjects discover law of equality of angle of incidence and angle of reflection.	*The Growth of Logical Thinking From Childhood to Adolescence*, Inhelder and Piaget (1958) pp. 3–19
'Equilibrium in the Balance'	At the concrete stage, subjects realize that equal weights at equal distance from the fulcrum balance each other and that a smaller weight a great distance from the fulcrum balances with a larger weight closer to the fulcrum on the other side. At the formal stage, subjects discover the proportional relationship between weights and distances from the fulcrum.	Inhelder and Piaget (1958), pp. 164–81
'Communicating Vessels'	At the concrete stage, subjects discovered that water levels return to a common level. At the formal stage, the subjects can predict what could happen in one container when the other is raised or lowered.	Inhelder and Piaget (1958), pp. 133–47
'The Projection of Shadows'	At the concrete stage, subjects discover that the size of shadow depends on size and distance from the screen; no inverse metrical relationship between size and distance discovered. At the formal stage the inverse metrical relationship between the size of the object and its distance from the screen is discovered.	Inhelder and Piaget (1958), pp. 199–209

*   Gratitude is extended to Professor R.P. Tisher of the University of Monash, Australia, for some of the above interpretations.

(b) *Measures of Moral Judgement (Kohlberg, 1958, 1971b)*

Kohlberg has empirically devised an instrument with which to measure moral judgment. Hypothetical moral dilemmas are presented, followed by a series of questions which ask the subject to resolve the dilemma and then probe into the reasons leading the subject to make his decision. It is the reasoning process which is of interest and Kohlberg has delineated criteria by which responses can be scored on a variety of dimensions according to a developmental scale of maturity of moral judgment. The moral judgment test has been designed so that it can be used either in written form or as a structural interview.

The selection of situations from Kohlberg's (1971b) Moral Judgement Interview was as follows:

Moral Form A

	Story	Conflict
iii	Heinz steals the drug	Law vs. Moral
iv	The Wife wants euthanesia	Law vs. Moral

Moral Form B

v	The captain orders a man to his death	Authority and Justice
vi	Choose the sick man or the troublemaker	Justice
vii	One brother steals, the other 'cons'	Law vs. Justice
viii	The reformed criminal hasn't served his jail term	Law vs. Justice

Scoring followed Kohlberg's 'Standard' or 'Short Form' Scoring procedure. A percentage of protocols were scored by a researcher at Harvard University and these formed the basis for all scoring procedures.

Procedure

Subjects were tested from three schools during 1973 and from the remaining three during 1974. Testing took place between the months of March and June in 1973 and April and May in 1974. Testing was completed within each school during a period not longer than four weeks. In all schools testing was arranged in accordance with the school timetable, two units of timetable being allotted for each testing session; this amounted to four sessions of one hour and twenty minutes each, in total, thereby allowing for the establishment of rapport, explanation and demonstration.

The order of administration of tests was kept throughout, as follows:

Session 1   The Standard Progressive Matrices, Sets A, B, C, D and E
             The Mill Hill Vocabulary Scale
Session 2   Moral Judgement Dilemmas III and IV
             Moral Judgement Dilemma VII
Session 3   The Piagetian Questionnaire
Session 4   Moral Judgement Dilemmas V and VI
             Moral Judgement Dilemma VIII

Situations VII and VIII were considered the most suitable dilemmas to divide between two sessions. Unlike the other two-situation units, they consist of two separate stories, not a continuation, and are relatively short.

Background information
Additional information obtained included:

> Date of birth;
> Position in the family — ages of brothers and sisters;
> Out-of-school-activities and interests;
> Ambitions for career

Statistical treatment of the data
Criterion for groups

The overall design for investigation involved the administration of Kohlberg's Moral Judgement Interview to populations contrasted in respect of Piagetian 'Concrete' and 'Formal' operativity (Tisher, 1962, 1971) and precision matched in terms of extraneous variables, namely IQ, age, sex and socioeconomic status.

The total sample of 231 subjects represented a range of intelligence levels, socioeconomic status categories, an age range from 14 to 15+ years and both sexes. Differing criteria (as defined below) were employed to establish matched-pair groups of varying sizes. This necessitated the inclusion of some subjects more than once.

Group 1 'Concrete' and 'Formal' (N = 35 + 35 = 70): represents groups contrasted according to lower ('Concrete') and upper ('Formal') levels of logical thinking (patterned after Tisher's Piagetian Questionnaire, *op. cit.*) and matched according to Raven's Categories (mean scores for 'Concrete' and 'Formal' = 51.0, 51.2, respectively); Mill Hill Vocabulary Categories (mean scores for 'Concrete' and 'Formal' = 50.5, 50.7, respectively); within 6 months of chronological age (mean age for 'Concrete' = 180.3 months and mean age for 'Formal' = 181.5 months); sex and socioeconomic status.

Group 2 'Concrete' and 'Formal' (N = 33 + 33 = 66): represents groups contrasted in terms of the lower ('Concrete') and upper ('Formal') regions of logical thinking scores (the cut-off point being established by cross-tabulation) and then matched on Raven's Categories (mean scores for 'Concrete' and 'Formal' = 49.9, 50.3, respectively); within six months of chronological age (mean age for 'Concrete' = 180.8 months and 'Formal' = 182.0 months); sex and socioeconomic status; all matched according to 'tight bands' within and across levels of logical thinking.

Group 3 'Concrete' and 'Formal' (N = 46 + 46 = 92): represents groups contrasted in terms of the lower ('Concrete') and upper ('Formal') regions of logical reasoning (the cut-off point being established by cross-tabulation) and matched according to Raven's Categories (mean scores for 'Concrete' and 'Formal' = 49.6, 50.1, respectively); within six months of chronological age (mean age for 'Concrete' and 'Formal' = 181.0, 181.8 months respectively); sex and socioeconomic status.

Group 4 'Concrete' and 'Formal' (N = 65 + 65 = 130): represents groups contrasted in terms of the lower ('Concrete') and upper ('Formal') of logical reasoning scores (following the 'weighting' procedures of the Australian Science Education Project, 1972, 1974). Subjects were then matched on the basis of five Raven's points (mean scores for 'Concrete' and 'Formal' = 47.7, 49.6, respectively); within 8 months of chronological age (mean ages for 'Concrete' and 'Formal' = 179.3, 180.7 months, respectively); sex and socioeconomic status.

Statistical treatment
The data were subjected to the following types of analysis:
   (a) Student's t-test;
   (b) Correlations coefficients; and
   (c) Stepwise Multiple Regression Analysis.

To test whether the performance of the Piagetian Stage groups were statistically different when compared with each other, Student's t-test was used. Table 1.1 shows the levels of probability values of t. It will be seen that Moral Maturity rejected the null-hypothesis of no difference for the performance of the Piagetian-Stage groups 1 and 2 at the 1 per cent significance level or below and groups 3 and 4 at the .1 per cent significance level or better. However, group 4 shows a highly significant difference on Mill Hill which could be due to relatively less precise matching.

The use of the matched groups technique introduces an element of selection and cannot therefore be considered representative. Correlations coefficients were therefore computed to indicate the strength or absence of associations between pairs of variables. These correlations coefficients, extracted from the main body of data, are presented in Tables 1.3 and 1.4 (the complete correlation matrix, Table 1.5 is likewise included). Means and standard deviations are presented in Table 1.2.

It will be seen (Table 1.3 that the 'Concrete' level of thinking is positively correlated to age (r = .202), Raven's (r = .482), Mill Hill (r = .462) and Moral Maturity (r = .429). Similar patterns are indicated for the 'Formal' level of thinking: age (r = .247), Raven's (r = .503), Mill Hill (r = .404) and Moral Maturity (r = .427). Sex shows no correlation (r = −.074), and r = −.008 for 'Formal'. Neither does SES, as measured by the Registrar General's Classification when compared with 'Formal' operativity (r = −.086). However, at the 'Concrete' level of thinking SES is negatively correlated (r = −.179).

Inspection of the correlations reported in Table 1.4 demonstrates that the variables of 'Concrete' and 'Formal' (combined) thinking are positively correlated to age (r = .255), Ravens (r = .548), Mill Hill (r = .469) and Moral Maturity (r = .472). Sex shows no correlation (r = −.036). Neither does SES indicate any significant relationship (r = −.132).

The most obvious danger of the correlational method is a tendency to infer causality when only association has been established.

Whereas the correlation coefficient measures the linear relationship between a dependent variable and one independent variable, multiple regression techniques measure the relationship of the dependent variable with several independent variables. The variables were included in a Stepwise Regression Analysis which might accurately predict Moral Maturity (Kohlberg). Summary Tables (1.6, 1.7) are reproduced for interpretation. The Moral Maturity Total was used as the dependent variable and 'Concrete', 'Formal', Mill Hill, SES, sex, age and Raven's variables were used as the independent variables. The independent variable (Table 1.6) which accounts for the greatest amount of variance is the one which has the highest correlation with the dependent variable. In this case, it is 'Concrete'. Stepwise Regression procedure then introduces the further variable which in combination with 'Concrete', accounts for the highest amount of variance. This combination is arrived at by elimination of intercorrelation between independent variables. In other words, that proportion of the second variable which measures essentially the same characteristics as the first is eliminated and only that part which measures a different characteristic is retained. Table 1.6 shows 'Formal' to be the best

Table 1.1: Comparisons between Piagetian-stage groups on Mill Hill and Moral Maturity scores

Group Designation	N	Age Mean	Age SD	Raven Mean	Raven SD	Mill Hill Mean	Mill Hill SD	Mill Hill t	Moral Maturity Mean	Moral Maturity SD	Moral Maturity t
1 'Concrete'	35	180.3	5.9	51.0	4.2	—	—	—	300.1	21.8	3.39**
'Formal'	35	181.5	5.9	51.2	4.3	—	—		318.5	24.4	
2 'Concrete'	33	180.8	4.9	49.8	5.7	48.8	9.2	.16	302.5	25.4	3.32**
'Formal'	33	182.0	4.8	50.3	5.3	48.6	7.4		321.1	21.0	
3 'Concrete'	46	181.0	5.4	49.6	6.2	48.5	8.6	1.08	302.3	24.1	3.82***
'Formal'	46	181.8	5.3	50.1	5.1	50.2	6.9		326.7	39.0	
4 'Concrete'	65	179.3	5.7	47.7	4.8	44.3	8.5	4.41***	297.2	20.3	4.68***
'Formal'	65	180.7	6.2	49.6	4.9	49.4	6.8		319.6	35.3	

Levels of probability values of t

* $< .05$
** $< .01$
*** $< .001$

all other t values not significant

Table 1.2: Means and Sds of the eight measures for the total sample (N = 231)

Variable / Name		Mean	SD
Var 1	Sex	—	—
Var 2	Age	180.186	6.976
Var 3	Social Class	—	—
Var 4	Ravens	48.208	6.445
Var 5	Mill Hill	47.225	8.509
Var 6	Concrete	10.333	2.474
Var 7	Formal	3.840	2.211
Vars 6 & 7	Combined	18.013	6.242
Var 8	Moral	307.913	32.014

Table 1.3: Correlations between operations (concrete / formal) and all other variables

	Sex Variable 1	Age Variable 2	SES Variable 3	Ravens Variable 4	Mill Hill Variable 5	Moral Variable 8
'Concrete' (Variable 6)	−.074	.202**	−.179*	.482**	.462**	.429**
'Formal' (Variable 7)	−.008	.247**	−.086	.503**	.404**	.427**

N =   231
**   Significant where p < .001
*   Significant where p < .005

Table 1.4: Correlations between Piaget total and all other variables

	Sex Variable 1	Age Variable 2	SES Variable 3	Ravens Variable 4	Mill Hill Variable 5	Moral Variable 8
Piaget Total ('Concrete' and 'Formal') (Var 6 and Var 7)	−.036	.255**	−.132	.548**	.469**	.472**

N =   231
**   Significant where p < .001
*   Significant where p < .005

Table 1.5: Correlation matrix of all variables

	Sex	Age	SES	Ravens	Mill Hill	'Concrete'	'Formal'	Moral
Sex		.017	.112	.014	-.197	-.074	-.009	-.087
Age			.204**	.260**	.287**	.202**	.247**	.171*
SES				-.157	-.198*	-.179*	-.086	-.021
Ravens					.549**	.482**	.503**	.306**
Mill Hill						.462**	.404**	.351**
'Concrete'							.609**	.429**
'Formal'								.427**
Moral								

N = 231

** Significant where $p < .001$

* Significant where $p < .005$

Summary table 1.6: Stepwise Regression Analysis (All − Unforced) Dependent Variable: Moral

Independent Variable	Multiple R	R Square	RSQ Change	Simple R	B	Beta
'Concrete'	.429	.184	.184	.429	2.288	.223
'Formal'	.477	.228	.044	.427	3.308	.228
Mill Hill	.497	.247	.019	.351	.580	.154
SES	.502	.252	.005	-.021	2.664	.074
Sex	.504	.254	.002	-.087	2.993	-.046
Age	.504	.253	.000	-.171	.041	.009
Ravens	.504	.254	.000	.306	.044	.009
(Constant)					227.463	

Summary table 1.7: Stepwise Regression Analysis (All − Unforced) Dependent Variable: Moral

Independent Variable	Multiple R	R Square	RSQ Change	Simple R	B	BETA
'Concrete' and 'Formal'	.472	.223	.223	.472	2.034	.397
Mill Hill	.494	.245	.022	.351	.610	.162
SES	.499	.249	.004	-.021	2.480	.070
Sex	.501	.251	.002	-.087	-3.143	-.049
Age	.501	.251	.000	.171	.037	.008
Ravens	.501	.251	.000	.306	.046	.009
(Constant)					233.185	

variable in combination with 'Concrete'. The table shows changes in R^2 occurring with successive independent variables included. The third variable is Mill Hill (vocabulary). This factor, however, accounts for a very small percentage increase in the value of R^2. The increase in value of R^2 associated with the addition of further variables is negligible. So that any characteristics these variables possess have already been accounted for by the combination already described (i.e. 'Concrete', 'Formal' and Mill Hill).

In this analysis therefore, a combination of the three cognitive factors, 'Concrete', 'Formal' and Mill Hill, effectively encompass the whole spectrum of Kohlberg moral judgment as measured by the remainder of the variables. An individual adolescent exhibiting a combination of such cognitive traits of verbal fluency, concrete and formal (abstract) operations is likely to be more morally mature than an adolescent with verbal deficits and poor reasoning.

Stepwise Regression need not yield the optimum combination of independent variables although it always produces a very good approximation. To discover whether better solutions existed it was decided to combine the 'Concrete' and 'Formal' variables: psychologically and statistically it was felt that the formal scores might be of greater importance and therefore appropriate for them to be weighted twice to the concrete scores; and further, to see whether a different combination of independent variables was produced. However, in operational terms, no differences were computed and the same combination and order of variables was exhibited as in the previous analysis. However, it will be observed that Multiple R for 'Formal' in combination with 'Concrete' in Table 1.6 is .477, whereas in Table 1.7 it is .472.

Quantitative discussion and qualitative observations of the overall Piagetian results in relation to other studies

Genevan results suggested that between 11 to 16 years the adolescent makes a gradual transition from the concrete to the formal mode, beginning on average at 11 or 12 years and forming a stable, formal system of thought structures about 14 or 15 years. The emergence of formal thought in the adolescent has not been so readily confirmed by replicatory studies, relative to other Piagetian levels, and as the formal stage becomes increasingly a focus of interest, it is subject to further debate. Piaget more recently (1972b) has acknowledged that the Genevan sample may have been based on a privileged population and that the formal stage may need review.

Results revealed that 5 per cent of boys and 9 per cent of girls are still at the early concrete level. Fifty-three per cent of boys and 53 per cent of girls are at the late concrete stage of operativity, with 39 per cent boys and 31 per cent girls revealing early formal thinking. Only three per cent of boys and six per cent of girls are categorized as reaching the equilibrium of formal thought. This can be considered as revealing little sex difference in logical thinking within this sample. When boys and girls are combined, the percentage of the total sample at the various operational levels are: early concrete, seven per cent; late concrete, 53 per cent; early formal, 36 per cent; and late formal, four per cent.

Ross (1974) for 'moderate achievers', mean age 15.10 years, on the basis of Tisher's Piagetian Questionnaire, employing three experiments, reported percentages of 10, 50, 40 and 0, for early concrete, late concrete, early formal and late formal, respectively. For 'high achievers', mean age 14.11 years, percentages of 0, 57, 39 and 4, were reported respectively. Tisher's (1962, 1971) investigation, employing the Questionnaire, reported for the 13.5 — 14.9 years age group, percentages of 63 per cent for combined early and late concrete categories and 41 per cent for combined early and late formal categories. For the 15.0 — 16.4 years age group, the percentages for the same categories were 54 per cent and 46 per cent respectively. These compare favourably with figures for the present investigation, although it has to be conceded that these are on the basis of the same Piagetian Questionnaire (in Ross's case, however, he used three of the four experiments). Jackson (1963) reported that 50 per cent of his 15-year-old subjects (IQs 90—110) were at the formal level, however, only 10 per cent at Stage IIIB. This would appear to be a slightly higher percentage than in the present investigation. Dulit's (1972) 14-year-old sample, selected at random, revealed a 10 per cent incidence of fully formal thinking on the 'Liquids' experiment, and 19 per cent when using 'relaxed' criteria. There were no incidences to report with respect to the 'Shadows' experiment. On the 'Pendulum' experiment alone, Somerville (1974) reported at 14 years, 54 per cent at early formal level and 25 per cent at late formal level.

Researches employing subjects at ages either in advance or beyond those of the subjects in the present investigation, include Field and Cropley (1969). Using Tisher's Questionnaire, among 178 subjects aged 16—18 years, they reported that of the females, 27 per cent reached the concrete level, 58 per cent the early formal and 15 per cent the late formal; for males, percentages were 9, 59 and 32 at corresponding stages, respectively. It would appear that these are considerably higher than in the present sample, although it needs to be recalled that Field and Cropley's sample comprised subjects with a mean IQ of 117, all of whom were enrolled in science courses. Tomlinson-Keasey (1972) among girls, mean age 11.9; female 'coeds', mean age 19.7; and women, mean age, 54 years; reported the percentages for early concrete, late concrete, early formal and fully formal as: 18, 47, 28, 4; 3, 28, 41, 26; and 13, 30, 36, 18; for the girls, 'coeds' and women, respectively. Allowing for differences in chronological age, these percentages would also appear to contain similar patterning to the present investigation and it is interesting to note the almost identical percentages at the early formal stage for 'coeds' and 'women' although the incidences at the late formal stage were considerably higher. Dulit among 'average' and 'gifted' adolescents, 16—17 years and 'average' adults, 20—55 years, recorded percentages at the fully formal level to be 35, 57 and 33 respectively for the 'Shadows' experiment and 17, 62 and 25 respectively for the 'Liquids'. At the early formal level, percentages for 'average' adolescents were 50 and 28 for 'Shadows' and 'Liquids' experiments respectively with percentages for 'average' adults being relatively lower.

Kuhn (1971) discussing formal operational thinking among four age ranges extending from 10 to 50 years, commented that on the basis of the pendulum problem, Stage IIIB thinking was about equally frequent among the age ranges 16—20, 21—30 and 45—50, but considerably less frequent among subjects of 10—15 years. With respect to the last age range, relevant to the present study, she concluded that the results indicated that beginnings of formal operational thought may begin to appear by early adolescence in most subjects (80 per cent of the 10—15 year group).

No significant sex differences in levels of logical operativity were identified in the present investigation which gives further credibility to the results reported by Tisher (*op. cit.*) and Case and Collinson (1962). These findings are however contrary to those described by Field and Cropley, Dulit, Ross and Graybill (1974) who demonstrated sex differences in favour of boys.

The analysis of the various Piagetian tests included in this investigation revealed that some proved to be more difficult than others with respect to the operational strategies involved. This finding is not at variance with observations made by other investigators. Three possible reasons can be forwarded for the variability: that there are differences in subjects interest and experience across content domains, which Piaget has suggested; that there are differences within the difficulty of the tasks or that formal operational ontogenesis is a relatively slow process of gradual application to different kinds of content. Somerville commented that Inhelder and Piaget suggest that certain of the 16 binary operations are easier for a child to discover than others, for example, the authors claim that it is easier for the child to deal with operations '... which state that which is, and establish true implications ... (than) those which exclude that which is not and deny the false implications', (Inhelder and Piaget, 1958, p. 75).

DISCUSSION AND INTERPRETATION OF THE RESULTS / *Hypothesis One*: 'That a relationship exists between Piagetian operativity and moral development.'

The hypothesis was confirmed using statistical measures which were all significant at the 1 per cent level and indeed the majority were significant at .1 per cent level or better. Tables 1.1, 1.3, 1.4, 1.5, 1.6 and 1.7 are relevant to the present hypothesis and the statistical evidence has been presented in a preceding section.

Caution needs to be exercised in the interpretation of the results: it is essential to recall that the results relate only to a narrow age range and that 'late concrete' and 'early formal' levels are of main concern with respect to Piagetian operativity and mainly Stages Two to Four are focused upon with respect to Moral Maturity. In the present study although the experimental procedures were aligned as closely as possible to Inhelder and Piaget's (1958) original conception, it can be hypothesized that results are not strictly comparable and when seen within the sphere of other replicatory studies, variations are bound to exist with respect to procedures in the presentation of the problems and / or evaluation of subjects' responses, together with the results being based upon different batteries of experimental tasks. However, within the confines of the study it is possible to originate interpretations of the results.

Integral to the study was the actualization in development of logical operations *per se* in particular, the actualization of 'formal' operations. Genevan results demonstrated that between 11 to 16 years the adolescent makes a gradual transition from the concrete to the formal mode, beginning on average at 11 or 12 years and forming a stable, formal system of thought structures about 14 or 15 years. Replicatory studies however report low percentages of fully emergent formal operations in the adolescent stage. Piaget (1972b, *op. cit.*) has acknowledged that the formal stage may require revision. However, there is sufficient evidence of the existence of the trends described by Inhelder and Piaget for comparative analyses to be expedient. This particular investigation revealed the patterning of logical development identified in the Genevan studies and compares favourably with other replicatory studies in the field.

Fairly extensive data are available regarding the development of moral judgment itself (Kohlberg, *passim*). Therefore the moral judgment data for this investigation are presented in accordance with a considerable body of earlier research establishing the hierarchy of moral judgment stages. However, it has to be conceded that only a limited range of stages has been identified due to the restricted age range investigated and the full realm of stages being an age-related developmental sequence. The frequencies of stage usage found in the present investigation are comparable to those obtained for other similar adolescent samples and the data essentially provide greater evidence for the hierarchy of moral judgment stages than for the age-related developmental sequence. Moral maturity scores in this investigation ranged from 225 (just falling within the 2(3)-Stage) to 491 (falling within Stage-5, the only subject reaching a pure-principled level) thereby indicating that the range generally represents Stages-2(3) to Stage-4 with small percentages of subjects indicating some principled thinking.

Present findings and related studies

Qualitative analyses indicated the stage relationships between levels of logical operativity and moral judgments for the four Piaget stage groups and for the total sample.

Subjects categorized as 'Formal' do not reveal any Stage-2 moral judgments [there is an exception of one subject in the total sample — further investigation reveals that the relevant stage score is 3(2)] . There is considerable overlap among subjects categorized as 'Concrete' and 'Formal' in relation to Stage-3 moral judgments. However, there is a trend for lower percentages at Stage-3 to be associated with subjects categorized as 'Formal'. Within the realm of Stage-4 moral judgments, higher incidences occur among the 'Formal' subjects. Any indications of Stage-5 moral judgments occur only among subjects categorized as 'Formal'.

Considerable momentum has been added to the discussion and interpretation of the findings for the present investigation by a comparison (1975, private communication) with the Kuhn *et al.* study (1971). The Kuhn study examined the development of formal operations in logical and moral judgment among 265 subjects of chronological ages ranging from 10 to 50 years, subdivided as follows: 10—15, 16—20, 21—30, 45—50 years. The main finding that fully emergent formal operations are a logical operational prerequisite to the emergence of principled moral reasoning but do not in themselves guarantee the emergence of principled reasoning, is only partly relevant to the present investigation, but the intermediary findings pertain to this present analysis. Kuhn reported that early formal operational subjects who show any principled moral reasoning are for the most part still at the predominantly conventional level. The subjects in the present investigation are in the main, at the early formal level and the low incidence of principled thinking would therefore receive credibility from the observations of Kuhn. However, it can be emphasized that any emergence of principled thinking that has been identified is associated with subjects at the early formal logical thinking stage, one at late formal. Kuhn's data further suggested in general, that the emergence of formal operations is a necessary condition for the consolidation of conventional moral judgment (i.e., pure Stage-4). She emphasizes however, that such a conclusion is much more tentative on both empirical and theoretical grounds. Empirically, it is tentative because of the small number of Stage-4 subjects (N = 22). Theoretically it is less tenable that certain logical operations are a necessary condition for the consolidation of reasoning that has already developed than that they are a necessary condition for the emergence of a new form of reasoning. In the present investigation Stages 3(4), 4(3), and 4 have been grouped within one category, however closer inspection of the protocol reveals that 4 subjects reveal pure Stage-4 judgments, of these 3 are at the early formal level. These figures do not provide any greater reliability than those obtained by Kuhn. Subjects categorized as 4(3), the next highest stage, produces a total of 9 subjects, all but one of whom are 'Early Formal' in logical thinking. When compared with Kuhn's figures for Stage-4(3), the present study indicates a more significant trend, for Kuhn reports from a total of 43 subjects at this moral judgment level, 24 subjects at the early formal level (19 at concrete).

Kuhn's data further indicate that the majority of subjects who are concrete operational or below show a level of moral judgment of predominantly Stage-3 or lower. Almost all of the concrete operational subjects show a moral judgment level of no higher than 4(3). Among subjects within the early formal logical stage, in contrast, almost half have moral stage scores of 4 or higher and a third show some principled reasoning. The present study provides further credibility for these findings: the majority of concrete operational subjects fall within the Stage-3 moral judgment category or lower. Further examination of the protocols reveals that of the percentages falling into the category of 3(4), 4(3) and 4, there is a representation of 16 concrete subjects, in the total sample, 14 of whom respond in the Stage-3(4) mode. Figures are not so comparable however with respect to the early formal category as a whole, for it cannot be confirmed that almost half have moral stage scores of 4 or higher and a third showing some principled reasoning. However, this may in part be due to Kuhn's sample comprising a wider age range.

The suggestion of a relationship between the emergence of formal operational thought and the consolidation of conventional moral judgment (for the present investigation specifically Stage 4(3), for Kuhn's study, Stage 4) receives some support from a study by Lee (1971). The latter reported, among subjects 5—17 years, an overall association between the use of formal operations and the use of a type of moral judgment (Level 4: Societal) roughly equivalent to Stage-4. It is of further interest that a study by Tomlinson-Keasey and Keasey (1974) involving girls of 12—13 years recorded that the transition to formal operations that begins at this age is accompanied in the moral realm by conventional moral reasoning (numbers were however small).

Décalage

Kuhn interprets the association between the attainment of formal operations and the consolidation of conventional moral judgment to be a reflection of the consistent *décalage* between levels of logical and moral judgment. As stated earlier, it is less likely that formal operations are a necessary condition for the development of a Stage-4 level of moral judgment, since many subjects show some Stage-4 usage, i.e. 4(3) and 3(4) without being at the formal operational stage (although this was not completely borne out by the present investigation). The high proportion of 45- to 50-year-olds at Stage-4 (25 per cent) suggested to Kuhn that there may be a point of fixation at the adult level: i.e., that the moral judgment level of many adults remains at Stage-4, although these adults have the logical operational potential for principled moral judgment. The fairly high percentages of 'Formal' subjects at the Stage-3 level in the present investigation can be taken to be indicative of a *décalage* between levels of attainment in the logical and moral domains. Tomlinson-Keasey and Keasey (*op. cit.*) also confirmed a *décalage* between the attainment of formal operations and its application to the area of moral reasoning and further that formal operations were not a sufficient condition for the emergence of principled (moral) reasoning among 24 college subjects. It will be recalled that Selman (1971) and Kohlberg and DeVries (1969) have also indicated a *décalage* between logical operativity and moral reasoning among subjects of younger ages.

Interpretations

The verification of a relationship between levels of logical operativity and moral development leads to speculation concerning the interrelationship of the two developmental sequences. Concrete logical reasoning appears to be a necessary condition for the appearance of Stage-2 moral thinking (Kohlberg and DeVries, *op. cit.*). Awareness of logical reciprocity or reversibility can be related to moral Stage-2 which presupposes a view of human beings as individuals each with his own distinguishable perspective, although instrumental. There would appear to be two conceptual developments that are prerequisites for moral Stage-3: firstly awareness of reciprocal role taking and secondly concepts of generalized patterns of interaction or relationships (Selman, *op. cit.*). The concept of relationship may be described as a kind of 'social conservation' integrating a notion of overall social patterning; however, it is confined at Stage-3 to a primary concern for the approval of others in such relationships to the self, with an emphasis on personal role-stereotypes. The moral Stage-4 conception of a social order requires the Piagetian first-stage of formal operations in which sets of relations are first conceived as invariant systems (the present investigation, together with the studies of Kuhn, Lee and Tomlinson-Keasey and Keasey, *op. cit.*). This conception generates a concern for the maintenance of a system of fixed rules and for the maintenance of a system of authority. Full formal operational reasoning leads to a concern with all possible hypothetical possibilities and to an awareness of a given rule system as only one of many logical possible rule-systems. This awareness provides the basis for the restructuring of society's rules into moral principles — Stages 5 and 6. (Based on discussion promoted by Rest, private communication, 1972 / 3, Harvard University, Laboratory of Human Development.)

Kuhn *et al.* have provided inspiration for interpretation of the results and the following analysis owes much to their speculations. It cannot be determined whether the stages of moral development reflect the application of successively more advanced logical operations in the moral domain or whether logical and moral stages constitute independent, though perhaps isomorphic developmental sequences. It can however be acknowledged that there is evidence suggesting that development in both the logical and moral domains occurs in terms of equilibrium process / auto-regulation mechanisms in which the inter-action of the individual's structures with the environment, feeds back to these structures in a way that promotes their reorganization. In the case of related structures in different domains, the hypothesis may be forwarded that it is the interaction of different, but partially overlapping, aspects of the individual's structures, with different, but partially overlapping sectors of external reality which leads to disequilibrium, reorganization and change in each of the domains: moral development may entail a somewhat (but not completely) different set of organization—environment interactions than does logical development. This leads to a further conjecture, that there are actually two kinds of interaction which are sources of developmental change. One is the interaction of the individual's structures with the structures comprising the environment. The other is the internal interaction among the structures themselves: in other words, the discrepancy between the level of development of the individual's operational structures in one domain and their level of development in another which may in itself be a source of disequilibrium, and hence change. Furthermore, each of these processes of interaction may influence and regulate the other. An interaction between a given mental structure and the environment, may stimulate a reorganization in the internal relationship or coordination of this structure and other related structures. This reorganization in turn may generate internal disequilibrium which leads to further interactions with the environment, involving both the original and related structures. Such relations are a complex form of that type which Flavell (1972) in his 'An analysis of cognitive-developmental sequence' (Genetic Psychology Monographs, volume 86, pp. 279–350), has labelled 'bidirectional' in his typology of all the possible relations between one developmental phenomenon and another.

That logical operations may possibly hold a more central position in the organization of operational structures becomes tenable through the observation that logical operations appear to serve as a 'pacing' mechanism in moral development, such that moral development never exceeds certain limits imposed by the individual's level of logical operations. Beyond these limitations however, there is considerable variability in the relations between subjects' logical and moral levels. Possible sources of this variability may include the extent to which logical and moral development may proceed independently: i.e. involve only partially overlapping sets of organism-environment interactions, e.g. general social experience, as indexed by chronological age may play a greater role in moral development than in logical development. Specific personal or social experience particular to the individual is a second source of variability: an individual's particular life experiences may contribute to the determination of his ultimate moral level in a way that is not the case for logical level. (The interpretations and analysis are essentially those as advanced by Kuhn *et al.*, 1971.)

SUBSIDIARY HYPOTHESIS /
Hypothesis Two: 'That measures of logical reasoning are relatively more effective indicators of moral maturity than a traditional measure of intelligence'.

The hypothesis was confirmed using statistical measures. Tables 1.3, 1.4, 1.5, 1.6 and 1.7 are relevant, the statistical evidence having been presented in a previous section. The correlations confirm that both the logical operational variables and the Raven's intelligence variable are indices of mental level related to moral judgment level. However, logical reasoning measures are relatively more related to the level of moral development than the psychometric index of intelligence.

Kohlberg (1969) reports that IQ scores have only moderate correlations with his moral judgment measures, that for some stages the correspondence was negligible and that the relationship seemed to be curvilinear rather than linear. Simon and Ward (1973) in an investigation of variables influencing pupils' responses on the Kohlberg schema of moral development focus on the disagreements concerning the relationship between moral judgment and intelligence and exploring the Raven's Matrices in relation to moral judgment, reported that intelligence level was a factor which was associated significantly with level of moral judgment. Among high, average, and low IQ groups the mean differences between each group were statistically significant at the .001 level. The present study reports the same correlation between Raven s and moral judgment (Value of r = .31) which Kohlberg himself gives for the correlation between Raven's and moral judgment. Likewise, Kuhn *et al.* (*op. cit.*) reported that in her main sample the correlation between IQ (WAIS, WISC) and moral score was .30 (significant p $<$ .01). However for the subsidiary sample, the correlation between IQ and moral score was only .11 (nonsignificant). Her correlations between the logical and moral variables were .27 for the main sample (significant, p $<$ .01) and .30 for sample two (significant, p $<$ .01).

It would be presumptuous to argue that the Piagetian tests measure real effective intelligence while the Raven's tests do not. With respect to traditional measures, Piaget (1947) in *The Psychology of Intelligence*, has argued: 'It is indisputable that these tests of mental age have on the whole lived up to what was expected of them: a rapid and convenient estimation of an individual's general level. But it is not less obvious that they simply measure a "yield" without reaching constructive operations themselves. As Pieron rightly pointed out, intelligence conceived in these terms is essentially a value judgment applied to complex behaviour'. Piaget (1957, and again in 1969, in *Science of Education and the Psychology of the Child*) has further elaborated his views that traditional tests are concerned with quantitative measures of behaviour and do not penetrate to the actual qualitative operational mechanisms which govern the behaviour. Piaget therefore indicates that his problem-solving tasks define basic and general thought processes and assess their level more adequately than psychometric tests.

One of the strongest contrasts of the Piagetian and traditional psychometric approaches to assessment was made by Pinard and Laurendeau (1964) in a paper entitled, 'A scale of mental development based on the theory of Piaget', published in the *Journal of Research in Science Teaching,* who consider that the traditional tests produce extremely artificial scales and can hardly serve to make known the child's intellectual growth much less intellectual evolution in general. Focusing on similar criticisms of standardized tests, Wolff (1974, in private communication) hypothesizes the consequences of the possible development of a 'Piaget Developmental Quotient.' Lester, Muir and Dudek (1970, p. 285) in a Paper: 'Cognitive structure and achievement in the young child', subsequently published in the *Canadian Psychiatric Association Journal* maintain, 'The Piaget tests seem to measure a range of structures wider than that of the traditional IQ tests. Orientational, spatial, and time concepts are involved but also the ability of the child to separate himself from the objective world to perceive himself from the objective world and to perceive himself as one element in an outside reality'. Stephens, McLaughlin, Miller and Glass (1972) maintain that Piagetian reasoning tasks involve abilities separate from those measured by standard tests of intelligence and achievement.

In commenting on the conceptual differences between Piagetian and psychometric conceptions of intelligence Elkind (1969) in a report: 'Piagetian and psychometric conceptions of intelligence', published in the *Harvard Educational Review*, maintains that the differences arise from the unique ways that each conception views intelligence and that they are focused on different aspects of intelligent behaviour, such as: (a) the type of genetic causality they presuppose; (b) the description of mental growth they provide, and (c) the contributions of nature and nurture which they assess. It may be important to acknowledge that these are conceptual similarities between Piagetian and psychometric conceptions of intelligence: both approaches share the assumption that mental ability is, at least in part, genetically determined; and both view intelligence as fundamentally rational in nature. Hathaway (in private communication, 1974, 1975) in an unpublished report: 'The degree, nature and temporal stability of the relations between traditional, psychometric and Piagetian developmental measures of mental development', using 21 traditional psychometric, 10 Piagetian measures and 10 scholastic achievement variables, concluded from his research that performance on Piagetian measures was related to but not identical with performance on traditional measures of mental development and that the degree of the relationship between the two types of measures, was moderate, positive and significant: the two types of measures were neither totally distinct nor totally identical.

Although the above statements tend to promote the view that Piagetian situations measure real effective intelligence it may be more appropriate to speculate rather that the Piagetian tests require the adolescent to assimilate what is for him a complex body of information and bring to bear on it an information processing strategy which (to him) is not immediately obvious, but is nevertheless necessary to account for all of the information. Although each problem in the Raven's Progressive Matrices is a system of thought and includes such problems as permutations of figures and resolution of figures with constituent parts, measuring fundamental aspects of cognitive performances it may be speculated that the Piagetian tasks involve relatively more complex forms of responding, assessing the development of an adolescent's knowledge of the physical world together with his logico-mathematical knowledge.

It is pertinent to acknowledge the Mill Hill relationships with moral maturity in view of the fact that Raven advocates their accompanying use with the Progressive Matrices. Likewise, the Mill Hill cannot be said to 'tap' the complex structures which the Piagetian measures assess. It can be suggested that Mill Hill is related to moral development in the sense of 'tapping' the individual's ability to recall and verbally communicate his reasoning processes.

As the moral judgment dilemmas also involve complex forms of responding it is not surprising to observe that Piagetian logical measures relate relatively more to the developmental moral maturity levels than Ravens. It is suggested that the logical variables reflect major, qualitative transformations or turning points (e.g., the transition from concrete to formal operations) which appear to be of significance for moral development and which are not reflected in a general psychometric index of mental advancement.

OTHER ANALYSES / *Relation of Tisher's Questionnaire to the Individual Piagetian Testing*

The Piagetian tasks, administered individually to 36 subjects selected at random included: 'Combinations of Coloured and Colourless Chemical Bodies', 'Equilibrium in the Balance' and 'The Oscillation of a Pendulum and the Operations of Exclusion', Inhelder and Piaget (1958, pp. 107—122, 164—81, 67—69, respectively). Interviews were conducted according to the clinical method developed by Inhelder and Piaget: further details of the experiments and the theoretical rationale for the distinction between stages are given in Modgil (1975). Subjects were seen individually, in a small room for the administration of the Piagetian tasks. Good rapport was established and all verbal responses were recorded verbatim. The subject was required to give a reason for each response and where necessary additional questions were asked for further clarification. Throughout the entire testing the investigator was aware of the need to avoid giving subjects any extraneous or inadvertent clues by gesture, expression or tone of voice. The subjects were classified into an overall level of development on the basis of two or more problems being designated to the same level and the resulting classification was compared with the stage level assigned for Questionnaire responses. Two comparison procedures were used: initially relating 'early' and 'late' categories for both concrete and formal stages and secondly relating 'global' concrete and formal categories. The following tables illustrate the resulting patterns:

Comparisons on the basis of the first procedure resulted in a percentage of agreement of 61 between the individual testing and the questionnaire. When overall stage (concrete / formal) was compared, the percentage of agreement was 83. Tisher (1962, 1971) reported a 77 per cent agreement using the latter method.

Comparisons of Piaget individual testing to Tisher Group Questionnaire (sub-stages)

	Substages	Individual Testing Higher	Questionnaire Higher	Subjects
Corresponding classifications	Early Concrete (2A)			4
	Late Concrete (2B)			11
	Early Formal (3A)			7
	Late Formal (3B)			0
Discrepancies	Early Concrete Concrete (2A) / Late (2B)	3	1	4
	Late Concrete (2B)/Early Formal (3A)	4	2	6
	Early Formal (3A) / Late Formal (3B)	0	4	4
			Total Subjects	36

Comparisons of Piaget individual testing to Tisher Group Questionnaire (Concrete / Formal)

	Stage	Individual Testing Higher	Questionnaire Higher	Subjects
Corresponding Classification	Concrete			19
	Formal			11
Discrepancies	Concrete/Formal	4	2	6
			Total Subjects	36

Relation of the group testing to individual testing — Kohlberg Moral Dilemmas

Dilemmas I, II, III and IV were administered to the subjects in the individual-interview situation in accordance with Kohlberg's 'standardized' probes to gain further credence for the group-testing situation.

The two, two-situation units were administered within one testing session, a break being permitted between each unit. All responses were recorded verbatim. Copies of the dilemmas and the respective probes are included in Modgil (1975).

Comparisons were made with respect to qualitative differences between the subjects' protocols obtained from the group testing and the individual testing. Dilemmas III and IV were administered in both testing situations and no significant differences were observed: the same essential responses were given with varying phraseology. With respect to Dilemmas I and II responses did not vary from the overall level of response given in the group testing situation. There was therefore no evidence that the group testing situation varied to any marked degree from the individual interviews.

IMPLICATIONS OF THE RESULTS AND INDICATIONS FOR FUTURE RESEARCH /
Implications of the results

The major overall implication of this investigation may be formulated as follows:

1. Studies of the interrelationship of different variables in adolescent development are still rare, yet most desirable if one is to develop a 'psychological theory' of human development as opposed to a 'cognitive' or 'social' or 'moral' theory of human development on an empirical basis. One ultimately seeks to comprehend the whole adolescent not just one facet of him. (Goldschmid, 1971, 1972, 1973, private communication expresses a similar contention). Specific detailing of the interlocking mechanisms in the formation of such a theory has yet to be spelled out. The present study has been just one attempt towards the fulfillment of such a challenging objective. If the study has but pointed toward a significant number of psychological directions it will have fulfilled its purpose. Theories are not static nor should they be (a point which is certainly in the spirit, if not the letter) of Piaget's and Kohlberg's theory and thinking.

2. The study has given support to the existence of a relationship between logical reasoning ability and moral maturity. This implies a differing role for cognitive development than has traditionally been the case: rather than cognitive actualization being important for intellectual

concerns alone, it may be seen as expedient for related developmental domains. It would seem therefore admissable for teachers in training and in practice to be made more aware of Piagetian concepts and to conceptualize cognitive development in terms of a more mobile set of criteria. By implication then, there is the need for greater diversification of the curricula content within colleges of education.

3. The study has provided credibility for the cognitive-developmental approach (Kohlberg, *passim*) and would therefore imply support for the aim of education as being the stimulation of the next stage of development, rather than as the transmission of information (intellectual) or indoctrination into the fixed values of the school or social values (moral). A cognitive-developmental approach would stress knowledge of the adolescent's stage of functioning and arousal of genuine cognitive and social conflict and disagreement about problematic situations involving exposure to the next higher level of thought: traditional education has stressed adult 'right answers', reinforcing and rewarding 'right answers' and 'behaving well'.

4. The suggested *décalage* between logical and moral development and the identification of a possible discrepancy between potential development and actualized ontogenesis would suggest a necessity to focus on preventing retardation and fixation in those adolescents beginning to lag behind. (Similar contentions have been expressed by Kuhn *et al., op. cit.*).

Indications for future research

This is the only known study of its kind which has attempted an investigation of logical reasoning in relation to moral judgment among 231 subjects aged 14 to 15 years. It must be conceded however, that the only other known closely-related study of Kuhn *et al.* (1971b, 1975 personal communication) comprised a more extensive age-range and gave a more comprehensive insight into the relationships under investigation. The two studies are, however, compatible and symbiotic in that the Kuhn *et al.* study provided a global analysis of the ages 10−50, and the present investigation a deeper insight into the 14 to 15 age range. The other partly related studies are Lee (1971) and Tomlinson-Keasey and Keasey (1974).

Although a range of intelligence levels, vocabulary levels, socio-economic status categories and both sexes have been included in the total sample and in the various Piaget stage groups, with suitable controls being exercised, further research may endeavour to look at a differing balance of subjects with employment of differing measures and more stringent criteria for categorization which may enhance the magnitude of differences observed.

Although appropriate statistical techniques were applied to the different types of data collected, the researcher has been aware that the investigation has been primarily correlational, making inferences of causal relations impossible. The most obvious danger of the correlational method is a tendency to infer causality when only association has been established. In such an investigation, an awareness of a number of influences in the physical and social environments of the adolescent need to be indicated. Thus, the amount of general social experiences particular to the individual constitute themselves as potent formative forces. Kohlberg (*passim*) stressed the centrality of role taking for moral judgment development, together with peer-group participation, communication, emotional warmth, sharing in decisions, receipt of awarding responses, the degree of the focusing on the consequences of action to others and the amount of parental encouragement of the adolescent's participation in discussion. All of these can be taken to be examples of extraneous variables. Attempts to control for these variables present an almost insurmountable methodological problem. The fact that both hypotheses were fully substantiated, involving a sample of 231 subjects with rather complex measures and that the trends of some of the findings tend to be largely in accord with theoretical and empirical expectation, suggest that the investigational measures were, to a large extent, suitable for tapping the different realms of behaviours investigated.

Although social-class categorizations in accordance with the Registrar General's Classification (1960) were controlled in the present study, a finer categorization of social class status would perhaps have led to more perfectly matched groups. However, no such controls were reported in either the Kuhn *et al.* or Keasey and Keasey studies (*op. cit.*), or further, in any studies investigating primarily, the existence of formal operations, e.g. Field and Cropley (1969), Dulit (1972) and Ross (1974) etc. and yet they confirm most of the present results. It can therefore be anticipated that a more analytical approach to e.g., family life-style, peer group participation or levels of aspirations with reference to career-after-school (Piaget emphasized the importance of the development of a 'life-plan' in relation to the emergence of formal operations, Inhelder and Piaget, 1958) may provide greater insight with respect to the relation of the developmental domains under consideration. Likewise, birth-orders and family-size (parent—child and sibling—sibling interactions) effects are unlikely to operate independently of other familial aspects. However, with a sample of 231 children in the present study it can be speculated that there is a representative sample of varying birth orders and family size and that this factor, if at all significant would only be of importance for future research.

The results obtained in the present study must be interpreted with the awareness that only 14- to 15+ year-old subjects were involved. Since responses to Piagetian tasks and Kohlberg's dilemmas are developmental in nature, it certainly would make sense to evaluate the results of a longitudinal study.

In a future study, a non-correlational study should be specifically designed to link moral development (of the kind studied here or other approaches to moral development measurement) to the logical reasoning development in children and adolescents across a number of cultures, in order to more adequately examine the effects of inhibitory or facilitatory socialization variables on the individual's auto-regulation mechanism. This endeavour requires careful long-range planning through series of preliminary investigations and may be best undertaken via corporate efforts at both national and international levels. This would seem a desirable amplification of the investigation for empirical generality.

If logical and moral judgment development is related as in the present investigation and further, there is a relation between moral judgment levels and moral behaviour Kohlberg (1971), then there must be ultimate links to be established between logical reasoning development, moral judgment and moral behaviour. It is encouraging to note that a research, currently in progress has come to the writer's attention — Stephens *et al.*, (1975, personal communication).

Integral to the study was the establishment of the existence of the concrete and formal operational stages identified by Piaget. It has been observed in this present exposition that the formal operational stage still requires further elaboration and review. Indeed Piaget himself (1972) has acknowledged that the 'period which separates adolescence from adulthood', raises a number of unsolved questions, e.g. more research into special aptitudes and professional specialization. Ross commenting on this paper by Piaget suggests that the way that research proceeds will be more complex and difficult than before. Assuming that the formal structures are manifested within a particular aptitude context, it will first be necessary to isolate the superior aptitude of each individual and then present a formal task congruent with that aptitude. Dulit (*op. cit.*) has suggested that there is a need to introduce into the model at least some concept as 'dropout rate' or 'branching into parallel tracks' one main track would be the formal stage, but only some modest proportion of the normal population would proceed in this direction. Other tracks would represent the development of alternative patterns of thought, those alternative patterns involving only partial or minimal development of the capacity for formal stage thought. Speculation concerning these recently stated requirements together with the preceding observations embodies a multidimensional spectrum of awaited research.

Whatever the direction future theory and research may assume, it is the writer's hope that the present study may offer a few rays of enlightenment.

SUMMARY / The investigation has attempted to show how Piagetian operativity relates to moral development. The particular relations that are found suggest specific aspects of logical reasoning which coexist with Kohlberg moral maturity and possibly enhance its development.
Results indicated that:

1. A relationship exists between Piagetian operativity and moral development.
2. Logical reasoning is a relatively more effective indicator of moral maturity than a traditional intelligence measure.

It is hoped that further research will serve to unravel and expound the experiential conditions responsible for the development of logical and moral schemas and more generally, contribute to the development of a comprehensive theory of maturation by clarifying the relation among different facets of adolescent development.

Egocentrism and the emergence of conventional morality in pre-adolescent girls
D.J. Moir, 1974

AIM / The strength of relationships between nonmoral and moral aspects of role taking behaviour was assessed.

SUBJECTS / N = 40. Eleven-year-old New Zealand girls participated in the study.

METHOD / The following tasks were administered:

(a) Nine moral-dilemma situations (patterned after Kohlberg, 1958).
(b) Nonmoral-role-taking tests (modelled after Flavell, 1968, pp. 45–55, 55–70 and 154–159; Selman, 1969; Schelling, 1960; and Fry, 1967). Scoring was patterned after Rothenberg (1970).

RESULTS / The prediction of an association between non-moral- and moral-role-taking measures was fully substantiated. The relationship was observed to be independent of the variance due to conventional verbal intelligence. Moir discusses the results and future research problems in the context of the Piagetian concept of *structure d'ensemble*. Some of the problems raised were ' . . . how role taking in one area generalizes to role taking in other areas. Whether the specific training of role taking is possible and what effect this has on moral development . . . ', p. 304.

The relationship between ego and moral development in adult lay and religious women
M.E. Moore, 1976

AIM / To investigate the relationship between Erikson's stages of ego development and Kohlberg's theory of moral development.

SUBJECTS / N = 143 Women between the ages of 25 and 74. Sixty-nine of the women were religious from a Roman Catholic Community of sisters and 74 were members of a Roman Catholic parish in the Chicago area.

METHOD / To evaluate ego development, Boyd's Self-Description Questionnaire was used. The instrument yields information concerning resolution of sequential ego stages and the pertinency of phase-specific ego stages. Rest's Defining Issues Test was employed to assess level of moral development. The test indexes moral development by locating a subject according to use of principled thinking.

RESULTS / Significant correlations between ego development and moral development scores were computed indicating that 'the totality of the positive and negative attitudes that have been incorporated into the personality is related to how one approaches a moral dilemma. A significant correlation was found between concern for the generativity crisis and moral development scores. There were also positive correlations between moral development and status as a lay or religious woman. When the effects of education were partialled, the correlation between status and moral development was negligible. Resolution of the eight stages of ego development served in the prediction of moral development scores. The contribution of the stages was found to be as follows: of the eight ego stages autonomy vs. shame and doubt emerged as the most important predictor of moral development scores with generativity vs. stagnation the second most important positive predictor. Two stages were weighted as negative predictors: industry vs. inferiority and ego integrity vs. despair. Resolution of the first developmental stage, trust vs. mistrust emerged as a moderate predictor in comparison more significantly than positive resolution of this stage.

Resolution of identity was the most difficult stage to interpret, in that both positive and negative resolution of this stage emerged as very important predictors of principled thinking. Lastly, resolution of initiative vs. guilt and intimacy vs. isolation emerged as the stages which contributed least in the prediction of adult moral development scores', (*ibid.*, p. 3580—B).

Moral judgments of aggression: personal and situational determinants
A.R. Nesdale, B.G. Rule, and M. Mcara, 1975

AIM / To assess whether adults' judgments were more responsive to intentions rather than outcomes or whether adults disregarded underlying intentions in their judgments when the consequences of the aggression were severe.

SUBJECTS / N = 128 female students.

METHOD / Ss read a transcript of an interview which described either an attractive or unattractive male interviewee who aggressed against another with either a good or bad intention and with mild or severe consequences for the victim. 'In fact, eight typewritten versions of one interview were prepared. The interviewee's attractiveness, his intentions in aggressing and the consequences of his aggression were manipulated within the context of the interview. In the attractive condition, the interviewee displayed pro-Canadian attitudes, indicating that he was favourably impressed by the standard of Canadian university education, the winter sports, the parliamentary system, the natural environment and the use people made of the environment. In the unattractive condition, the interviewee displayed anti-Canadian attitudes, taking the opposing position on each of these questions and expressing much dislike for Canada and things Canadian. During the interview, the interviewee also outlined a situation in which he aggressed against another person over a wallet containing a sum of money they had jointly found. In the good intention condition, the interviewee indicated that the aggressive act stemmed from the conflict between his desire to return the wallet and money to the rightful owner and the other person's wish to retain the money and wallet for himself. In the bad intention condition, the interviewee indicated that the aggressive act stemmed from the clash between the other person's wish to return the wallet and the money to the rightful owner and the interviewee's desire to retain the money for himself. The transcripts also contained two versions of consequences of the aggressive act. In the mild consequences condition, the victim was "a bit shaken up but otherwise unmarked". In the serious consequences condition, the victim was hit in the eye, which "seemed to swell up quickly",' Nesdale, Rule and Mcara (1975, p. 342).

RESULTS / An attractive person who committed aggression and had good intentions was judged more favourably than was aggression committed by an unattractive person and by one who had bad intentions. An unattractive aggressor was seen as more likely to aggress again when his intentions were bad rather than good, 'whereas little difference due to varying intentions was seen in the probability of an attractive person's future aggression. However, the corresponding prediction that attractiveness would interact with intentions to affect moral judgments of aggression was not supported. The finding of an intention rather than consequence effect on judgments was discussed in terms of an attributional approach and Piaget's notions concerning moral development', (*ibid.*, p. 339).

A study of the relationship of transcendental meditation to Kohlberg's stages of moral reasoning
S.I. Nidich, 1976

AIM / To find if a positive relationship existed between the practice of transcendental meditation and moral reasoning.

SUBJECTS / N = 96 meditators, divided into six subgroups, ranging from one to three and a half years since beginning transcendental meditation, 20 nonmeditators, and 10 pre-meditators. Ss ranged in age from 18 to 24 years.

METHOD / Kohlberg's Moral Judgment Interview was administered to the students and all tests were sent to Harvard's Moral Development Center to be scored.

RESULTS / Students who practised transcendental meditation performed at the higher levels than nonmeditators on Kohlberg's moral development scale. Longer term meditators did not score higher on Kohlberg's scale than shorter term meditators. That there would be no significant difference between nonmeditators, not predisposed to beginning transcendental meditation, and premeditators interested in immediately beginning transcendental meditation, was substantiated. Nidich concluded that a positive relationship exists between the practice of transcendental meditation and moral development, as measured by Kohlberg's scale. 'Education and rehabilitation institutions were encouraged to begin to look into transcendental meditation as a means for facilitating moral development', Nidich (1976, p. 4362—A).

Conflict and moral judgment
C. Peterson, J. Peterson and N. Finley, 1974

AIMS / These were that '(a) more intentional judgments are made on the child—adult conflict pair (ill-intentioned child-low damage versus well-intentioned adult-high damage) than on the adult—child, adult—adult, and child—child pairs; (b) adults make more intentional judgments than second graders who, in turn, make more than pre-schoolers; and (c) more intentional judgments on the child—child pair are made in response to the question "Which person was naughtiest?" than to the question "who did the worst thing?"', p. 66.

SUBJECTS / Twenty children within the age range from two years 10 months to five years nine months; 50 second grade Ss; and 25 college students.

METHOD / A conflict procedure in which reliance on adult values was opposed to reliance on damage as a measure of blame was utilized. This opposition was accomplished by varying the age of the characters in intentionality story pairs similar to the kind Piaget used. 'Thus in the conflict pair a well-intentioned adult doing large damage was contrasted with an ill-intentioned child whose damage was small, and the conflict was assumed to result from the fact that the high-damage act, which the moral realist views as wrong, was that of an adult, whose actions he tends to view as always right. A control pair contrasting an ill-intentioned-low-damage adult with a well-intentioned-high-damage child was included to allow for the effects of comparing characters of different ages. For additional control, a conventional child—child pair and a corresponding adult—adult pair were also used.'

RESULTS / The conflict procedure in which reliance on adult values was opposed to reliance on damage as a measure of blame was found to enhance second grade subjects' use of intention in making moral judgments of story pairs. Conflict had no effect on the judgments of pre-school children or adults. Question wording affected adults but not second grade children.

The effect of age, sex, intelligence, and social class on children's moral

judgments: an examination of Piaget's theory in cross-cultural perspective
H.R. Rawan, 1975

AIM / To study the effect of age, sex, intelligence, and social class on children's moral judgments; an examination of Piaget's theory in cross-cultural perspective.

SUBJECTS / N = 160 Afghanistan Ss. Forty at each of four age levels — seven, nine, 11 and 13.

METHOD / Four areas of moral judgment were studied: intention versus consequence; solution to transgression, immanent justice; and meaning of rules — all patterned after Piaget (1932). Children's level of intellectual functioning was assessed through the administration of the Goodenough-Harris Drawing Test. SES was measured by the combination of a rating of subject's father's occupational level with a rating of place of residence.

RESULTS / Age was positively and significantly related to moral maturity but not to immanent justice; IQ and SES were positively and significantly related to both moral maturity and immanent justice. However, sex showed no such relation. Age contributed most to the prediction of moral maturity, and intelligence improved prediction significantly. A comparison of the Afghanistan children's results was made with those reported by Piaget. In the areas of intention versus consequence, solution to transgression, and meaning of rules, it was observed that Afghan children demonstrated generally slightly less maturity than the Swiss children. In the area of immanent justice the difference in developmental maturity was greater. 'While seven- and nine-year-olds tended to give responses comparable to those of Piaget's sample, 11- and 13-year-olds tended to give responses considerably less mature than those given by Piaget's sample.'

The modification of age-specific expectations of Piaget's theory of development of intentionality in moral judgements of four- to seven-year-old children in relation to use of puppets in a social (imitative) learning paradigm
J.M. Reeves, 1972

AIMS / The author formulated three objectives: '(1) Was there an age difference in the objectivity (focusing on immediate consequences of an accident irrespective of intent of the subject — immature reaction) vs. subjectivity (intentionality or a purposeful act reflecting a mature moral choice) continuum of intentionality choices between children aged four to five years and six to seven years? (2) How effective would the treatment (a colour and sound 16 mm film — mediated performance of a puppet which imitates the actions of the characters in Piaget-type stories of accidental—intentional themes and receives vicarious reinforcement from a six-year-old peer) be in producing change from objective to subjective judgments? (3) Would there be an interaction between treatment effects and age level?'

SUBJECTS / N = 80 within the age range from four to seven years selected after pre-test.

METHOD / Subjects were assigned to one of eight treatment conditions. Bandura and McDonald's (1963) imitative learning paradigm which had utilized adult models was adapted and administered. '. . . an adaptation of the social learning paradigm involved the introduction of a 20-minute film (a) using glove-type, hand-manipulated puppets as models to act out Piaget-type stories, which provided a natural plot or dramatization, and (b) affording vicarious reinforcement from a six-year-old peer throughout the treatment in an effort to maximize the resultant acquisition of those moral judgments that involve the distinction between social acts of intentionality or accident'.

RESULTS / Moral development was promoted through the use of the film and the immediate and post-test afforded a basis for casting doubt on the age-specific expectations of Piaget's theory. 'The results of this experiment seem to provide an obvious extension to educational television. While the simulated television production provides the treatment for the experimental group, it could also be an example for relating educational and socialization objectives to television programming'.

Moral compatibility in married couples: a study of marital satisfaction as related to stage of moral development of spouses
M.C. Register, 1976

AIM / To compare two sets of stage pairings of married couples with an assessment of their marital satisfaction based on Kohlberg's postulation that two individuals at non-similar and non-adjacent stages of development do not agree with each other's reasoning in moral dilemma situations.

METHOD / Stage level of moral judgment, was determined by the Kohlberg Moral Maturity Scale and marital satisfaction, by the Locke–Wallace Short Marital Adjustment Test and a modified form of the Barrett–Lennard Relationship Inventory.

RESULTS / 'The hypothesis that partners at the same stage of adjacent stages of moral development would be more satisfied with their marriages than partners at non-similar or non-adjacent stages was supported at the .05 level of significance by only the Barrett–Lennard Relationship Inventory. One scale of the Relationship Inventory, the "Willingness to be known" scale discriminated the two groups at the .01 level of significance.'

Judging the important issues in moral dilemmas – an objective measure of development
J. Rest, D. Cooper, R. Coder, J. Masonz, and D. Anderson, 1974

AIMS / The authors formulated the following hypotheses: '(a) Are there differences in the way people choose the most important issues of moral dilemmas? . . . (b) Do groups that can be presumed to be at different developmental levels . . . show significant differences? . . . (c) Is preference for the higher stage statements showing a "blind" preference for complexity, or is there evidence that appreciation goes along with comprehension? (d) Does the way that a S chooses the most important issue of hypothetical moral dilemmas relate to his stance on current real social–moral–political controversies, or is the Defining Issues Test just tapping value–neutral conceptualization tendencies? (e) What is the degree of correlation between Kohlberg's present scale and the Defining Issues Test?', p. 493.

SUBJECTS / N = 193 from junior high, senior high, college and graduate school.

METHOD / The following tests were administered: (a) Defining Issues Test in which a S read a moral dilemma and was presented with 12 issues or considerations bearing upon that situation. Using Kohlberg's moral stages (1958), statements were written to exemplify stage characteristics; (b) Comprehension of social–moral concepts in which the S read a paragraph and then was asked to pick from among four statements which one best interpreted the main idea of the paragraph. The S was asked to match one of the statements with the paragraph, not to match a statement with his own ideas; (c) Attitude tests: two attitude tests were used. The Law and Order Test was comprised of 15 public policy issues. The second attitude test was the Libertarian Democracy devised by Patrick (1971) for use in studying democratic political orientation; (d) Kohlberg's moral judgment scale (1958); (e) IQ aptitude test and the Iowa Tests of Basic Skills (Cooper, 1972); and (f) Demographic variables included father's level of education and father's occupation was indexed on its socioeconomic status level using Duncan's scale (Reiss, 1961). (Fuller details of the battery of tests is also described in Rest *et al.*, 1974, pp. 493–495).

RESULTS / 'The importance attributed to principled (Stages five and six) moral statements (the P score) evidenced developmental trends: The P score differentiated student groups of varied advancement – junior high, senior high, college, and graduate students (F > 48.5); P correlated in the .60s with age, comprehension of social–moral concepts, and Kohlberg's scale – and less so but significantly with IQ. The way subjects chose important issues was not only an intellectual skill but also value related: P correlated in the .60s with attitude measures. A second student sample and an adult sample provided replications. Test–retest correlation of the P score was .81', p. 491.

A comparison of the effects of selective Catholic and public high schools on the moral development of their respective students
B.A. Robinson, 1976

AIM / To assess the success and failure of Catholic and public schools' environments in the area of moral development.

SUBJECTS / N = 630 selected from six high schools.

METHOD / An empirical assessment of morality was undertaken through the administration of the BAR Mental Measure Test. The test provided the S an opportunity to cheat. Each S, at the conclusion of a short form examination, had a cheat score based on the number of times he or she cheated. A 30-item questionnaire which provided feedback on students' moral behaviour and attitudes was also administered. A measurement of the student's moral reasoning abilities was obtained through the administration of Kohlberg's Moral Interview (1958).

RESULTS / The study concluded that changes in moral development were more likely to occur in the Catholic high schools. 'These changes in a global sense were mostly in a negative direction. However, in the breakdown of the data by individual schools, there are several instances of significant positive moral development. This is particularly true of specific Catholic high schools where measurable improvements occur in various value category scores. The general findings for public schools is that few significant changes occur in the character development of students from the freshman to senior years. In every category considered, the senior's moral behaviour and attitudes are almost indistinguishable from the freshman's. Significant distinctions in the moral reasoning abilities of the students from the two school systems are apparent. This difference favouring the Catholic high schools indicates that the students from this learning environment have better moral reasoning abilities. This distinction, however, does not correlate with their actions. There was also no correlation found between students who cheated and other negative moral behaviour', Robinson (1976, p. 3622–B).

The relationship between moral judgement, egocentrism, and altruistic behaviour
K.H. Rubin, and F.W. Schneider, 1973

AIM / The authors were intent to verify the hypothesis that there is a positive relationship between young children's scores on measures of communicative skill (lack of egocentrism) and moral judgment and the incidence of their altruistic behaviour.

SUBJECTS / Subjects with a mean age of 89.7 months and the Peabody Picture Vocabulary Test (Dunn, 1965), IQ mean of 100 − 89, SD = 18.70.

METHOD / Testing was done in two sessions. During the first session each subject was individually administered the Peabody Picture Vocabulary Test. This was followed by the administration of a communicative egocentrism task adapted from Glucksberg and Krauss (1967). 'The task required that two persons communicate with one another about novel, low-encodable, graphic designs'.

Two opportunities were provided to demonstrate altruistic behaviour: (a) to distribute sweets to poor children and (b) to help a younger child complete a task. These were administered in the form of simple games.

Each child was also evaluated on a measure of moral judgment. This was patterned after Kohlberg's (1964) moral-judgment stories and administered as adapted by Lee (1971). Three 'authority versus altruism' situations and three 'poor versus altruism' situations were read to each subject.

(Fuller details of the experimental procedures of moral judgment, egocentrism, and altruistic behaviour are described in Rubin and Schneider, 1973, pp. 662–663.)

RESULTS / The authors conclude, 'Success on the two cognitive measures was positively correlated with the incidence of altruistic behaviour in both altruism conditions. With mental age partialled out the correlations between the cognitive measures and donating candy were significantly lower than the correlation between the cognitive measures and helping. The difference between the correlations was accounted for by the fact that only in the candy donation were there cues that helped the subject attend to the possibility of emitting an altruistic act. Finally, the communicative and moral judgement measures were significantly correlated', p. 661.

Altruism and cognitive development in children
J.P. Rushton and J. Wiener, 1975

AIMS / The authors were intent to explore further the role of cognitive developmental variables in accounting for the generosity of children; to test the notion of 'generalized levels' in cognitive development; and to examine generalities across altruistic behaviours.

SUBJECTS / N = 60 seven- and 11-year-olds, divided evenly between the sexes. The sample was of average ability (verbal IQ: mean 7 = 99.9, SD = 11.8; mean 11 = 106.6, SD = 14.6; non-verbal IQ: mean 7 = 104.3, SD = 15.7; mean 11 = 109.6, SD = 13.5) (The National Foundation for Educational Research Intelligence Test No. 3).

METHOD / The cognitive tasks comprised:

(a) Role-taking task: Board game (Flavell, 1968, pp. 82–102);
(b) Role-taking task: Cylinders (Flavell, 1968, pp. 55–70);
(c) Conservation task (Bruner *et al.*, 1966);
(d) Person perception photo-grouping task (adapted after Olver and Hornsby, 1966);
(e) Cognitive simplicity – cognitive complexity measure (Olver and Hornsby, 1966);
(f) Person perception Kelly – Grid-type-construct task ('devised by J. Wiener');
(g) Egocentricity score. 'The constructs generated by the above measure were scored for sizes of egocentricity. This was a yes / no

categorization based on whether the construct was made with direct reference to the subject. The subject's egocentricity score consisted of the absolute number of egocentric statements out of the 30 possible', p. 343.

The behavioural tasks comprised:

(a) Competitive racing game (adapted from Rutherford and Mussen, 1968);
(b) Generosity to a charity (Rosenhan and White, 1967);
(c) Generosity to a friend (patterned after Rutherford and Mussen, 1968).

(Full details of the experimental procedures are given in Rushton and Wiener, 1975, pp. 342–344.)

RESULTS / Highly significant age differences were found on all cognitive tasks. Likewise, the 11-year-olds were significantly more altruistic than were the seven-year-olds. Some generality emerged across altruistic behaviours. However, no such generalities emerged either between the cognitive measures themselves or between the cognitive measures and altruism.

Achievement and morality: a cross-cultural analysis of causal attribution and evaluation
F. Salili, M.L. Maehr, and G. Gillmore, 1976

AIMS / The study was conducted 'to determine whether the presumably universal patterns suggested by Weiner and Peter (1970) do, in fact, hold up in a different cultural context, namely, that provided in Iran. Do the three dimensions serve as differential determinants of evaluations in achievement and morality in Iran as well as the US? Do the overall patterns vary similarly with age . . . to determine how such patterns or how progress through the stages may vary as a function of subcultural factors', p. 328. Further, 'to determine whether the "regression" in the achievement domain noted by Weiner and Peter with US subjects is societally based or perhaps a universal intrinsic in the nature of achievement', p. 329.

SUBJECTS / N = 291, aged seven to 18 years selected from government primary, intermediate, and high schools in Tehran.

METHOD / Procedures followed those developed and employed by

Weiner and Peter (1973). 'After extensive explanation of and
instruction in procedure, subjects were presented with moral and
achievement judgment situations, stories in which a child was variously
characterized according to ability (present or absent) and effort (trying
or not trying) and which eventuated in different outcomes (task
completion or success, incompletion or failure). Subsequently, subjects
were asked to evaluate the behaviour of the child by assigning one to
five gold (reward) or red (punishment) stars. Unlike the Piagetian
procedure... which is the obvious prototype here, these situations /
stories were designed to be presented in a standardized manner and in a
group setting', p. 329. (Fuller details of the experimental procedure are
given in Salili, Maehr, and Gillmore, 1976, pp. 329–330.)

RESULTS / Important discrepancies with Weiner and Peter were
found. 'A first such point of difference relates to the role of ability in
the determination of moral judgments. Weiner and Peter found high
ability to be rewarded, while low ability was punished. Weiner and
Peter claim surprise at this finding and blame it on the unique
characteristics of the story. An opposite result was found in the present
study... A second point of difference occurs in the case of
achievement judgments. In contrast to Weiner and Peter, ability had a
significant effect, suggesting that the existence of ability is more
positively valued in Iran than in the US. That is, competence,
independent of what one does with it, seems to be an inherent good in
Iran — but not in the US... A third... point of difference between
the two studies is that the "regression" in the achievement domain
noted by Weiner and Peter does not occur here... All in all then, there
are important differences in the pattern of judgments exhibited in the
two studies. Conceivably, one may interpret these differences within a
cognitive-developmental framework referring to culturally inspired
"acceleration" or "regression" in proceeding through presumably
universal stages. But one can just as readily interpret these findings as
fundamental evidence against such a point of view. We leave the matter
open. The fact is that this study, along with Weiner and Peter, clearly
demonstrates the importance of cultural learning experiences. Admit-
tedly, cognitive maturation is bound to provide a structure which
influences the way moral and achievement behaviour is actualized. This
would probably serve to establish certain similarities in behavioural
patterns across widely divergent cultural groups. Thus the young child,
irrespective of culture, is not as likely as the older child to look beyond
the outcome of an event in evaluating it. But whereas cognitive growth
provides the capacity to go beyond outcome, it probably does not
insure that this would actually occur. And therein, at least, lies an
important role for cultural learning', (*ibid.*, pp. 335–336).

Moral judgment level and conformity behaviour
H.D. Saltzstein, R.M. Diamond and M. Belenky, 1972

AIMS / The authors formulated the aims as follows: I. 'Major hypothesis: To the extent that subjects at the higher stages (four, five, and perhaps three) conform, these responses occur more frequently in the interdependent situation than in the independent situation; subjects at the lowest stages (one and two) do not conform more in one situation than in the other ... II. Minor hypothesis: Stage three subjects in general conform more than those at other stages, either lower or higher', p. 330.

SUBJECTS / N = 63, with an upper-middle class background.

METHOD / Moral judgment levels were obtained through individual interviews. Hypothetical moral dilemmas and the scoring of responses were patterned after Kohlberg (1963). Subjects in the experimental group sessions were assessed for conformity behaviour in a modified Ash-type (1956) group-influence situation, under both interdependent and independent goal conditions. (Details of the moral dilemmas, stimulus materials used and the stage-placements of subjects are described in Saltzstein, Diamond and Belenky, 1972, pp. 330–331.)

RESULTS / 'Frequency of conforming responses did not differ significantly between the two conditions. Nor was there an interaction effect between moral judgement level, conformity, and goal condition. There was, however, a curvilinear relationship between moral judgement level and overall frequency of conformity. Stage three children (so called "good boy, good girl, approval seeking" morality) were more likely to conform than children at either higher or lower moral judgments ... very few of the higher level subjects (those at Stages four or five) made any conforming response', p. 327.

Father absence, perceived maternal behaviour, and moral development in boys
J.W. Santrock, 1975

AIMS / That father-absent boys will be less advanced in moral development than father-present boys; that boys from divorced homes will display a lower level of moral development than boys from widowed homes; and 'perceived maternal induction and affection are related positively to moral development, whereas power assertion and love withdrawal are negatively related', p. 754).

SUBJECTS / N = 120 boys, half from father-absent homes and half from father-present homes. 'One-third of the father-absent boys were from homes in which the father had died when the boy was between six- and 10-years-old, another one-third were from homes in which the parents were divorced before the boy was six-years-old, and a final one-third were from homes in which the parents were divorced when the boy was between six- and 10-years-old', p. 754. The Ss were selected from the fifth and sixth grades.

METHOD / The tasks administered were as follows:

(a) Resistance-to-temptation task one (patterned after Grinder, 1962).
(b) Resistance-to-temptation task two.
(c) Resistance-to-temptation task three.
(d) The guilt measure comprised two story-completion items (modeled after Hoffman, 1971).
(e) Moral judgment was evaluated by the administration of three stories (adapted from Kohlberg, 1958).
(f) Self-criticism, reparation and self-reward (Aronfreed, Cutick and Fagen, 1963).
(g) Altruism.
(h) Trust and paranoid blame.
(i) Delay of gratification (Followed Mischel, 1961).
(j) Teacher ratings.
(k) Maternal discipline — four concrete examples of transgressions (patterned after Hoffman, 1971).
(l) Maternal affection.

(Full details of the experimental procedures are described in Santrock, 1975, pp. 755–756.)

RESULTS / Few differences were computed between father-absent and father-present boys when IQ, SES, CA and sibling status were held constant. However, father-absent boys were reported by their teachers as less advanced in moral development than father-present boys. The sons of the divorced women indicated more 'social deviation', but were more advanced in level of moral judgment than were the sons of widows, according to their teachers. Divorced women, according to their sons' reports, disciplined with more power assertion than widows.

Moral judgments, behaviour and cognitive style in young children
M. Schleifer and V.I. Douglas, 1973

Study One

AIM / To examine moral judgments, behaviour and cognitive style in young children.

SUBJECTS / N = 29, with a mean age of six years and eight months.

METHOD / Piaget-type stories (1932) were read so as to elicit moral judgments. The reflection—impulsivity test (Kagan *et al.,* 1964) and the Peabody Picture Vocabulary Test (Dunn, 1965) were administered, as was the field-independence test (Karp and Konstadt, 1963). Teachers completed the Pupil Personality Evaluation Form (Sutherland and Goldschmid, 1971) for each child.

Study Two

SUBJECTS / N = 72 from middle class backgrounds, ranging in age from three years two months to six years.

METHOD / Films designed to test moral judgments were shown, adapted from Piaget-type stories (1932). The Beller Rating Scale (reliability provided by Emmerich, 1966) were completed. This is a social behaviour scale in which items are directly related to the child's interactions with peers and teachers, especially regarding the child's level of aggression, dependency and autonomy. The Early Childhood Familiar Figures Test and the Early Childhood Embedded Figures Test were also administered modeled after Banta (1968).

RESULTS / In the six-year-old children, the level of moral maturity related to the cognitive styles of reflection-impulsivity and field dependence-independence, but not to verbal intelligence. Ss characterized as immature in their moral judgments tended to be impulsive and more field-dependent. Children performing at the higher moral judgment levels were rated as more attentive and more reflective by their teachers. Pre-school Ss performing at the higher levels of moral maturity were seen as less aggressive by their teachers. These were also least impulsive in cognitive style and some were more field-independent.

Moral education in the primary grades: an evaluation of a developmental curriculum
R.L. Selman and M. Lieberman, 1975

AIM / To evaluate the effects of a semistructural group discussion approach to moral education on the level of usage of the concept of moral intentionality.

SUBJECTS / N = 68 second grade children and were divided equally by sex. Half of the subjects were from middle and half from lower socioeconomic status school districts. 'In School I, one of three second grade classes was randomly assigned to one of three treatments: experienced leader, informed lay teacher-led, and control. In School 2, one class was assigned to the experienced leader group and one class to the informed lay-led group. To estimate and control for carry-over effects from treatment classroom children who communicate casually with control group children, a second control group was drawn from a third school geographically but not demographically different from the second', p. 713.

METHOD / A programme of dilemmas, using the method of sound filmstrips, was designed aimed at stimulating development in primary grade children as follows: '1.) They present dramatic stories which are involving to watch for children of this age. 2.) They present a conflict between two or more moral values understood by children of this age. 3.) They are open — children of this age disagree about what is right and have difficulty making up their minds. 4.) Without giving "right answers", they present a range of levels of reasoning: below, at, and slightly above the level of most of the children in the class, which may help stimulate the child to make his own reasoning more adequate . . . The evaluation consisted of a comparison of the moral reasoning of children exposed to the filmstrip programme in classes run by lay teachers versus those run by developmentally trained discussion leaders, as well as a comparison of these groups with a control group receiving no intervention', p. 713. (Fuller details of the experimental procedure are given elsewhere, Selman and Lieberman, 1975, pp. 713–715.)

RESULTS / Children in the experimental condition demonstrated higher level usage of the concept of moral intentionality on post — and follow-up testing than did the control group. The authors however caution that due to the small number of classrooms involved, results 'could not be definitively attributed to programme effects rather than to teacher effects, and conclusions must be interpreted within the context of a pilot evaluation research', p. 712.

Some relationships between sociopolitical ideology and moral character among college youth
S.R. Snodgrass, 1975

AIM / The author was intent to clarify the relationship, observed in studies using Kohlberg's moral character model, between the character of college youth and their ideology.

SUBJECTS / N = 118 students (41 males and 77 females).

METHOD / All Ss were administered the following measures:

(a) Moral judgment: Form A of the Survey of Ethical Attitudes (SEA) developed by Hogan (Hogan, 1970; Hogan and Dickstein, 1972)

(b) Socialization: The Socialization Scale of the California Psychological Inventory (Gough, 1969; Gough and Peterson, 1952).

(c) Empathy: An abridged version of the Hogan Empathy Scale comprising of 39 items from the California Psychological Inventory (Grief and Hogan, 1973; Hogan, 1969)

(d) General liberalism − conservatism: 'There were three general measures of ideology included in the questionnaire. (a) A self-description on a seven-point scale ranging from "very liberal" to "very conservative" (LC Self-rating). (b) A 12-item Likert-type scale of liberalism − conservatism (LC), composed of items from several published liberalism − conservatism scales. The scale contained four items in each of the three areas of economics, civil liberties, and foreign policy. (c) A similarly constructed supplementary scale of nine liberalism − conservatism items (SLC) covering a variety of more current and specific issues (e.g., bussing, defense spending, women's rights, foreign aid). The LC and SLC scales were scored individually and then combined into a 21-item composite liberalism − conservatism (CLC)', Snodgrass (1975, p. 199).

(e) Law and order ideology: An eight-item Likert-type scale dealing with issues such as capital punishment, marijuana penalties, and draft amnesty (Law and Order).

(f) Severity of sentencing: 'A scale involving sentencing (from 0 to 50 years) in 22 hypothetical cases (covering the major categories of crime) described in brief paragraphs. Most of these descriptions were slightly modified versions of actual newspaper accounts. Examples were chosen that would divide the subjects; therefore, with an occasional exception, trivial infractions and particularly heinous offenses were avoided. A composite sentencing score (Median Sentence) was calculated for each subject', (*ibid.*, p. 199).

RESULTS / The results demonstrated, 'that respect for the utility of rules as a means of regulating human conduct (not socialization or empathy) is the moral character foundation of student ideology. On the basis of correlations between the SEA and several standard personality inventories, Hogan (1970, 1973) described the conservative and punitive adherents to an ethics of social responsibility as possessing a combination of positive and negative characteristics. They are on the one hand "reasonable, helpful, and dependable; on the other hand . . . conventional and resistant to change" (1973, p. 225). Conversely, proponents of an ethic of personal conscience were depicted (dialectically) as both independent and opportunistic, innovative and irresponsible. Such a mixed set of personality correlates point out the difficulty of making any judgments about the relative moral maturity of the two groups. The distinction between these two orientations has conceptual similarities to the distinction between Kohlberg's stages five and six (Hogan, 1970). Nonetheless, Hogan argued on theoretical grounds that a moderate position should be considered most mature. In an empirical test of that assumption, however, he found differences favouring the ethics-of-conscience group', (*ibid.*, p. 202).

Long-term cultural change in cognitive development
C. Tomlinson-Keasey and C.B. Keasey. 1972

Experiment One

AIM / The authors hypothesized that animistic thinking and thinking about specific moral dilemmas have been affected by cultural events over the years.

SUBJECTS / N = 73, within the age range of six years five months to nine years.

METHOD / Each child was questioned individually as follows: (a) 'Does a table feel anything if I hit it with a hammer? Does a table know if you move it? Why? (b) Does a motor know when it goes? Can a motor feel anything when it goes very fast? Why? (c) Does the wind know when it is blowing? Does the wind feel anything when it blows against a mountain? Why? (d) Does the sun feel anything? What? (e) What things can know and feel?', p. 136. Responses were scored according to the four steps that Piaget maintains a child takes in acquiring stable notions about consciousness.

Experiment Two

SUBJECTS / N = 144. The sample was predominantly Caucasian and of average intelligence (22 from fifth grade and 122 from sixth grades).

METHOD / Seven of Kohlberg's (1958) moral dilemmas were administered. These dilemmas focused on issues like breaking a promise, reporting a reformed criminal, stealing, euthanasia and slavery.

RESULTS / Children in the fifth and sixth grades demonstrated significantly higher levels of moral reasoning about slavery than on the six other dilemmas. 'Cognitive progress then seems to be positively affected by cultural changes which are long term and which allow the child time to consolidate the information and experience provided', p. 135. The authors cite the work of Russell (1940) which showed 'children's responses showed less animistic thinking than in 1929 but more animistic thinking than in the present study. The trend . . . from 1929 to the present, has been toward fewer animistic responses. This kind of comparison across studies neglects the slightly different methodology used in the three studies (the third study refers to Piaget, 1929). These differences and other methodological issues in studies of animism have been reviewed by Looft and Bartz (1969). Nevertheless, the response levels indicate that today's child may well have profited conceptually from the long-term attention the culture has given to scientific phenomena', p. 138.

The mediating role of cognitive development in moral judgment
C. Tomlinson − Keasey and C.B. Keasey, 1974

AIMS / The authors formulated the following four hypotheses:

(a) 'That there is a substantial and predictable relationship between formal operations and principled moral reasoning'.
(b) 'that formal operations are a necessary condition for the development of principled moral reasoning'.
(c) 'that there is a *décalage* between the attainment of formal operations and its application to the area of moral reasoning'.
(d) 'that formal operations are not a sufficient condition for the emergence of principled moral reasoning'.

SUBJECTS / N = 54. Thirty were sixth grade girls and 24 college students of average and above average intelligence, respectively.

METHOD / Subjects were administered the following tasks:

(a) Six moral dilemmas (patterned after Kohlberg, 1958, 1969).
(b) Three formal operational tasks of pendulum, balance, and flexibility (modelled after Inhelder and Piaget, 1958, pp. 67—79, 164—181, 46—66, respectively).

Scoring of the moral and the formal-operations tasks followed Kohlberg (1958) and Inhelder and Piaget (1958), respectively.

RESULTS / The first hypothesis (a) stated above, was fully substantiated. Concerning hypothesis (b) above, the resultant patterns demonstrated a parallel growth between formal operations and principled moral reasoning. ' . . . the hypotheses concerning the relationship and the *décalage* between formal operations and moral development were unequivocally supported. That formal operations are not a sufficient condition for the emergence of principled moral reasoning was demonstrated. The necessity of formal operations prior to principled moral reasoning was upheld in the majority of subjects', p. 296.

A cognitive-developmental analysis of achievement and moral judgements
B. Weiner and N. Peter, 1973

AIM / The authors examine the determinants of achievement judgment and 'compares the developmental sequence of judgment observed within an achievement-related context with that displayed in an ethical situation', p. 291.

SUBJECTS / N = 300 children between the ages of four and 18 years.

METHOD / A moral and an achievement situation was appraised — moral and achievement judgments were evaluated through 16 situations. To discover the determinants of adult achievement, Weiner and Kukla's (1970) modification of a paradigm was employed. The achievement and a moral situation were presented to subjects in counterbalanced order. The situations differed according to the intent (effort) and ability of the person being judged and in the objective consequences of the behaviour. 'The achievement-related situation involved a child working at a puzzle task. The child was characterized according to ability (present or absent), "trying" (yes or no), and the consequences of the action (completion and success or incompletion and failure). . . . The moral situation had to be portrayed with the ability, effort, and outcome dimensions used in the achievement condition. Further, the story contents had to be interpretable as either a positive or a negative moral action. The majority of themes used to investigate morality involve moral transgressions in which not engaging in an action is judged as moral . . . it was decided to use a social moral situation, in contrast to the asocial achievement theme . . . The moral incident chosen was a variant of the "lost child" theme used by Piaget . . . A lost child was depicted as seeking help to get home in time for dinner. An older child in the story either did or did not know the correct directions (ability) did or did not want to help (intent), and the lost child either did or did not get home in time (outcome)', p. 293.

RESULTS / Weiner and Peter conclude, ' . . . the three evaluative dimensions of intent, ability, and outcome are used systematically in both achievement and moral appraisal. Further there were highly significant age trends. In both the achievement and the moral conditions subjective intent replaced objective outcome as the main determinant of judgment. However, after the age of 12 years in the achievement context objective outcome again became the more important determinant of evaluation. It is contended that society reinforces this more "primitive" developmental stage. The sequence of evaluative stages in the moral and achievement situations was identical across racial and sex groupings . . . the data strongly supported the position that achievement strivings are maintained primarily by social reward, while moral behaviour is controlled primarily by social punishment', p. 290.

Kohlberg and Piaget: aspects of their relationship in the field of moral development
H. Weinrich, 1975

Weinrich states that Kohlberg and his 'disciples' stand at the current end of a line of research which was first begun by Piaget in 1932, the framework of which, although receiving some modification of interpretation, has not essentially departed in any significant sense in description. However, Kohlberg's examination and elaboration has led to the development of a more or less new system.

Examining Piaget's system of moral growth and the extent to which subsequent research has validated it, thereby placing Kohlberg in an historical context, Weinrich examines the ways in which Kohlberg extends or departs from Piaget's system. She indicates that Kohlberg elaborates the Piagetian notion and considers justice to be the key principle. It is Weinrich's opinion that 'despite the global nature of the definition of justice used by Kohlberg, there are many aspects of moral development, encompassed by his own scheme, which can be more adequately conceptualized by other notions than justice, and furthermore, his apparent attempt to use "the sense of justice" as a motivating force seems a concession to Piaget's view that the pressure of the peer-group acts as a causative agent in moral growth in later-childhood. This is a view to which Kohlberg does not wholly ascribe'.

Weinrich in further analysis emphasizes that in many ways Kohlberg's findings and interpretations depart considerably from Piaget and 'it should be noted that Kohlberg was influenced by "character development" theorists, in the tradition of McDougall, as well as by Piaget'. His first 'two types' have some similarity to Piaget's heteronomous and autonomous stages, but depart from them in some important aspects. Weinrich focuses on the difficulty of demonstrating the relationship of Piaget's third stage to Kohlberg's data; 'it is an oversimplification to say that the latter four types are subtypes of an equity-based morality because equity is firstly only one factor of many in each of the stages, and secondly, equity is too general a term for the rather fine differentiations of different types of justice which were found to develop at later stages. But it is clear that Kohlberg's work must be regarded as a confirmation and extension of Piaget's thinking, rather than a refutation of it'. She concludes that a body of research has confirmed the general 'parameters of the system', not departing from the basic framework derived from Piaget in major respects. However, the conception of 'stage' and the relationship between moral and cognitive growth are issues remaining in both systems.

Weinrich gives a full exposition to the concept of stages and the nature and processes of stage development (pp. 206–10) and in this context the relationship between Kohlberg's moral development and Piaget's cognitive development (pp. 210–12). She concludes: 'In the way in which each stage overcomes the deficiencies in the previous one, there can be seen a structural parallel between moral and cognitive growth. However, the most significant fact may be that Kohlberg finds two or three sub-types within both "concrete" and "formal" levels, even though Piaget's own study, with a narrower range of age, does not clearly follow the pattern of pre-operational-concrete-formal thought. Although as stated before, there cannot necessarily be assumed a one-to-one parallel between intellectual and moral growth, it is possible to argue that the processes are fundamentally the same, at least in terms of functions operating in the organization of the environment. A test of this is not whether a one-to-one relationship can be found, but whether the criteria of stage-wise development and of logical functioning which is applied to intellectual functioning, can also be applied to moral growth. The tentative conclusion that emerges from examining the logic of Kohlberg's scheme and the data derived from it, is that it seems possible and fruitful to do so'.

*Heteronomy and the child's emerging sense of justice**
M. Whelan, 1975

In this paper I shall review Jean Piaget's stages of development in justice and authority, examine those stages as logical, natural developments of the child's growing awareness of himself and of society, and suggest the educational implications of this developmental process.

In his study of children's moral judgment Piaget concluded that there exists two kinds of morality, a morality of heteronomy and a morality of autonomy. The morality of heteronomy is based on unilateral respect, while the morality of autonomy has its basis in relationships of mutual respect. He found that as solidarity between children grows the notion of justice, which for the young child is defined in terms of adult commands, gradually emerges in almost complete autonomy to an understanding of justice in terms of equity. Unlike moral rules which are imposed from without, Piaget feels, the rule of justice 'is a sort of immanent condition of social relationships, or a law governing their equilibrium', and that its development is largely independent of adult influences, (Piaget p. 195).

Several aspects of justice were examined by Piaget in order to piece together a comprehensive description of children's notions of justice. The factors that relate to this paper include children's notions of retributive justice, defined by due proportion between acts and punishment, and children's notions of distributive justice, defined by equality. Piaget found that younger children up to about age nine had notions of justice that related to their attitudes toward authority. Their understanding of what is just and what is fair focuses on retributive justice, particularly expiatory punishment. These children believe that every rule violation must be punished, if not by ordinary means, then by some extraordinary fortuitous event, hence a strong belief in immanent justice. When given choices of punishments for dilemma subjects, younger children always choose the most painful punishment precisely because it will hurt.

As children mature their understanding of justice expands and retributive punishment gives way to distributive justice. As these developing notions of justice come into conflict with adult authority,

* Published by the kind permission of the author.
Gratitude is extended to Dr Mariellen Whelan of Rosemount College, Pennsylvania.

adult authority diminishes in importance and influence, and justice gains ascendancy. It is this development that we will discuss.

Piaget states 'that justice has no meaning except as something that is above authority', (Piaget, p. 280) By probing children's reasoning in situations where fairness conflicted with obedience to authority, Piaget found three broad stages of development to the autonomy required for justice. The youngest children insist on obedience, 'what is just is not differentiated from what is in conformity to authority', (Piaget, p. 279). At this stage any adult command is fair and should be obeyed. At a later age these children are able to distinguish between what is just and what is commanded, but the command nevertheless should be obeyed, even if it is unfair. At the next stage equality overrules obedience. If commands are unfair the children commanded should not obey them. Obedience and even friendliness are outweighed by equality. The third stage is a stage of equity 'which consists in never defining equality without taking into account the way in which each individual is situated', (Piaget, p. 285). The following table illustrates the stages of justice and authority which Piaget found.

Table I: Stages of justice and authority

Ages	5	6	7	8	9	10	11	12	13	14
Equity- considers other factors								XXXXXXXXXX		
Equality outweighs obedience, even friendliness				XXXXXXXXXXXXXXX						
Just is what is commanded	XXXXXXXXXXX									

In this first stage, where the child defines justice as 'that which is commanded' and likewise believes that 'whatever is commanded is fair', the child is typically Piaget's egocentric child. Adult authority is the most influential factor in the child's judgment. There may be occasions with his peers where he will demonstrate concern for equality, but if an adult inserts a suggestion or a command, this will capture the focus of the young child and he will judge that suggestion or command as the just and fair thing to do. At this stage the child's strong belief in punishment as the means of restoring the bond that connects him to those on whom he is dependent, biases his judgment of what is fair and unfair in punishment in favour of the punishment that will hurt the most.

Younger children at this stage then define justice in terms of authority and they do not make any distinctions in adult commands, all of them are fair. Older children in stage one can distinguish just from unjust commands, but they are not sufficiently independent of adult authority to consider any alternative other than obedience. Thus, the stage one child obeys all adult commands, even those he judges unfair.

As the child matures cognitively and socially, his recognition of himself as a person distinct from other persons and other aspects of the environment emerges strongly. Judgments in questions of justice in this period are based on a strict interpretation of what is fair to him as a person. His position is almost a reactionary one. After years of heteronomous submission, he now assumes a radical stance *vis a vis* authorities. He has an understanding of himself apart from the adult rules and commands that have governed his life. He no longer defines fair punishment as that which is most painful, but believes rather that punishment should be related to the offense. Requests for him to turn off a light if he did not turn it on, or to close a door if he was not the last one in, are judged unfair, and if a command is unfair it should not be obeyed. The sole criterion for justice then is equality.

I know a mother of eight who has lived through this stage many times, who now forms meat patties in a cup, carefully pressed down and measured out, so hamburger size will not be an issue at the dinner table for whichever of her children is experiencing his newly discovered sense of justice.

As painful as this stage may be for the adults involved, it is important to remember that it is a stage of development. Prior to this period the child has no sense of himself apart from the adults in his life. Though the first stage is an easier stage for adults, because the child obeys their commands, one must hope that the child will develop beyond the dependence that motivates his response at the first stage, to higher reasons for responding.

At this stage then justice is defined by strict equality unaffected by attenuating circumstances and relationships.

As the child continues to mature cognitively and socially his perspective on justice expands beyond strict equality to include considerations of equity. His judgments now are not based on what is fair for him as a person, but on what is fair in terms of each person involved, and of the specific circumstances. Thus, he might consider turning the light off, or closing the door, because it would be the nice thing to do in these circumstances, or for this person. He takes into consideration such relationships as affection, age and physical condition. Unlike the child at the first stage, the child at the third stage is not motivated by obedience or fear of punishment, but rather by recognition of the responsibilities of his relationship to other people and groups. He can and does judge commands unfair, but that is not the exclusive criterion in questions of justice.

More complex relationships require a revision of his definition of justice. To judge in terms of strict equality on the basis of fairness to himself is no longer adequate, he perceives too many other factors that should be considered. At this time then justice is situation specific. The child has liberated himself from adult authority and the narrowness of street equality, and in that sense he is autonomous.

Socially the development of justice can be viewed as movement from unawareness, to awareness of self, to awareness of self as a member of society. Cognitively it can be viewed as movement from pre-operational, to concrete operations, to formal operations. Both movements are necessary conditions for development to autonomy.

Now let us look at the educational implications of Piaget's theory of the development of justice and its conflict with authority.

It is important to remember that this is a developmental process. Piaget states that the development of justice 'is largely independent of adult influences . . . ', (Piaget, p. 198). It is not a process then of imprinting a rule by modeling, lecturing, punishing and rewarding, but rather a process of cognitive restructuring, and the role of the educator is to facilitate that restructuring. Let us look at the assumptions of a developmental theory.

1. Development involves basic transformations of structure, that is the shape, pattern and organization of a response. This is evident in each of the stages that has been described, for example, the transformation of structures necessary to go from stage one heteronomy to stage two equality. Development is not a change of position on a specific issue, but a change in one's perspective on all such problems.
2. The direction of development is toward greater equilibrium in the interaction with the environment. As the stage one child experiences unfairness from adults, his single classification system 'that all adult commands are fair' does not fit some adult commands. A number of these experiences leads to the disequilibrium that transforms the basic structure to one that is more adequate.

What are the implications of developmental stages of justice and authority for those who are involved with the child on a regular basis?

In the first stage the young child's perspective is severely limited by heteronomy and his unilateral respect. It is important for him to have many opportunities for peer interaction and cooperative activities removed from superior—inferior relationship. It is only apart from adult influence that the child can establish relationships of mutual respect in communities of adults and children, like the family, heteronomy will receive less support if structures for cooperative governance are established that limit the necessity for authoritarian roles. This type of family and classroom facilitates the liberation of the child from heteronomy and provides the environment for the development of mutual respect. I am speaking specifically about families where the children participate in establishing the rules for the good order of the house and community living, and classrooms where the teacher and children establish the rules and procedures for a group working and living together.

Care should be taken in the exercise of authority with these children, precisely because they judge every adult command as fair and they will not rebel. This is not to say that they are humbly submissive at all times, but they judge themselves as being out of step, not the rules as being unfair.

The child at this stage believes strongly in punishments that hurt, that affect him physically; he does not think that verbal reprimands are efficacious. It would seem appropriate in the area of punishment to try to stimulate the child to consideration of the second stage, that is, to view punishment as an action related to the offence. One aspect of heteronomy is a belief in punishment for punishment's sake, and too often we reinforce that, for example, by having him copy a poem twenty five times because he did not do his arithmetic homework. He considers that punishment fair because it is troublesome to write that much, but his belief that punishment is a mystical ritual is reinforced. A more educative action would be to select a punishment more closely related to the specific homework that was not done.

The child at the second stage needs support during this period when he is freeing himself from adult authority. He judges on the basis of strict fairness. He will frequently retort with 'No, why should I clean it up, or pick it up, (or whatever), I didn't leave it that way', or a similar retort that provokes adult disequilibrium and arouses latent dictatorial tendencies. If, however, you assume the perspective of this age child, which is limited to judging the fairness of the concrete instance with which he is confronted, such as bringing in the newspaper because his brother is not home yet, or cleaning the blackboards because the one whose turn it is forgot, you may be able to understand his sense of justice. He does not consider, and cognitively is not capable of considering, extenuating circumstances, such as affection for his father, or the friendliness of his teacher.

It is important at this stage for adults to distinguish requests from commands, and in those instances where the adult need is one that is beyond the call of duty in terms of the established rules of the house or classroom, the command should be a request that conveys to the child that he is being asked a favour and that he has the right to refuse. The child at this stage can be helped to expand his perspective on justice in discussions of reasons of affection or friendliness or age that could be considered in his judgment of fairness on a specific issue. The focus should not be on changing behaviour, but on stimulating reasoning. You want to liberate him from the narrowness of his reasoning about justice.

In terms of punishment, this age child believes that the only fair punishments are ones that are related to the offense. Arbitrary punishment should be avoided. To stimulate consideration of the perspective of the next stage, those punishments that emphasize the effects of the misbehaviour on the community should be selected. Thus, temporary exclusion from the social group or censure focused on helping him realize how he has broken a bond of solidarity would be appropriate.

It is important to support the child at the second stage of development as he gradually liberates himself from adult authority. He should not be confronted with adult power as a reason for action. He may indeed respond to this superior force, but such authoritarianism does not modify his judgment. As a matter of fact to pose to him the threat of adult authority, is to appeal to him at a stage of reasoning lower than his own, and that is not attractive to him.

Though the child at the third stage is attracted by such considerations as 'the nice thing to do', 'the friendly thing to do', it is important to stress that this is the structure for reasoning about questions of justice, it may or may not result in action that conforms to that thought. The cognitive aspect of moral judgment is significant, but we do not always feel like being nice, our physical and emotional set are also factors.

The stage three child can and does judge some commands unjust, though he may carry them out. It is important to periodically discuss with him considerations of fairness in your relationship, so that you have an understanding of the commands or rules that are considered unfair. In questioning a sixth grader who from her responses appeared to be a stage three, about some aspects of justice in the classroom, she told me about the jobs that were valued, such as messenger and paper passer, and the ones that were disliked, board washer and basket emptier. She thought the teacher's system for assigning jobs was unfair, because they did not rotate fast enough. I feel certain the teacher has not given too much thought to the rank order of the classroom jobs, and, therefore, to a rotation system that would move the children out of the disliked jobs faster. In another classroom of younger children, probably stage two, the teacher did discuss elements of fairness in the classroom procedures and it was revealed to her that many children felt she was calling on a few children more frequently than others. This is a good example of the children demanding equality in distribution of the teacher's attention. This teacher, however, wanted empirical data from the children to support their claim. She had each child keep a card on the top of his desk in the right hand corner, and each time a child was called on during the day he was to mark his card. At the end of each day these marks were tallied and compared. I do not remember whether the teacher was vindicated, I like to think they win sometimes, but she certainly established with the children her interest in fair procedures.

In summary then we see the process of reason working over a heteronomous rule of justice, taking it from 'whatever is commanded is fair' to more complex considerations. Piaget quoting from M. Bovet explains how personal autonomy comes to be conquered. 'Reason works over moral rules, generalizing them, making them coherent with each other, and above all extending them progressively to all individuals until universality is reached', (Piaget, p. 376). It is the work of Lawrence Kohlberg that describes the process beyond Piaget's stage three, of extending the notion of justice progressively to all individuals until universality is reached.

Moral development in Bahamian school children: a cross-cultural examination of Kohlberg's stages of moral reasoning
C.B. White, 1975

AIMS / That the Bahamian children would evidence advances in moral reasoning with advanced age. Additionally, the relationship concerning sex differences was examined.

SUBJECTS / N = 134 Bahamian school children between the ages seven and 14 years.

METHOD / Three of the standard Kohlberg moral dilemmas (1958) were presented individually to each subject.

RESULTS / The author concluded, 'The present findings of an age trend in moral development are supportive of previous cross-cultural research utilizing the Kohlberg system. With regard to the age of the present sample and the stages of moral development in evidence, the male—female difference at the 13- to 14-year-old age level is consistent with previous findings in the US. These sex differences may reflect greater role-taking experience in males and females (Kohlberg, 1964) or may be seen as reflecting a systematic sex bias in the Kohlberg measure.

Such a sex difference may be an artifact of having only male characters in the major roles in the moral dilemmas used to assess the stage of moral reasoning. Longitudinal data is needed to provide evidence of the sequential developmental nature of the Kohlberg stages beyond age trends in the present sample. Whether or not the sex differences will persist also remains to be investigated longitudinally', White (1975, pp. 535—536).

ABBREVIATIONS USED IN THE BIBLIOGRAPHY
(under the series *Piagetian Research*, Vols. 1–8)

Acta Psychol.	Acta Psychologica (Holland)
Adol.	Adolescence
Aging and Hum. Develop.	Aging and Human Development
Alberta J. Ed. Res.	Alberta Journal of Educational Research
Am. Ed. Res. Assoc.	American Educational Research Association
Am. Ed. Res. J.	American Educational Research Journal
Am. J. Ment. Def.	American Journal of Mental Deficiency
Am. J. Orthopsych.	American Journal of Orthopsychiatry
Am. J. Psych.	American Journal of Psychology
Am. J. Soc.	American Journal of Sociology
Am. Psych.	American Psychologist
Am. Psych. Assoc.	American Psychological Association
Am. Soc. Rev.	American Sociological Review
Ann. Rev. Psych.	Annual Review of Psychology
Arch. Dis. Child.	Archives of the Diseases of Childhood (UK)
Archiv. Gen. Psychiat.	Archives of General Psychiatry
Arch. de Psychol.	Archives de Psychologie
Aust. J. Psych.	Australian Journal of Psychology
Aust. J. Soc. Issues	Australian Journal of Social Issues
Brit. J. Clin. & Soc. Psych.	British Journal of Clinical and Social Psychology
Brit. J. Ed. Psych.	British Journal of Educational Psychology
Brit. J. Psych.	British Journal of Psychology
Brit. J. Stat. Psych.	British Journal of Statistical Psychology
Brit. J. Psych. Stat.	British Journal of Psychology – Statistical Section
Brit. J. Soc.	British Journal of Sociology
Brit. Med. Bull.	British Medical Bulletin
Brit. J. Med. Psych.	British Journal of Medical Psychology
Bull. Danish Inst. for Ed. Res.	Bulletin of the Danish Institute for Educational Research
Calif. J. Ed. Res.	Californian Journal of Educational Research
Can. Educ. Res. Dig.	Canadian Educational and Research Digest
Can. J. Behav. Sci.	Canadian Journal of Behavioural Science
Can. J. Psych.	Canadian Journal of Psychology
Can. Psychol.	Canadian Psychology
Child. Developm.	Child Development (USA)
Child Study Journ.	Child Study Journal
Childhood Psych.	Childhood Psychology (UK)
Cogn.	Cognition
Cogn. Psych.	Cognitive Psychology
Contemp. Psych.	Contemporary Psychology (USA)
Dev. Psych.	Developmental Psychology (USA)

Diss. Abstr.	Dissertation Abstracts (USA)
Educ. of Vis. Handicap.	Education of the Visually Handicapped
Educ. & Psych. Measmt.	Educational and Psychological Measurement (USA)
Ed. Res.	Educational Research (UK)
Ed. Rev.	Educational Review (UK)
Educ. Stud. Maths.	Educational Studies in Mathematics
El. Sch. J.	Elementary School Journal (USA)
Eug. Rev.	Eugenics Review (UK)
Excep. Child.	Exceptional Children
Forum Educ.	Forum Education
Gen. Psych. Mon.	Genetic Psychological Monographs (USA)
Harv. Ed. Rev.	Harvard Educational Review
Human Developm.	Human Development (Switzerland)
Hum. Hered.	Human Heredity
Inst. Child Welf. Monogr.	Institute of Child Welfare Monographs
Int. J. Psych.	International Journal of Psychology (France)
Int. Rev. Educ.	International Review of Education (Germany)
Int. Soc. Sci. Bull.	International Social Science Bulletin (France)
Jap. J. Ed. Psych.	Japanese Journal of Educational Psychology
Jap. Psych. Res.	Japanese Psychological Research
J. Abnorm. Soc. Psych.	Journal of Abnormal and Social Psychology (USA)
Journ. Amer. Acad. Child Psychiat.	Journal of American Academy of Child Psychiatry
J. Am. Stat. Assoc.	Journal of American Statistical Association
J. App. Psych.	Journal of Applied Psychology (USA)
J. Compar. Psychol.	Journal of Comparative Psychology
J. Comp. and Physiolog. Psych.	Journal of Comparative and Physiological Psychology
J. Child Psych. Psychiatr.	Journal of Child Psychology and Psychiatry
J. Clin. Psych.	Journal of Clinical Psychology (USA)
J. Consult. Psych.	Journal of Consultant Psychology (USA)
J. Cross. Cult. Psych.	Journal of Cross-Cultural Psychology (USA)
J. Ed. Psych.	Journal of Educational Psychology (USA)
J. Ed. Res.	Journal of Educational Research (USA)
J. Ed. Stud.	Journal of Educational Studies (USA)
J. Exp. Child Psych.	Journal of Experimental Child Psychology (USA)
J. Exp. Educ.	Journal of Experimental Education
J. Exp. Psych.	Journal of Experimental Psychology

J. Gen. Psych.	Journal of Genetic Psychology (USA)
J. Gerontol	Journal of Gerontology
J. Home Econ.	Journal of Home Economics
Journ. Learn. Disabil.	Journal of Learning Disabilities
J. Math. Psych.	Journal of Mathematical Psychology
J. Ment. Sub.	Journal of Mental Subnormality
J. Negro Ed.	Journal of Negro Education (USA)
J. Pers.	Journal of Personality (USA)
J. Pers. Soc. Psych.	Journal of Personality and Social Psychology (USA)
J. Pers. Assessm.	Journal of Personality Assessment (USA)
J. Psych.	Journal of Psychology (USA)
J. Res. Maths. Educ.	Journal of Research in Mathematics Education
J. Res. Sci. Teach.	Journal of Research in Science Teaching (USA)
J. Soc. Iss.	Journal of Social Issues (USA)
J. Soc. Psych.	Journal of Social Psychology (USA)
J. Soc. Res.	Journal of Social Research
J. Spec. Ed.	Journal of Special Education (USA)
Journ. Struct. Learn.	Journal of Structural Learning
J. Teach. Ed.	Journal of Teacher Education (USA)
J. Verb. Learn. Verb. Behv.	Journal of Verbal Learning and Verbal Behaviour (UK/USA)
J. Youth Adolesc.	Journal of Youth and Adolescence
Math. Teach.	Mathematics Teacher (USA)
Maths. Teach.	Mathematics Teaching
Merr.-Palm. Quart.	Merrill-Palmer Quarterly (USA)
Mon. Soc. Res. Child Dev.	Monographs of the Society for Research in Child Development (USA)
Mult. Beh. Res.	Multivariate Behavioural Research
New Zealand Journ. Educ. Stud.	New Zealand Journal of Educational Studies
Ped. Sem.	Pedagogical Seminary
Pedag. Europ.	Pedogogica Europaea
Percep. Mot. Skills	Perceptual and Motor Skills
Psych. Absts.	Psychological Abstracts
Psych. Afric.	Psychologica Africana
Psych. Bull.	Psychological Bulletin (USA)
Psych. Iss.	Psychological Issues
Psych. Mon.	Psychological Monographs (USA)
Psych. Mon. Gen. and Appl.	Psychological Monographs: General and Applied (USA)
Psychol. Rec.	Psychological Record
Psych. Rep.	Psychological Reports (USA)
Psych. Rev.	Psychological Review (USA)
Psychol. Sch.	Psychology in Schools
Psych. Sci.	Psychological Science (USA)
Psychomet.	Psychometrika
Psy.-nom. Sc.	Psychonomic Science
Psy. Today	Psychology Today
Publ. Opin. Quart.	Public Opinion Quarterly (USA)

Quart. J. Exp. Psych.	Quarterly Journal of Experimental Psychology (UK/USA)
Rev. Educ. Res.	Review of Educational Research
R. Belge de Ps. Ped.	Review Belge de Psychologie et de Pédagogie (Belgium)
Rev. Suisse Psych.	Revue Suisse de Pschologie (Switzerland)
Scan. J. Psych.	Scandinavian Journal of Psychology
Sch. Coun. Curr. Bull.	Schools Council Curriculum Bulletin
Sch. Sci. Maths.	School Science and Mathematics
Sci.	Science
Sci. Americ.	Scientific American
Sci. Ed.	Science Education (USA)
Scot. Ed. Stud.	Scottish Educational Studies
Sem. Psychiat.	Seminars in Psychiatry
Soc. Psychi.	Social Psychiatry
Soviet Psych.	Soviet Psychology
Teach. Coll. Contr. Ed.	Teachers' College Contributions to Education (USA)
Theo. into Pract.	Theory into Practice
Times Ed. Supp.	Times Educational Supplement
Train. Sch. Bull.	Training School Bulletin
Vita. Hum.	Vita Humana
WHO Mon.	World Health Organization Monographs
Wiener Arb. z. pad. Psychol.	Wiener Arbeiten zur pädagogischen Psychologie (Austria)
Yearbook Journ. Negro Educ.	Yearbook of the Journal of Negro Education
Zeitschr. f. ang. Psychol.	Zeitschrift für angewandte Psychologie und Charakterkunde (Germany)
Zeitschr. f. pad. Psychol.	Zeitschrift für pädagogische Psychologie und Fugendkunde (Germany)

ABEL, T. (1941) 'Moral judgements among subnormals', *J. Abnorm. Soc. Psych.*, 36, 378—92.

ADELSON, J., GREEN, B. and O'NEILL, R. (1969) 'Growth of the idea of law in adolescence,' *Dev. Psych.*, 1, 4, 327—32.

ALDRICH, C.C. (1976) 'Observations of transgressions and a child's differential reaction to adult chastisement: effects on children's moral / person judgments', *Diss. Abstr.*, 36, 8, 3687B—4237B (p. 4123B).

ALLINSMITH, W. (1966) 'Moral standards: the learning of moral standards'. In: MILLER, D.R., and SWANSON, G.E. (Eds.) *Inner Conflict and Defense*. New York: Wiley.

ALMY, M., CHITTENDEN, E., and MILLER, D. (1966) *Young Children's Thinking*. New York: Teachers College Press.

ALSTON, W.P. (1971) 'Comments on Kohlberg's "From is to Ought"'. In: MISCHEL, T., (Ed.), *Cognitive Development and Epistemology*. New York and London: Academic Press.

AMBRON, S. R., and IRWIN, D.M. (1975) 'Role taking and moral judgment in five- and seven-year-olds', *Dev. Psych.*, 11, 1, 102 (Abstract).

ARBUTHNOT, J. (1974) 'Cognitive style and modification of moral judgment', *Psych. Rep.*, 34, 273—274.

ARBUTHNOT, J. (1975) 'Modification of moral judgment through role playing', *Dev. Psych.*, 11, 3, 319—24.

ARMSBY, R.E. (1971) 'A re-examination of the development of moral judgements in children', *Child Developm.*, 42, 1241—48.

ARONFREED, J. (1961) 'The nature, variety and social patterning of moral responses to transgression', *J. Abnorm. Soc. Psych.*, 63, 223—40.

ARONFREED, J., CUTICK, R.A., and FAGEN, S.A. (1963) 'Cognitive structure, punishment and nurturance in the experimental induction of self-criticism', *Child Developm.*, 34, 283—94.

ASCH, S.E. (1956) 'Studies of independence and submission to group pressure. I. A minority of one against a unanimous majority', *Psych. Monogs.*, 70, (9, whole No. 416).

ATTFIELD, D. (1976) 'Moral thinking in religion — a note on Goldman', *Educ. Stud.*, 2, 1, 29—32.

AUSTRALIAN SCIENCE EDUCATION PROJECT (1972, 1974) Private communication with L.G. Dale.

BALDWIN, C.P. and BALDWIN, A.L. (1970) 'Children's judgments of kindness', *Child Developm.*, 41, 29—47.

BALDWIN, J.M. (1906) *Social and Ethical Interpretations in Mental Development.* London: Macmillan.

BANDURA, A. (1969) 'Social learning of moral judgments', *J. Person. Soc. Psych.*, 11, 275—279.

BANDURA, A., and McDONALD, F. (1963) 'Influence of social reinforcement and the behaviour of models in shaping children's moral judgments', *J. Abnorm. Soc. Psych.*, 67, 274—281.

BANTA, T.J. (1968) 'Tests for the evaluation of early childhood education: The Cincinnati Autonomy Test Battery (CATB)'. In: HELMUTH, J. (Ed.), *Cognitive Studies*, Volume One. Seattle: Special Child Publications.

BARNES, E. (1894) 'Punishment as seen by children', *Ped. Sem.*, 3, 235—45.

BARNES, E. (1902) 'Growth of social judgement', *Studies in Education*, 2, 203—17.

BAR-YAM, M., and KOHLBERG, L. (1971) 'Development of moral judgment in the kibbutz,' In: KOHLBERG, L. and TURIEL, E. (Eds.), *Moralization: A Cognitive-Developmental Approach to Socialization,* To be published, 1976.

BERG-CROSS, L.G. (1975) 'Intentionality, degree of damage, and moral judgments', *Child Developm.*, 46, 970—974.

BERNDT, T.J., and BERNDT, E.G. (1975) 'Children's use of motives and intentionality in person perception and moral judgment', *Child Developm.*, 46, 904—912.

BIELBY, D.D.V., and PAPALIA, D.E. (1975) 'Moral development and egocentrism: their development and interrelationship across the life span', *Aging Hum. Develop.*, in press.

BLATT, M. (1969) 'The effects of classroom discussion on the development of moral judgement'. In: KOHLBERG, L. and TURIEL, E. (Eds.), *Moralization: A Cognitive-Developmental Approach to Socialization.* New York: Holt-Blond. To be published 1976.

BLATT, M., and KOHLBERG, L. (1971) 'The effects of classroom discussion on the development of moral judgement.' Unpublished Paper. To be published in KOHLBERG, L., and TURIEL, E. (Eds.), *Moralization: A Cognitive-Developmental Approach to Socialization.* New York: Holt. To be published 1976. (Unpublished paper obtainable from Harvard University).

BOBROFF, A. (1960) 'The stages of maturation in socialized thinking and in ego development of two groups of children', *Child Developm.*, 31, 321—38.

BOEHM, L. (1957) 'The development of independence: a comparative study', *Child Developm.*, 28, 85—92.

BOEHM, L. (1962) 'The development of conscience: a comparison of American children of different mental and socio-economic levels', *Child Developm.*, 33, 575—90.

BOEHM, L. (1962a) 'The development of conscience: a comparison of students in Catholic parochial schools and in public schools', *Child Developm.*, 33, 591—602.

BOEHM, L., and NASS, M.L. (1962) 'Social class differences in conscience development', *Child Developm.*, 33, 565—74.

BORSHTEIN, N., ETZION, D. (1973) 'Behavioural validity of resistance to temptation scores'. Unpublished manuscript, Bar Ilan University.

BRENNAN, W.K. (1962) 'The relation of social adaptation, emotional adjustment and moral judgement to intelligence in primary school children', *Brit. J. Ed. Psych.*, 32, 200—4.

BREZNITZ, S., and KUGELMASS, S. (1967) 'Intentionality in moral judgement: developmental stages', *Child Developm.*, 38, 469—79.

BROOKS-WALSH, I., and SULLIVAN, E.V. (1973) 'The relationship between moral judgement, causal reasoning and general reasoning,' *J. Moral Ed.*, 2, 2, 131—36.

BROWN, A.M., MATHENY, A.P., Jr., and WILSON, R.S. (1973) 'Baldwins' kindness concept measure as related to children's cognition and temperament: a twin study', *Child Developm.*, 44, 193—195.

BROWN, M., FELDMAN, K., SCHWARTZ, S., and HEINGARTNER, A. (1969) 'Some personality correlates of conduct in two situations of moral conflict', *J. Pers.*, 37, 1.

BRUNER, J. *et al.* (1966) *Studies in Cognitive Growth*. New York: Wiley.

BUCHANAN, J.P. and THOMPSON, S.K. (1973) 'A quantitative methodology to examine the development of moral judgment', *Child Developm.*, 44, 186—189.

BULL, N.J. (1969) *Moral Judgement from Childhood to Adolescence*. London: Routledge and Kegan Paul.

BURTON, R.V. (1963) 'The generality of honesty reconsidered', *Psych. Rev.*, 70, 481—500.

CAUBLE, M.A. (1975) 'Interrelations among Piaget's formal operations, Erikson's ego identity, and Kohlberg's principled morality', *Diss. Abstrs.*, 36, 2, 579—1131A (p. 7773—A).

CHANDLER, M.J., GREENSPAN, S., and BARENBOIM, C. (1973) 'Judgments of intentionality in response to videotaped and verbally presented moral dilemmas: the medium is the message', *Child Developm.*, 44, 315—320.

CLAYTON, V. (1975) 'Erikson's theory of human development as it applies to the elderly', *Human Developm.*, 18, 119—128.

COOPER, D. (1972) The analysis of an objective measure of moral development. Unpublished PhD dissertation, University of Minnesota.

COOPER, R.G., and FLAVELL, J.H. (1972) 'Cognitive correlates of children's role-taking behaviour'. Unpublished report, Institute of Child Development, University of Minnesota.

COSTANZO, P.R., COIE, J.P., GRUMET, J.F., and FARNILL, D. (1973) 'A reexamination of the effects of intent and consequences on children's moral judgments', *Child Developm.*, 44, 154—161.

COURIER-EXPRESS (1974) 'Ex-flier replacing church painting destroyed in war', p. 1, *Courier Express*, Buffalo, April 4th.

COUSINS, D. (1972) An investigation of young children's perspective skills. Unpublished PhD dissertation, George Washington University, Washington, DC.

COWAN, P.A. (1966) 'Cognitive egocentrism and social interaction in children', *Am. Psych.*, 21, 623.

COWAN, P.A., LANGER, J., HEAVENRICH, J., and NATHANSON, M. (1969) 'Social learning and Piaget's cognitive theory of moral development', *J. Person. Soc. Psych.*, 11, 261—274.

CRAIG, R.P. (1976) 'Durkheim and others: some philosophical influences on Piaget's theory of moral development'. Paper read at the Sixth Annual Seminar of Piagetian Theory and its implications for the Helping Professions. Los Angeles, California: University of Southern California, Jan. 30th. Also personal communication.

D'ARCY, E. (1963) *Human Acts: an Essay on their Moral Evaluation*. Oxford: Oxford University Press.

DECARIE, T.G. (1965) *Intelligence and Affectivity in Early Childhood*. New York: International Universities Press.

DEUTSCH, F. (1974) 'Observational and sociometric measures of peer popularity and their relationship to egocentric communication in female preschoolers', *Dev. Psych.*, 10, 5, 745—747.

DEUTSCH, F. and MADLE, R. (1975) 'Empathy: historic and current conceptualizations, measurement and a cognitive theoretical perspective'. *Human Developm.* 18, 267—87.

DE VILLIERS, P.A., and DE VILLIERS, J.G. (1974) 'On this, that, and the other: nonegocentrism in very young children', *J. Exp. Child Psych.*, 18, 438—447.

DIENSTBIER, R.A., HILLMAN, D., LEHNHOFF, J., HILLMAN, J. and VALKENAAR, Mc. (1975) 'An emotion-attribution approach to moral behaviour: interfacing cognitive and avoidance theories of moral development', *Psych. Rev.*, 82, 4, 299—315.

DISTEFANO, A. (1975) Teaching moral reasoning about sexual interpersonal dilemmas. Unpublished PhD thesis, Boston University.

DOCKERELL, W.B. (Ed.), (1970) *On Intelligence: The Toronto*

Symposium on Intelligence, 1969. London: Methuen.

DREMAN, S.B. (1976) 'Sharing behaviour in Israeli school children: cognitive and social learning factors', *Child Developm.*, 47, 186–194.

DREMAN, S.B., and GREENBAUM, C.W. (1973) 'Altruism or reciprocity: sharing behaviour in Israeli kindergarten children', *Child Developm.*, 44, 154–161.

DUDEK, S.Z. (1972) 'A longitudinal study of Piaget's developmental stages and the concept of regression II', *J. Pers. Assessm.*, 36, 5, 468–78.

DULIT, E. (1972) 'Adolescent thinking à la Piaget: the formal stage,' *J. Youth Adolesc.*, 1, 4, 281–301.

DURKHEIM, E. (1960) *Moral Education.* New York: The Free Press.

ELKIND, D. (1968) 'Always changing, always the same', *Childhood Educ.*, 44, 292–294.

ERICKSON, V.L. (1974) 'Psychological growth for women', *Counselling and Values*, 18, 2, 102–116.

ERICKSON, V.L. (1975) 'Deliberate psychological education for women: From Iphigenia to Antigone', *Couns. Educ. Superv.*, 14, 4, 297–309.

FARNILL, D. (1974) 'The effects of social-adjustment set on children's use of intent information', *J. Pers.*, 42, 276–289.

FIELD, T.W., and CROPLEY, A.J. (1969) 'Cognitive style and science achievement', *J. Res. Sci. Teach.*, 6, 2–10.

FLAPAN, D. (1968) *Children's Understanding of Social Interaction.* New York: Teachers College Press.

FLAVELL, J.H. (1972) 'An analysis of cognitive-developmental sequences', *Gen. Psych. Mon.*, 86, 279–350.

FLAVELL, J.H., BOTKIN, P.T., FRY, C.L., WRIGHT, J.W., and JARVIS, P.E. (1968) *The Development of Role-taking and Communication Skills in Children.* New York: Wiley.

FODOR, E.M. (1969) 'Moral judgment in negro and white adolescents', *J. Soc. Psych.*, 79, 289–91.

FODOR, E.M. (1972) 'Delinquency and susceptibility to social influence among adolescents as a function of level of moral development', *J. Soc. Psych.*, 86, 257–60.

FONTANA, A.F., and NOEL, B. (1973) 'Moral reasoning in the University', *J. Pers. Soc. Psych.*, 27, 3, 419–29.

FRANK, H. (1976) 'Identification, moral character and conceptual organization', *Gen. Psych. Monogs.*, 93, 129–53.

FREINET, C. (1960) *L'education du Travail.* Neuchatel: Delachaux et Niestlé.

FRY, C.L. (1967) 'A developmental examination of performance in a tacit coordination game situation', *J. Person. and Soc. Psych.*, 5, 277–281.

GALLAGHER, M.J. (1975) 'A comparison of Hogan's and Kohlberg's theories of moral development', *Diss. Abstr.*, 36, 5, 1979B—2534B.

GASH, H. (1976) 'Moral judgment: a comparison of two theoretical approaches', *Gen. Psych.*, 93, 91—111.

GIL, B., ARYEE, A.F., and GHANSAH, D.K. (1964) *1960 population census of Ghana, special report 'E': Tribes in Ghana.* Accra: Census Office.

GILLIGAN, C., KOHLBERG, L., LERNER, J., and BELENSKY, M. (1971) 'Moral reasoning about sexual dilemmas: an interview and scoring system'. Technical Report of the Commission on Obscenity and Pornography, 141—74.

GLASSCO, J.A., MILGRAM, N.A., and YOUNISS, J. (1970) 'Stability of training effects on intentionality in moral judgement in children', *J. Pers. Soc. Psych.*, 14, 4, 360—5.

GLUCKSBERG, S., and KRAUSS, R.M. (1967) 'What do people say after they have learned how to talk? Studies of the development of referential communication', *Merr.-Palm. Quart.*, 13, 309—316.

GOLDMAN, R. (1964) *Religious Thinking from Childhood to Adolescence.* London: Routledge and Kegan Paul.

GORHAM, D.R. (1956) *Clinical Manual for the Proverbs Test.* Psychological Test Specialists.

GOUGH, H. (1969) *Manual for the California Psychological Inventory.* Revised Edition. Palo Alto, California: Consulting Psychologists Press.

GOUGH, H. and PETERSON, D. (1952) 'The identification and measurement of predispositional factors in crime and delinquency', *J. Consult. Psych.*, 16, 207—212.

GRAHAM, D. (1972) *Moral Learning and Development: Theory and Research.* London: Batsford.

GRAYBILL, L.A. (1974) 'A study of sex differences in the transition from concrete to formal thinking patterns', *Diss. Abstr.*, 34, 7, 3613A—4477A, (3988—A).

GRIEF, E., and HOGAN, R. (1973) 'The theory and measurement of empathy', *J. Counsel Psych.*, 20, 280—284.

GRIMES, P. (1974) Teaching moral reasoning to eleven year olds and their mothers: a means of promoting moral development. Unpublished PhD thesis, Boston University.

GRIMLEY, L.K. (1974) 'A cross-cultural study of moral development', *Diss. Abstr.*, 34, 7, 3613A—4477A (3988A), Xerox University Microfilms.

GRINDER, R.E. (1962) 'Parental childrearing practices, conscience and resistance to temptation of sixth-grade children'. *Child Developm.*, 33, 803—20.

GRINDER, R.E. (1964) 'Relations between behavioural and cognitive dimensions of conscience in childhood', *Child Developm.*, 35, 881—891.

GUILLILAND, S.F. (1971) Effects of sensitivity groups on moral judgment. Unpublished PhD dissertation, Boston University.

GUTKIN, D.C. (1972) 'The effect of systematic story changes on intentionality in children's moral judgments', *Child Developm.*, 43, 187—95.

GUTKIN, D.C. (1973) 'An analysis of the concept of moral intentionality', *Human Developm.*, 16, 371—81.

GUTKIN, D.C. (1975) 'Maternal discipline and children's judgments of moral intentionality', *J. Gen. Psych.*, 127, 55—61.

HAAN, N., SMITH, M.B., and BLOCK, J. (1968) 'Moral reasoning of young adults: political—social behaviour, family background, and personality correlates, *J. Pers. Soc. Psych.*, 10, 3, 183—201.

HARDEMAN, M. (1972) 'Children's moral reasoning', *J. Gen. Psych.*, 120, 49—59.

HARRIS, H. (1970) 'Development of moral attitudes in white and negro boys', *Dev. Psych.*, 2, 3, 376—83.

HARROWER, M.R. (1934) 'Social status and the moral development of the child', *Brit. J. Ed. Psych.*, 4, 75—95.

HARTSHORNE, H., and MAY, M.A. (1928—30) *Studies in the Nature of Character:* Vol. 1, Studies in Deceit, 1928; Vol. 2, Studies in Service and Self-control, 1929; Vol. 3, Studies in the Organisation of Character, 1930, (with F.K. Shuttleworth). New York: Macmillan.

HAVIGHURST, R.J., and NEUGARTEN, B.L. (1955) *American Indian and White Children: A Sociopsychological Investigation.* Chicago: University of Chicago Press.

HEBBLE, P.W. (1971) 'The development of elementary school children's judgment of intent', *Child Developm.*, 42, 1203—1215.

HEWITT, L.S. (1975) 'The effects of provocation, intentions and consequences on children's moral judgments', *Child Developm.*, 43, 540—544.

HOFFMAN, M.L. (1970) 'Moral development'. In: MUSSEN, P. (Ed.), *Carmichael's Manual of Child Development.* New York: Wiley.

HOFFMAN, M.L. (1971) 'Father absence and conscience development', *Dev. Psych.*, 4, 400—6.

HOFFMAN, M.L. (1975) 'Developmental synthesis of affect and cognition and its implications for altruistic motivation', *Dev. Psych.*, 11, 5, 607—622.

HOGAN, R. (1969) 'Development of an empathy scale', *J. Consult. Clin. Psych.*, 33, 307—316.

HOGAN, R. (1970) 'A dimension of moral judgment', *J. Consult. Clin. Psych.*, 35, 205—212.

HOGAN, R. (1973) 'Moral conduct and moral character: a

psychological perspective', *Psych Bull.*, 79, 217—232.

HOGAN, R. (1974) 'Dialectical aspects of moral development', *Human Developm.*, 17, 107—117.

HOGAN, R., and DICKSTEIN, E. (1970) 'Moral judgment and perceptions of injustice', *J. Pers. Soc. Psych.*, 23, 3, 409—413.

HOLSTEIN, C.B. (1971) 'Parental determinants of the development of moral judgment'. In: KOHLBERG, L. and TURIEL, E. *Moralization: A Cognitive-Developmental Approach to Socialization.* New York: Holt, to be published 1976.

HOLSTEIN, C.B. (1973) 'Moral judgment change in early adolescence and middle age: a longitudinal study', *Soc. Res. Child Develop.*, Philadelphia, Pa.

HOLSTEIN, C.B. (1976) 'Irreversible, stepwise sequence in the development of moral development: a longitudinal study of males and females', *Child Developm.*, 47, 51—61.

HOOPER, F.H. (1975) 'Life-span analyses of Piagetian concept tasks'. In: RIEGEL, K., and MEACHAM, J. *The Developing Individual in a Changing World*, Vol. I. The Hague: Mouton.

HUIZINGA, R.J. (1971) The relationship of the Illinois Test of Psycholinguistic Abilities to the Stanford-Binet Form L—M and the Wechsler Intelligence Scale for children. Unpublished PhD dissertation, University of Arizona.

INHELDER, B., and PIAGET, J. (1958) *The Growth of Logical Thinking from Childhood to Adolescence.* New York: Basic Books.

INHELDER, B., and PIAGET, J. (1964) *The Early Growth of Logic in the Child.* London: Routledge and Kegan Paul.

INHELDER, B., and SINCLAIR, H. (1969) 'Learning cognitive structures'. In: MUSSEN, P., LANGER, J., and COVINGTON, M. (Eds.), *Trends and Issues in Developmental Psychology.* New York: Holt, Rinehart and Winston.

IRWIN, D.M. (1973) The relation between moral judgment and role-taking in five-year-olds. Unpublished PhD., Minnesota University.

IRWIN, D.M., and MOORE, S.G. (1971) 'The young child's understanding of social justice', *Dev. Psych.*, 6, 3, 406—410.

JACKSON, D.N. (1956) 'A short form of Witkin's Embedded-figures Test', *J. Abnorm. Soc. Psych.*, 53, 254—255.

JACKSON, S. (1963) The growth of logical thinking in normal and subnormal children. Unpublished MEd thesis, University of Manchester.

JAHODA, G. (1958) 'Immanent justice among West African children', *J. Soc. Psych.*, 47, 241—8.

JENSEN, L., and HUGHSTON, K. (1971) 'The effects of training children to make moral judgements that are independent of sanctions', *Dev. Psych.*, 5, 2, 367.

JENSEN, L., and LARM. C. (1970) 'The effects of two training procedures on intentionality in moral judgments among children', *Dev. Psych.*, 2, 2, 310.

JOHNSON, R.C. (1962) 'Early studies of children's moral judgements', *Child Developm.*, 33, 603—5.

JURD, M. (n.d.) 'A critical survey of research on the development of social science concepts during adolescence.' Research Paper No. 1, National Committee on Social Science Teaching (Australia) no date.

KAGAN, J., ROSEMAN, B., DAY, D., ALBERT, J., and PHILLIPS, W. (1964) 'Information processing in the child: significance of analytic and reflective attitudes', *Psych. Mon.*, 78, 1, (whole No. 578).

KANE, K.R. (1970) 'A study of children's concepts of lies', *Diss. Abstr.*, 1971A, 242.

KANE, M.H. (1975) 'The phenomemology and psychodynamics of moral development', *Diss. Abstr.*, 36, 6, 2535—B—3134B.

KARP, S., and KONSTADT, N. (1963) *Children's Embedded Figures Test.* Brooklyn: Cognitive Tests.

KAY, W. (1968) *Moral Development.* New York: Schocken Books.

KEASEY, C.B. (1971) 'Social participation as a factor in the moral development of preadolescents, *Dev. Psych.*, 5, 2, 216—20.

KEASEY, C.B. (1973) 'Experimentally induced change in moral opinions and reasoning', *J. Pers. Soc. Psych.*, 26, 30—38.

KING, M. (1971) 'The development of some intention concepts in young children', *Child Developm.*, 42, 1145—1152.

KOHLBERG, L. (1958) The development of modes of moral thinking and choice in the years ten to sixteen. Unpublished doctoral dissertation, University of Chicago.

KOHLBERG, L. (1963) 'Moral development and identification.' In: STEVENSON, H. (ed.), *Child Psychology.* National Society for the Study of Education, 62nd Year book, pp. 277—332.

KOHLBERG, L. (1963a) 'The development of children's orientation towards a moral order, I: Sequence in the development of moral thought', *Vita Hum.*, 6, 11—33.

KOHLBERG, L. (1964) 'Development of moral character and moral ideology'. In: M. and L. HOFFMAN (Eds.) *Review of Child Development Research*, I. New York: Russell Sage Foundation.

KOHLBERG, L. (1964a) 'Sex differences in morality'. In: MAC-COBY, E.L. (Ed.), *Sex Role Development.* New York: Social Science Research Council.

KOHLBERG, L. (1966) 'Moral education in the schools: a developmental view', *The School Review*, 74, 1—30.

KOHLBERG, L. (1968) 'The child as a moral philosopher', *Psych. Today*, 2, 4, 25—30.

KOHLBERG, L. (1968a) 'Moral development', In: *International Encyclopaedia of the Social Sciences*. New York: Crowell, Collier and Macmillan, Inc.

KOHLBERG, L. (1969) 'Stage and sequence: the cognitive-developmental approach to socialization'. In: GOSLIN, D. (Ed.), *Handbook of Socialization Theory and Research*. New York: Rand McNally.

KOHLBERG, L. (1969a) 'The relations between moral judgment and moral action: a developmental view'. Paper presented as a colloquium at the Institute of Human Development, University of California Berkeley, March.

KOHLBERG, L. (1970) 'The moral atmosphere of the school'. In: OVERLEY, N. (Ed.), *The Unstudied Curriculum*. Monograph of the Association for Supervision and Curriculum Development, Washington, DC. January 9th 1969. Offprint available from Harvard. Printed in AASC Yearbook, 1970.

KOHLBERG, L. (1971) 'From is to ought: how to commit the naturalistic fallacy and get away with it in the study of moral development'. In: MISCHEL, T. (Ed.), *Cognitive Development and Epistemology*. New York and London: Academic Press.

KOHLBERG, L. (1971a) 'The concepts of developmental psychology as the central guide to education: examples from cognitive, moral and psychological education'. Proceedings of the Conference on Psychology and the Process of Schooling in the Next Decade: Alternative Conceptions. Bureau for Educational Personnel Development. US Office of Education: A publication of the Leadership Training Institute/Special Education. Offprint available from Harvard University.

KOHLBERG, L. (1971b) 'Moral Judgement Interview and Procedures for Scoring'. University of Harvard, Unpublished.

KOHLBERG, L. (1973) 'Continuities in childhood and adult moral development revisited'. In: BALTES and SCHAIE, *Life-Span Developmental Psychology: Personality and Socialization*. New York: Academic Press.

KOHLBERG, L. (1973a) 'Collected papers on moral development and moral education'. Cambridge, Massachusetts: Laboratory of Human Development, Harvard University.

KOHLBERG, L., and KRAMER, R. (1969) 'Continuities and discontinuities in childhood and adult moral development', *Human Developm.*, 12, 93–120.

KOHLBERG, L., and MAYER, R. (1972) 'Development as the aim of education', *Harv. Ed. Rev.*, 42, 449–496.

KOHLBERG, L., and TURIEL, E. (1971) *Moralization: A Cognitive-Developmental Approach to Socialization*. Holt: To be published 1976.

KOHLBERG, L., and TURIEL, E. (1971a) 'Moral development and moral education'. In: LESSER, G. (Ed.), *Psychology and Educational Practice.* Chicago: Scott Foresman.

KOTALAWALA, D.E.M. (1971) An investigation of the development of moral judgment in a group of 10–14 year old British and Ceylonese children. PhD thesis, University of London.

KRAMER, R. (1968) Changes in moral judgment response pattern during late adolescence and young childhood: retrogression in a developmental sequence. Unpublished PhD thesis, Chicago University.

KREBS, D.L. (1970) 'Altruism – an examination of the concept and a review of the literature', *Psych. Bull.,* 73, 258–302.

KREBS, R.L. (1967) Some relationships between moral judgement, attention and resistance to temptation. Unpublished Doctoral Dissertation, University of Chicago.

KUHN, D. (1974) 'Inducing development experimentally: comments on a research paradigm', *Dev. Psych.,* 10, 5, 590–600.

KUHN, D., LANGER, J., KOHLBERG, L., and HAAN, N.S. (1971) 'The development of formal operations in logical and moral judgment', Unpublished paper, Columbia University. Also personal communication.

KUPFERSMID, J.H. (1975) 'The relationship between moral maturity and selected characteristics of mental health among young adults', *Diss. Abstr.,* 36, 6, 3169A–4081A (p. 3516–A).

LANGFORD, P.E. (1974) 'Development of concepts of infinity and limit in mathematics', *Arch. de Psycholog.,* 42, 311–22. Also personal communication.

LANGFORD, P.E., and GEORGE, S. (1975) 'Preconditions for the development of moral judgement', personal communication.

LAURENDEAU, M., and PINARD, A. (1962) *Causal Thinking in the Child.* New York: International Universities Press.

LaVOIE, J.C. (1974) 'Cognitive determinants of resistance to deviation in seven-, nine- and eleven-year-old children of low and high maturity of moral judgment', *Dev. Psych.,* 10, 3, 393–403.

LEE, L.C. (1971) 'The concomitant development of cognitive and moral modes of thought: a test of selected deductions from Piaget's theory', *Gen. Psych. Mon.,* 83, 93–146.

LeFURGY, W.G., and WOLOSHIN, G.W. (1969) 'Immediate and long-term effects of experimentally induced social influence in the modification of adolescents' moral judgements', *J. Soc. Psych.,* 12, 2, 104–10.

LEMING, J.S. (1973) 'Adolescent moral judgment and deliberation on classical and practical moral dilemmas'. Unpublished PhD dissertation, University of Wisconsin-Madison.

LEMING, J.S. (1974) 'An empirical examination of key assumptions underlying the Kohlberg rationale for moral education'. Paper presented at Annual Meeting of the American Education Research Association, April.

LEMING, J.S. (1976) 'An exploratory inquiry into the multi-factor theory of moral behaviour', *J. Moral Educ.*, 5, 2, 179—188.

LEPPER, R.M. (1971) 'Dissonance, self perception and the generalization of moral behaviour', *Diss. Abstr.*, 1, 32.

LERNER, E. (1937) 'The problem of perspective in moral reasoning', *Am. J. Soc.*, 43, 249—69.

LESTER, E.P., MUIR, R., and DUDEK, S.Z. (1970) 'Cognitive structures and achievement in the young child', *Can. Psychiatr.*, 15, 279—287.

LUI, CHING-HO. (1950) 'The influence of cultural background on the moral judgement of children', doctoral dissertation, Columbia University.

LOCKWOOD, A.L. (1972) *Moral Reasoning — the Value of Life*. Harvard Project Social Studies. Middleton, Conn.: American Educational Publications.

LOCKWOOD, A.L. (In press) 'Stage of moral development and reasoning about public policy issues'. In: KOHLBERG, L., and TURIEL, E. (Eds.), *Moralization: The Cognitive-Development Approach*. New York: Holt, Rinehart and Winston. To be published 1976.

LOOFT, W.R., and BARTZ, W.H. (1969) 'Animism revived', *Psych. Bull.*, 71, 1—19.

LYDIAT, M. (1973) 'Development of moral judgments in children', *J. Moral Educ.*, 3, 1, 367—377.

MACCOBY, E.E. (1968) 'The development of moral values and behaviour in childhood'. In: CLAUSEN, *Socialization and Society*. Boston: Little Brown.

MACKIE, P. (1974) Teaching counselling skills to low achieving high school students. Unpublished PhD thesis, Boston University.

MAGUIRE, D.C. (1974) 'Death by Chance, Death by Choice', *Atlantic*, 333, 56—65.

MANN, L. (1973) 'Attitudes toward My Lai and obedience to orders: an Australian Survey', *Aust. J. Psych.*, 25, 1, 11—21.

McCANN, J., and BELL, P. (1975) 'Educational environment and the development of moral concepts', *J. Moral Educ.*, 6, 1, 63—70.

McGEORGE, C. (1974) 'Situational variation in level of moral judgment', *Brit. J. Ed. Psych.*, 44, 2, 116—22.

McGEORGE, C. (1975) 'Susceptibility to faking of the Defining Issues Test of Moral Development', *Develop. Psych.*, 11, 1, 108.

McGHEE, P.E. (1974) 'Moral development and children's appreciation of humor', *Dev. Psych.*, 10, 4, 514—525.

McKECHNIE, R.J. (1971) 'Between Piaget's stages: a study in moral development', *Brit. J. Ed. Psych.*, 213—17.

McKECHNIE, R.J. (1971a) The influence of story structure and behavioural area on the moral judgement of the child. MSc thesis, Leeds University.

McRAE, D. (1954) 'A Test of Piaget's theories of moral development', *J. Abnorm. Soc. Psych.*, 49, 14—18.

MAGOWAN, S.A., and LEE, T. (1970) 'Some sources of error in the use of the projective method for the measurement of moral judgement', *Brit. J. Psych.*, 61, 535—43.

MANN, L. (1973) 'Attitudes toward My Lai and obedience to orders,' *Aust. J. Psych.*, 25, 11—21.

MEACHAM, J.A. (1975) 'A dialectical approach to moral judgement and self-esteem', *Human Developm.*, 18, 159—170.

MEAD, G.H. (1934) *Mind, Self, and Society.* Chicago: University of Chicago.

MEDINNUS, G.R. (1959) 'Immanent justice in children: a review of the literature and additional data', *J. Gen. Psych.*, 94, 253—62.

MEDINNUS, G.R. (1961) 'The relation between several parent measures and the child's early adjustment to school', *J. Ed. Psych.*, 52, 153—6.

MEDINNUS, G.R. (1962) 'Objective responsibility in children: a comparison with Piaget data', *J. Gen. Psych.*, 101, 127—33'

MEDINNUS, G.R. (1966) 'Behavioural and cognitive measures of conscience development', *J. Gen. Psych.*, 109, 147—50.

MERCHANT, R.L., and REBELSKY, F. (1972) 'Effects of participation in rule formation on the moral judgment of children', *Gen. Psych. Mon.*, 85, 287—304.

MILLER, P.E. (1966) The effects of age and training on children's ability to understand certain basic concepts. Unpublished PhD thesis, Teachers College, Columbia University, New York.

MISCHEL, W. (1961) 'Delay of gratification, need for achievement and acquiescence in another culture', *J. Abnorm. Soc. Psych.*, 62, 543—52.

MISCHEL, W. (1973) 'Toward a cognitive social learning reconceptualization of personality', *Psych. Rev.*, 80, 252—283.

MISCHIO, G.S. (1976) 'Moral judgment and role-taking of young retarded children', *Diss. Abstr.*, 36, 8, 4813A—5602A (p. 5199—A).

MODGIL, C. (1975) Piagetian operations in relation to moral development. Unpublished MPhil Thesis, University of Surrey.

MODGIL, S. (1969) The relation of emotional adjustment to the conservation of number. Unpublished Masters Thesis, University of Manchester.

MODGIL, S. (1974) *Piagetian Research: A Handbook of Recent Studies.* Slough: NFER.

MODGIL, S. (1974a) The patterning of cognitive development in relation to parental attitude. PhD Thesis, Kings' College, London University.

MODGIL, S., DUDEK, S.Z., and GERMAIN, G. (1975) 'The Personality of the Child and the Use of Operational Thought.' In Press.

MODGIL, S., LANGFORD, P.E., MODGIL, C (1976) 'Parental attitude and conceptual growth in the early school years', In press.

MOIR, D.J. (1974) 'Egocentrism and the emergence of conventional morality in preadolescent girls', *Child Developm.*, 45, 299—304.

MOORE, M.E. (1976) 'The relationship between ego and moral development in adult lay and religious women', *Diss. Abstr.*, 36, 7, 3135B—3685B (p. 3580B).

MORRIS, J.F. (1958) 'The development of moral values in children', *Brit. J. Ed. Psych.*, 94, 253—62.

MOSHER, R.L., and SPRINTHALL, N.A. (1971) Psychological education: a means to promote personal development during adolescence', *The Counsell. Psych.*, 2, 4.

MOSHER, R.L., and SULLIVAN, P.R. (1976) 'A curriculum in moral education for adolescents', *J. Moral Educ.*, 5, 2, 159—172.

NAJARIAN-SVAJIAN, P.H. (1966) 'The idea of immanent justice among Lebanese children and adults', *J. Gen. Psych.*, 109, 57—66.

NATALE, S. (1972) *An Experiment in Empathy.* Windsor: NFER.

NESDALE, A.R. RULE, B.G., and McARA, M. (1975) 'Moral judgments of aggression: personal and situational determinants', *Europ. J. Soc. Psych.*, 5, 3, 339—349.

NIDICH, S.I. (1976) 'A study of the relationship of transcendental meditation to Kohlberg's stages of moral reasoning'. *Diss. Abstr.*, 36, 7, 4083A—4512A (p. 4361A).

OLIM, E.G., HESS, R.D., and SHIPMAN, V.C. (1967) 'Role of mother's language style in mediating the preschool children's cognitive development', *The School Review* 75 (No. 4, Winter), University of Chicago Press.

OLVER, R.R., and HORNSBY, J.R. (1966) 'On equivalence'. In: BRUNER, J.S. *et al. Studies in Cognitive Growth.* New York: Wiley.

ORR, J.B. (1974) 'Cognitive-developmental approaches to moral education: a social ethical analysis'. Paper presented at the 4th Annual Conference on Piaget and the Helping Professions, Los Angeles, California, Feb. 15th. Also personal communication.

OVERTON, W.F., and REESE, H.W. (1973) 'Models of development: methodological implications'. In: NESSELROADE and REESE, *Life-Span Developmental Psychology: Methodological Issues.* NY: Academic Press.

PAOLITTO, D. (1975) Role-taking opportunities for early adolescents: a programme in moral education. Unpublished PhD thesis, Boston University.

PAPALIA, D.E., and BIELBY, D.D.V. (1974) 'Cognitive functioning in middle and old age adults: a review of research based on Piaget's theory', *Human Developm.*, 17, 424–443.

PATRICK, J. (1971) 'Political education and democratic political orientations of ninth-grade students across four community types'. Unpublished manuscript, Indiana University.

PECK, R.F., and HAVIGHURST, R.J., *et al.* (1960) *The Psychology of Character Development*. New York: Wiley.

PETERS, R.S. (1971) 'Moral development: a plea for pluralism.' In: MISCHEL, T. (Ed.), *Cognitive Development and Epistemology*. New York and London: Academic Press.

PETERS, R.S. (1974) *Psychology and Ethical Development*. London: Allen and Unwin Ltd.

PETERSON, C., PETERSON, J., and FINLEY, N. (1974) 'Conflict and moral judgment', *Dev. Psych.*, 10, 1, 65–69.

PIAGET, J. (1926) *The Language and Thought of the Child*. London: Routledge and Kegan Paul.

PIAGET, J. (1928) *Judgement and Reasoning in the Child*. London: Routledge and Kegan Paul.

PIAGET, J. (1929) *The Child's Conception of the World*. New York: Harcourt, Brace.

PIAGET, J. (1932) *Moral Judgment of the Child*. New York: Harcourt, Brace.

PIAGET, J. (1950) *The Psychology of Intelligence*. New York: Harcourt, Brace.

PIAGET, J. (1952) *The Origins of Intelligence in Children*. New York: International University Press.

PIAGET, J. (1960) 'The definition of stages of development'. In: TANNER, J. and INHELDER, B. (Eds.), *Discussions in Child Development*, Vol. 4. New York: International University Press.

PIAGET, J. (1962) 'The relation of affectivity to intelligence in the mental development of the child', *Bull. of the Menninger Clinic*, 26, 3, 129–137.

PIAGET, J. (1964) 'Development and learning'. In: RIPPLE, R.E., and ROCKCASTLE, V.N., (Eds.), *Piaget Rediscovered: a report of the Conference on cognitive studies and curriculum development*. Ithaca, NY.: Cornell University Press.

PIAGET, J. (1967) *Six Psychological Studies*. New York: Random House.

PIAGET, J. (1969) *The Child's Conception of Physical Causality*. Totowa, NJ: Littlefield, Adams.

PIAGET, J. (1970) 'Piaget's theory'. In: MUSSEN, P.H. (Ed.), *Carmichael's Manual of Child Psychology.* New York: Wiley.

PIAGET, J. (1972) *Essai de Logique Operatorie.* (2nd rev. ed.), Paris: Dunod.

PIAGET, J. (1972a) *Inconscient Affectif et Inconscient Cognitif. Problems de Psychologie Genetique.* Paris: Editions Denoel.

PIAGET, J. (1972b) 'Intellectual evolution from adolescence to adulthood', *Human Developm.,* 15, 1—12.

PIAGET, J. (1972c) 'Piaget now, Parts 1, 2 and 3. (Piaget in discussion with B. Hill), *Times Ed. Supp.,* 11 Feb., 18 Feb., and 25 Feb., pp. 19, 19, 21, respectively.

PIAGET, J. (1972d) *The Principles of Genetic Epistomology.* London: Routledge and Kegan Paul.

PIAGET, J. (1973) *Main Trends in Psychology.* London: George Allen and Unwin.

PIAGET, J. (1973a) 'The neglected years: early childhood, "How a child's Mind Grows"', United Nations Children's Fund, pp. 21—36.

PIAGET, J. (1973b) *To Understand is to Invent: the Future of Education.* New York: Grossman Publishers.

PIAGET, J. (1974) 'The future of developmental child psychology', *J. Youth Adolesc.,* 3, 2, 87—93.

PIAGET, J., and INHELDER, B. (1941) *Le Développement des Quantités chez l'Enfant.* Paris: Delachaux and Niestle.

PIAGET, J., and INHELDER, B. (1947) 'Diagnosis of mental operations and theory of intelligence', *Am. J. Mental Deficiencies,* 51, 401—406.

PINARD, A., and LAURENDEAU, M. (1964) 'A scale of mental development based on the theory of Piaget: description of a project', *J. Res. Sc. Teach.,* 2, 253—260.

PITTEL, S.M. and MENDELSOHN, G.A. (1966) 'Measurement of moral values: a review and critique', *Psych. Bull.* 66, 1, 22—35.

PODD, M.H. (1972) 'Ego identity status and morality: the relationship between two developmental constructs', *Dev. Psych.,* 6, 497—507.

PORTER, N. (1972) 'Kohlberg and moral development', *J. Moral Educ.,* 1, 2, 123—28.

PORTEUS, B.D., and JOHNSON, R.C. (1965) 'Children's responses to two measures of conscience development and their relation to sociometric nomination', *Child Developm.,* 36, 703—11.

PURCELL, K. (1958) 'Some shortcomings in projective test validation', *J. Abnorm. Soc. Psych.,* 57, 115—8.

RAVEN, J.C. (1943) *The Mill Hill Vocabulary Scales.* London: Lewis and Company Limited.

RAVEN, J.C. (1960) *Guide to the Standard Progressive Matrices, Sets A, B, C, D and E.* London: Lewis and Company Limited.

RAWAN, H.R. (1975) 'The effect of age, sex, intelligence, and social-class on children's moral judgments: an examination of Piaget's theory in cross-cultural perspective', *Diss. Abstr.*, 35, 7, 3941A–4780A (4259–A).

REEVES, J.M. (1972) 'The modification of age-specific expectations of Piaget's theory of development of intentionality in moral judgments of four- to seven-year-old children in relation to use of puppets in a social (imitative) learning paradigm', *Diss. Abstr.*, 6815A (order No. 72–17502), Xerox University Microfilms.

REGISTER, M.C. (1976) 'Moral compatibility in married couples: a study of marital satisfaction as related to stage of moral development of spouses. *Diss. Abstr.*, 36, 8, 3687B–4237B (p. 4176B).

REISS, A.J. (1961) *Occupations and Social Status*. New York: The Free Press of Glencoe.

REST, J. (1969) Developmental hierarchy in preference and comprehension of moral judgement. Unpublished doctoral dissertation, University of Chicago.

REST, J., TURIEL, E., and KOHLBERG, L. (1969) 'Relations between level of moral judgement and preference and comprehension of the moral judgment of others', *J. Pers.* 37, 225–52.

REST, J., COOPER, D., CODER, R., MASONZ, J., and ANDERSON, D. (1974) 'Judging the important issues in moral dilemmas – an objective measure of development', *Dev. Psych.*, 10, 4, 491–501.

RIEGEL, K.F. (1973) 'Developmental Psychology and Society: some historical and ethnical considerations'. In: NESSELROADE and REESE, *Life-Span Developmental Psychology: Methodological Issues*. New York: Academic Press.

RIEGEL, K.F. (1975) 'Adult life crises: a dialectic interpretation of development'. In: DATAN and GINSBERG, *Life-Span Developmental Psychology: Normative Life Crises*. New York: Academic Press.

ROBINSON, B.A. (1976) 'A comparison of the effects of selective Catholic and public high schools on the moral development of their respective students', *Diss. Abstr.*, 36, 7, 3135B–3685B (p. 3622–B).

ROSENHAN, D.L. (1972) 'Prosocial behaviour of children'. In: HARTUP, *The Young Child: Reviews of Research*, Volume 2. Washington: National Association for the Education of Young Children.

ROSENHAN, D.L., and WHITE, G.M. (1967) 'Observations and rehearsal as determinants of prosocial behaviour', *J. Pers. Soc. Psych.*, 5, 424–431.

ROSS, R.J. (1974) 'The development of formal thinking for high and average achieving adolescents'. Paper presented at the 4th Annual Conference at University of Southern California and Los Angeles

Children's Hospital, 15th Feb. Also, at the University Affiliated Programme Conference on Piaget, Los Angeles, Feb. 15th, 1973. Also personal communication.

ROTHENBERG, B.B. (1970) 'Children's social sensitivity and the relationship to interpersonal comfort and intellectual level', *Dev. Psych.*, 2, 335–50.

RUBIN, G. (1970) Reduction of egocentrism in chronic schizophrenic patients as a function of a conservation learning task. Unpublished PhD thesis, University of Maryland.

RUBIN, K.H., and SCHNEIDER, F.W. (1973) 'The relationship between moral judgement, egocentrism, and altruistic behaviour', *Child Developm.*, 44, 661–65.

RULE, B.G. and DUKER, P. (1973) 'Effects of intentions and consequences on children's evaluations of aggressors', *J. Pers. Soc. Psych.*, 27, 184–89.

RUSHTON, J.P., and WIENER, J. (1975) 'Altruism and cognitive development in children', *Brit. J. Soc. Clin. Psych.*, 14, 341–349.

RUSSELL, R.W. (1940) 'Studies in animisms, IV, An analysis of concepts allied to animism', *J. Gen. Psych.*, 57, 83–91.

RUSTAD, K., and ROGERS, C. (1975) 'Promoting psychological growth in a high school class', *Couns. Educ. Superv.*, 14, 4, 277–85.

RUTHERFORD, E., and MUSSEN, P. (1968) 'Generosity in nursery school boys', *Child Developm.*, 39, 755–765.

SALILI, F., MAEHR, M.L., and GILLMORE, G. (1976) 'Achievement and morality: a cross-cultural analysis of causal attribution and evaluation', *J. Pers. Soc. Psych.*, 33, 3, 327–37.

SALTZSTEIN, H.D., DIAMOND, R.M., and BELENKY, M. (1972) 'Moral judgment level and conformity behaviour', *Dev. Psych.*, 7, 3, 327–36.

SANTROCK, J.W. (1975) 'Father absence, perceived maternal behaviour and moral development in boys', *Child Developm.*, 46, 753–57.

SCHAEFFER, P. (1974) Moral judgment: a cognitive developmental project. PhD thesis, University of Minnesota.

SCHALLENBERGER, M. (1894) 'Children's rights', *Ped. Sem.*, 3, 87–96.

SCHELLING, T.C. (1960) *The Strategy of Conflict*. Cambridge, Mass.: Harvard University Press.

SCHLEIFER, M., and DOUGLAS, V.I. (1973) 'Moral judgments, behaviour and cognitive style in young children', *Can. J. Behav. Sci. Rev. Can. Sci. Comp.*, 5, 2, 145–51.

SCHONBERG, R.B. (1975) 'Figurative language as a means of investigating Piaget's and Erikson's concepts of adolescence', *Diss. Abstr.*, 35, 8, pp. 3677B to 4295B, (p. 4195B).

SEARS, R., RAU, I., and ALPER, R. (1965) *Identification and Child Rearing*. Stanford: Stanford University Press.

SEGALL, M.H., CAMPBELL, D.T., and HERSKOVITS, M.J. (1965) *The Influence of Culture on Visual Perception*. Indianapolis: Bobbs Merrill.

SELLERS, W. (1941) 'The production of film for primitive people', *Overseas Education*, 13, 221.

SELMAN, R.L. (1969) Role-taking and the development of moral judgment in children. Unpublished doctoral dissertation, Boston University.

SELMAN, R.L. (1971) 'Taking another's perspective: role-taking development in early childhood', *Child Developm.*, 42, 1721—34.

SELMAN, R.L. (1971a) 'The relation of role-taking to the development of moral judgment in children', *Child Developm.*, 42, 79—91.

SELMAN, R.L. (1975) 'Level of social perspective taking and the development of empathy in children: speculations from a social-cognitive viewpoint', *J. Moral Ed.*, 6, 1, 35—43.

SELMAN, R.L. (1975a) 'The relation of perspective-taking levels to stages of moral judgment: theoretical and empirical analysis'. Paper presented to the Eastern Psychological Association, New York City, New York, April 6.

SELMAN, R.L. (forthcoming) 'The development of social cognitive understanding: a guide to educational and clinical practice'. To appear in T.L. LICKONA (Ed.), *Morality: Theory, Research and Social Issues*. New York: Holt, Rinehart and Winston.

SELMAN, R.L. and BYRNE, D. (1974) 'A structural analysis of levels of role-taking in middle childhood', *Child Developm.*, 803—07.

SELMAN, R.L., and DAMON, W. (1975) 'The necessity (but insufficiency) of social perspective taking for conceptions of justice at three early levels'. In: DEPALMA, D., and FOLEY, J. (Eds)., *Contemporary Issues in Moral Development*. Hillsdale, NJ: Erlbaum Associates.

SELMAN, R.L., and LIEBERMANN, M. (1975) 'Moral education in the primary grades: and evaluation of a developmental curriculum', *J. Ed. Psych.*, 67, 5, 712—716.

SELTZER, A.R. (1969) 'The relationship between moral development and the development of time perception and time conceptualization in lower class negro children', *Diss. Abstr.*, 31, 1524.

SERAFICA, F. (1969) 'Object concept in deviant children'. Paper presented at the Meetings of the Eastern Psychological Association.

SHANTZ, C. (in press) 'The development of social cognition'. In: HETHERINGTON, E.M. (Ed.), *Review of Child Development Research*. Volume 5. Chicago: University of Chicago Press.

SHANTZ, D.W., and VOYDANOFF, D.A. (1973) 'Situational effects on retaliatory aggression at three age levels', *Child Development.*, 44, 149—153.

SHARRAN, R., and DECARIE, T.G. (1973) 'Short term stability of infants' response to strangers'. Paper presented at the meeting of the Soc. Res. Child Develop., Philadelphia, March.

SIMON, A., and WARD, L.O. (1973) 'Variables influencing pupils' responses on the Kohlberg schema of moral development', *J. Moral Educ.*, 2, 3, 283—86.

SIMON. F. (1976) 'Moral development: some suggested implications for teaching', *J. Moral Ed.,* 5, 2, 172—178.

SIMPSON. E.L. (1974) 'Moral development research: a case study of scientific cultural bias', *Human Developm.*, 17, 81—106.

SMEDSLUND, J. (1961) 'The acquisition of conservation of substance and weight in children', *Scand. Journ. Psych.*, 6, 85—9.

SNODGRASS, S.R. (1975) 'Some relationships between sociopolitical ideology and moral character among college youth', *Youth and Adoles.*, 4, 3, 195—204.

SOMERVILLE, S.C. (1974) 'The pendulum problem: patterns of performance defining developmental stages', *Brit. J. Ed. Psych.*, 44, 3, 266—281.

SPRINTHALL, N.A. (1973) 'A curriculum for secondary schools: counsellors as teachers for psychological growth', *Sch. Couns.*, 5, 3, 361—369.

STANLEY, S. (1975) The justice structure of the family: a focus for education and counselling. Unpublished PhD, Boston University.

STEPHENS, W.B., MILLER, C.K., and McLAUGHLIN, J.A. (1969) 'The development of reasoning, moral judgment, and moral conduct in retardates and normals'. Report on Project No—RD—2382—P, Philadelphia, Pennsylvania: Temple University, May. Personal communication.

STEPHENS, W.B., McLAUGHLIN, J.A., MILLER, C.K., and GLASS, G.V., (1972) 'Factorial structure of selected psycho-educational measures and Piagetian reasoning assessments', *Dev. Psych.*, 6, 2, 343—348.

STRAUSS, A.L. (1954) 'The development of conceptions of rules in children', *Child Developm.*, 25, 193—208.

STUART, R.B. (1967) 'Decentration, age and intelligence in the development of children's moral judgement', *Diss. Abstr.*, 27 (8B) 2864—5.

SUTHERLAND, A., and GOLDSCHMID, M.L. (1971) 'Teacher expectation effects on cognitive development under normal classroom conditions'. Paper presented at the Canadian Psychological Association, Annual Meeting, St. John's, Newfoundland.

SWAINSON, B.M. (1949) The Development of Moral Ideas in Children and Adolescents. Unpublished PhD thesis.

TAPP, J.L. (1970) 'A child's garden of law and order', *Psych. Today*, December.

TAPP, J.L., and KOHLBERG, L. (1971) 'Developing senses of law and legal justice', *J. Soc. Iss.*, 27, 2, 65–91.

THOMPSON, L. (1948) 'Attitudes and acculturation', *Am. Anthrop.*, 50, 200–15.

TISHER, R.P. (1962) The development of some science concepts: a replication of Piaget's studies with pupils in a New South Wales county high school. Unpublished BA (Honours) thesis, University of New England, Armidale, New South Wales. Personal communication.

TISHER, R.P. (1971) 'A Piagetian questionnaire applied to pupils in a secondary school', *Child Developm.*, 42, 1633–1636.

TOMLINSON, P. (1975) 'Political education: cognitive developmental perspectives from moral education', *Oxf. Rev. Educ.*, 1, 3, 241–267.

TOMLINSON-KEASEY, C. (1972) 'Formal operations in females from 11 to 54 years of age', *Dev. Psych.*, 6, 2, 364.

TOMLINSON-KEASEY, C., and KEASEY, C.B. (1974) 'The mediating role of cognitive development in moral judgment', *Child Developm.*, 45, 291–98.

TURIEL, E. (1969) 'Developmental processes in the child's moral thinking'. In: MUSSEN, P., LANGER, J., and COVINGTON, M. (Eds.), *New Directions in Developmental Psychology*. New York: Holt.

TURIEL, E. (1974) 'Conflict and transition in adolescent moral development', *Child Developm.*, 45, 14–29.

TURNURE, C. (1975) 'Cognitive development and role-taking ability in boys and girls from seven to 12', *Dev. Psych.*, 11, 2, 202–09.

UGUREL-SEMIN, R. (1952) 'Moral behaviour and moral judgement of children', *J. Abnorm. Soc. Psych.*, 47, 463–74.

VON WRIGHT, J.M., and NIEMALA, P. (1966) 'On the ontogenetic development of moral criteria', *Scand. Journ. Psycholog.*, 7, 65–75.

WARD, L.O. (1965) An investigation into the attitudes of pupils in a girl's grammar school to the moral aspects of historical events. MA dissertation, University of Wales.

WECHSLER, D. (1949) *Wechsler Intelligence Scale for Children*. New York: The Psychological Corporation.

WEINER, B. (1973) 'From each according to his abilities: the role of effort in a moral society', *Human Developm.*, 16, 53–60.

WEINER, B., and KUKLA, A. (1970) 'An attributional analysis of achievement motivation', *J. Pers. Soc. Psych.*, 15, 1–20.

WEINER, B., and PETER, N. (1973) 'A cognitive-developmental analysis of achievement and moral judgments', *Dev. Psych.*, 9, 3, 290–309.

WEINREICH, H.E. (1970) A replication and evaluation of a study by Lawrence Kohlberg of the development of moral judgment in the adolescent. Unpublished MPhil thesis, University of Sussex.

WEINREICH, H.E. (1974) 'The structure of moral reason', *J. Youth Adolesc.*, 3, 2, 135–43.

WEINRICH, H.E. (1975) 'Kohlberg and Piaget: aspects of their relationship in the field of moral development', *J. Moral Educ.*, 4, 3, 201–13.

WEISBROTH, S.P. (1970) 'Moral judgment, sex and parental identification in adults', *Dev. Psych.*, 2, 3, 396–402.

WHELAN, M. (1975) 'Heteronomy and the child's emerging sense of justice', personal communication. Also Paper presented at the Fifth Invitational Interdisciplinary Seminar Piagetian Theory and its implications for the Helping Professions, January 24th.

WHITE, C.B. (1975) 'Moral development in Bahamian school children: a cross-cultural examination of Kohlberg's stages of moral reasoning', *Dev. Psych.*, 11, 4, 535–36.

WHITEMAN, P.H., and KOSIER, K.P. (1964) 'Development of children's moralistic judgements: age, sex, IQ and certain personal-experiental variables', *Child Developm.*, 35, 843–50.

WILSON, R.S., BROWN, A.M., and · MATHENY, A.P., Jr. (1971) 'Emergence and persistence of behavioural differences in twins', *Child Developm.*, 42, 1381–1398.

WOZNIAK, R.H. (1975) 'Dialecticism and structuralism: the philosophical foundation of Soviet and Piagetian developmental theory'. In: RIEGEL, K., and ROSENWALD, *Structure and Transformation: Developmental and Historical Aspects.* New York: Wiley.

WRIGHT, D. (1971) *The Psychology of Moral Behaviour.* Harmondsworth: Penguin.

ZIV, A. (1976) 'Measuring aspects of morality', *J. Moral Educ.*, 5, 2, 189–201.

INDEX

Abel, T., 25
Adelson, J., 89
Aldrich, C.C., 34, 99, 100
Almy, M., 38, 119
Alston, W.P., 72, 73
Ambron, S.R., 37, 38, 100
Anderson, D., 83, 84, 171
Arbuthnot, J., 84, 85, 100, 101
Armsby, R.E., 29, 44, 103
Aronfreed, J., 46, 178
Attfield, D., 45

Baldwin, A.L., 20, 41, 56, 105
Baldwin, C.P., 20, 41, 56, 105
Baldwin, J.M., 83
Bandura, A., 31, 42, 50, 103, 117, 118, 169
Banta, T.J., 39, 179
Barenboim, C., 103
Barnes, E., 24
Bartz, W.H. 183
Bar-Yam, M., 94
Belenky, M., 83, 177
Bell, P., 44, 128, 129
Berg-Cross, L.G., 32, 102
Berndt, E.G., 32, 103
Berndt, T.J., 32, 103
Bielby, D.D.V., 97, 98
Blatt, M., 63, 66, 67, 83, 94, 95
Block, J., 71
Bobroff, A., 27
Boehm, L. , 30, 36, 37, 41, 42, 43, 44, 48, 49
Bovet, M.P., 20
Brennan, W.K., 27, 41
Breznitz, S., 29, 30, 39, 56
Brooks-Walsh, I., 38, 104
Brown, A.M., 41, 105
Brown, M., 70
Bruner, J.S., 174
Buchanan, J.P., 31, 105
Bull, N.J., 37, 42, 43, 45, 46
Burton, R.V., 46, 58

Case, D., 149
Cauble, M.A., 87, 106
Chandler, M.J., 103, 104
Coder, R., 83, 84, 171

Coie, J.P., 34
Collinson, J., 149
Cooper, D., 83, 84, 171, 172
Costanzo, P.R., 34
Cowan, P.A., 50, 118
Craig, R.P., 53, 107
Cropley, A.J., 148, 149, 162
Crowley, P.M., 50, 51, 103
Cutick, R.A., 178

Damon, W., 39, 111, 112
Dennis, W., 25, 26, 49
Deutsch, F., 91
DeVries, R., 153
Dewey, J., 108
Diamond, R.M., 177
Dickstein, E., 90, 181
Dienstbier, R.A., 78
Distefano, A., 97
Douglas, V.I., 39, 47, 179
Dreman, S.B., 48
Dudek, S.Z. 156
Duker, P., 31, 34, 119
Dulit, E., 148, 149, 162, 163
Dunn, L.M., 39, 173, 179
Durkheim, E., 20, 53, 108, 109, 110, 111
Durkin, D., 27, 30, 34, 36, 43
Dworkin, E.S., 50

Erikson, E.H., 82, 87, 106, 165

Fargen, S.A., 178
Farnill, D., 34, 104
Field, T.W., 148, 149, 162
Finley, N., 51, 168
Flavell, J.H., 37, 100, 155, 164, 174
Fodor, E.M., 71, 81
Fontana, A.F., 89
Frank, H., 88
Freinet, C., 44, 129
Freud, S., 53, 71,
Fry, C.L., 164

Gallagher, M.J., 91, 112
Gash, H., 91, 113
George, S., 82, 86, 127
Gilligan, C., 83

GROWING THINGS AND OTHER STORIES

By Paul Tremblay

A chilling short story collection by the Bram Stoker Award-winning author of *A Head Full of Ghosts* and *The Cabin at the End of the World,* bringing his short stories to the UK for the first time. Unearth nineteen tales of suspense and literary horror, including a new story from the world of *A Head Full of Ghosts*, that offer a terrifying glimpse into Tremblay's fantastically fertile imagination.

Intricate, humane, ingenious and chilling, embrace the *Growing Things.*

"One of the key writers who have made modern horror exciting again" Adam Nevill, author of *The Ritual*

"Both wildly entertaining and deeply unsettling, Paul Tremblay's writing has a way of sneaking under your skin and messing with your head. Superb. Can't rate it highly enough" Sarah Lotz, author of *The Three, Day Four* and *The White Road*

"This collection proves again that in any form, at any length, Tremblay is a must-read" Chuck Wendig, *New York Times* bestselling author of *Wanderers* and *Invasive*

SOON
By Lois Murphy

On winter solstice, the birds disappeared, and the mist arrived.

The inhabitants of Nebulah quickly learn not to venture out after dark. But it is hard to stay indoors: cabin fever sets in, and the mist can be beguiling, too.

Eventually only six remain. Like the rest of the townspeople, Pete has nowhere else to go. After he rescues a stranded psychic from a terrible fate, he's given a warning: he will be dead by solstice unless he leaves town – *soon*.

"Exquisitely written" Paul Tremblay

"Charms and beguiles right up to the end—with an ending that might stop your heart" Alma Katsu

"Like a combination of Josh Malerman's *Bird Box* and the brilliant crime novels of Jane Harper" Mark Morris

"Disarming... I had to carry on reading through the night" Aliya Whiteley

TITANBOOKS.COM

For more fantastic fiction, author events,
exclusive excerpts, competitions, limited editions and more

VISIT OUR WEBSITE
titanbooks.com

LIKE US ON FACEBOOK
facebook.com/titanbooks

FOLLOW US ON TWITTER AND INSTAGRAM
@TitanBooks

EMAIL US
readerfeedback@titanemail.com